AROUND AND ABOUT PARIS

NEW HORIZONS:
HAUSSMANN'S ANNEXATION

THIRZA VALLOIS

Around and About Paris

NEW HORIZONS:
HAUSSMANN'S ANNEXATION

THE 13TH, 14TH, 15TH, 16TH, 17TH, 18TH,
19TH & 20TH ARRONDISSEMENTS

ILIAD BOOKS

First Published in 1997

Reprinted 1999

Copyright © 1997, Thirza Vallois

ISBN 0 9525378 2 6

Iliad Books
5 Nevern Road
London SW5 9PG
Tel: 0973 325 468
Internet: http://www.wfi.fr/vallois

Designed and produced by Kitzinger, London
Printed in Canada by Webcom Limited

To my Parents and Nathaniel
with love

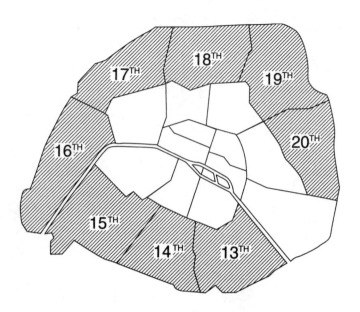

CONTENTS

In memory of Ella

ACKNOWLEDGEMENTS

I would like to express my deepest gratitude to Masha Schmidt, the illustrator of this book, who has captured so faithfully its atmosphere.

I would like also to thank the people who have worked with me specifically on this third volume of *Around and About Paris*. They are listed in alphabetical order:

Ingrid Cranfield who has given me invaluable advice in editing the book, Nicolas Georget who has designed the maps, Pat Doyle who has offered all her expertise to the design of the cover, Tony Kitzinger who has designed the book with so much commitment and care.

Special thanks also to all my friends and colleagues who, in one way or another, have given me their support during this long adventure. They include:

Helen Braverman, Roselyn Dery, Fifi Dosoruth, Ann Dowling, Richard Dunn, Linda Ellis, Amy Ellzey, Debby Franklin, Baba Gamet, Fleurette Havranek, Raymond Howard, Prina Kass, René Lacombe, Eve Lauhouti, Ena Langman, Adrian Leeds, Dan Levy, Guy Livingston, Danielle Michel-Chiche, Hilary Moore, Gloria Moss, John Price, Susan Rosenberg, Ellie Santos, Eve Saulais, Ron Shepping, Gerry Silverman, Alan Smalley, Stephen Solomons, Brian Spence, Linda Thalmann, Philippe Valéry, Barbara-Sue White, George Whitman, Caroline, Elizabeth and Peter Wilson

INTRODUCTION

Ce n'est pas Paris tout a fait;
Ce n'est pas non plus la campagne;
Et le soir, lorsque l'ombre gagne,
On ne sait pas trop où l'on est.

This is not exactly Paris
Nor is this the country;
And in the evening, when dusk encroaches,
One does not quite know where one is.

Rosemonde Gérard

On 1 January 1860 the toll walls encircling Paris were no more and the 24 'villages' dotted around them were gobbled up by a city seeking to widen its horizons as far as the defence walls (*les fortifications*), which became the city's new boundary. These were built by Adolphe Thiers in 1841 and ran along what is now known as the Boulevards Extérieurs or Boulevards des Maréchaux. The expanding city carved out for itself 8 new arrondissements, to be added to its 'snail-shell' layout, at times ignoring the natural boundaries of the suburban 'villages', often incurring their hostility to the annexation project. Further opposition arose from the fear of being subjected to the city toll. True, those inhabitants living more favourably in the west could anticipate economic growth and a rise in the value of real-estate, but the majority, although they could rejoice at no longer being strangulated between two walls, as had been the case for the past 20 years, worried that the authorities would be unwilling to relinquish this substantial source of revenue and would extend the toll to the newly annexed territory. Their misgivings proved right when the gates of the defence walls were converted into checkpoints for this purpose. Initially Thiers had built the walls against a potential Prussian assault but they were to prove totally useless, both against the Prussians in 1870 and the Germans in 1914. They were equally useless against Thiers's own forces during the civil war of the *Commune* in 1871, when he found himself in the preposterous situation of having to assault his own defence system! The walls were consequently torn down in 1919, and, for the first time, Paris ceased to be a walled city. The toll, however, was doggedly maintained until 1930 and levied at its former gates (*portes*), of which no more is left but their names. The last to vanish was the tax on petrol, when the authorities finally faced the fact that measuring the petrol in each incoming car was more trouble than it was worth.

It was now too late to bring remedy to the territory which (except in the west) was economically too vulnerable to resist the burden of the new tax and the advance of industrialisation. Whereas before 1860 most of its inhabitants were of modest means, by the dawn of the 20th century they were downright destitute! Meanwhile Haussmann's bulldozer relentlessly ploughed through these countrified parts, bringing about the same radical changes as in central Paris, preparing the ground for the takeover by the automobile in decades to come. Those town planners who trampled through the territory a century later, however, wreaked even worse ravage with their enormous blocks of concrete into which were fitted the growing numbers of working- and even middle-class residents (except in the west, rich enough to resist, and Montmartre, thanks to its steep hill) leaving little space for the old village life.

The little that has survived is worth the detour – it is a journey into the less well-known face of Paris that does not necessarily make its way into the pages of history books, but where so much of the city's lifeblood has run. It is also a journey into timeless, quintessential France, all the more precious as so little of it has survived, all the more exciting as it demands an effort to find. Do not come here in winter nor on a dull day – the palette of nature bathed in sunlight is an essential part of the experience.

A NOTE ON THE TEXT

So as to facilitate the reading of French names and titles, the use of capital letters follows English rules. When they are italicised, however, French rules have been retained

Because Paris is a city of change, some of the places or exhibits mentioned in the text may have since disappeared or been transformed. If this is the case, please bear with the author.

THE 13TH ARRONDISSEMENT

A stroller forty years ago penetrating beyond La Salpêtrière
by way of the Boulevard de l'Hôpital . . . would have come to
a region where Paris seemed to disappear.

Les Misérables, Victor Hugo, 1862

ONLY a few years ago most people would have agreed with
Victor Hugo – some may do to this day. Despite its conspicuous
high-rise buildings, to many, the 13th has remained a 'no man's
land'. Few outsiders venture here; guidebooks hardly mention the
area, except for the Gobelins workshops, which are on the northern edge of the arrondissement and mercifully close to the 'civilis-
ed' 5th. In short, an uninviting neighbourhood most Parisians
avoided until recently and most tourists have never heard of.

Many would still agree with the rest of Victor Hugo's description: 'By day the place was ugly. In the evening it was melancholy.
At night it was sinister.' The waves of Far East Asian war refugees
who arrived in Paris in the mid-1970s did not pay attention to such
details. A dismal high-rise compound of concrete in the south-east
of the arrondissement, repugnant to the conservative French who
had not yet come to terms with American-style urbanisation, was a
godsend to them. In no time they turned the area bounded by the
Avenues d'Ivry and Choisy and the Boulevard Masséna into the
biggest Chinatown in Paris, Le Triangle Jaune as it has come to be
known, with a population of 30,000 out of the arrondissement's
total of 190,000. With their multitude of inexpensive, no-nonsense
restaurants, they brought the out-of-the-way, unsightly 13th to the
attention of Parisians, livened up its bleak arteries and almost
overnight put it on the map.

In pre-industrial days this was a land of green pastures, of scattered
windmills, and of vineyards watered by the meandering Bièvre as
reported by one of its inhabitants:

> *Le liquide puisé au tonneau d'Ivry*
> *me chatouille d'une maniere suave*

> The liquid drawn from the wine-cask at Ivry
> gently titillates my palate.

A few other villages already stood here in the early Middle Ages – Gentilly, Arcueil and Saint-Marceau (or Marcel). Later the great Renaissance poet Ronsard used to meet his poet friends under the bowers of Saint-Marcel or take a leisurely stroll through the countryside to Arcueil. Ronsard was pining at the time after the young but married Geneviève, a native of the future arrondissement, and it was for the love of her that he drank his fill so as to forget his pangs:

> Go to Harcueil hereafter,
> Put the table as close as may
> By the fountain.
> Put hither the bottle full,
> Then for ever
> Pour wine into my glass,
> To strangle the memory
> Of my troubles after drinking.

Geneviève's husband was either the owner of one of the area's *guinguettes* (open-air taverns) or the concierge of the prison of the borough of Saint-Marceau. It was named after Marcel, the ninth bishop of Paris in the 5th century, when it was still a very small village, but by the second half of the 12th century it was a sizeable borough and was even confirmed as an independent borough by a parliamentary decree in 1296. As such it was exempted from Parisian taxation and entitled to its own prison.

It had begun as one of the very early Christian settlements of Paris, as revealed in the 17th century by excavations undertaken in the vicinity of the present Gobelins cross-roads of a Christian cemetery with 1,000 graves, dating from the 3rd century. Indeed, lying on the southern gateway of Paris, this was where the early Christians settled having made their way through France from the Mediterranean shores. Two centuries later Marcel was the inspiring leader of the Christian community of Paris. Born next to Notre-Dame in 360 AD, he had played an active role in the conversion of heathens. His natural ascendancy was such that even a monstrous dragon was forced into submission by him. In *Le Miroir historial* Vincent de Beauvais reports that the horrific beast made its way

4

into the above-mentioned Christian cemetery, sowing terror among the inhabitants. However, the charismatic Bishop Marcel came to their rescue and prayed on their behalf, after which 'the dragon lowered its head and applauded with its tail with great humility, imploring mercy.' At this point Marcel dealt him three strokes on the head with his crook and led him three miles out of town. He then admonished 'the enemy from hell' to disappear: '*Ou t'en vas au désert, ou t'en vas jeter à la mer*' ('either you clear off into the desert or you throw yourself into the sea'). The beast plunged into the river at once '*et de lui jamais plus ne fut nouvelle*' ('and was never heard of again'). Soon pictures of the holy man were hung on gables and street corners and when he died on 1 November 436, huge throngs streamed to the chapel of Saint-Clément, just south of the present Boulevard Saint-Marcel, where his body was exposed, all the more so, as he continued to heal the sick even after his death. No wonder he was offered a magnificent reliquary, as Madame de Sévigné reported in the 17th century. On Ascension Day, she wrote, the reliquary would be carried by the goldsmiths' guild to Notre-Dame, together with the reliquary of Saint Geneviève, the Patron of Paris, '*la plus belle chose du monde*' ('the most beautiful thing in the world'), according to Sévigné, covered with more than 2,000 gems. The memory of the evil dragon was still alive as recently as the 18th century, when sweets were sold outside the Hôtel-Dieu hospital (next to Notre-Dame) in a dragon-shaped wicker basket. The holy man's name not only honours a boulevard and a Métro station, but his bishop's mitre also decorates the coat of arms of the 13th arrondissement, despite this being a secular administration.

This land of bucolic retreat, through which Rabelais led Pantagruel on his way to the library of Saint-Victor, where J.J. Rousseau liked to gather plants and which Watteau immortalised in his idyllic landscapes, notably in his famous painting *Voyage à Cythère*, had nonetheless been marked for doom already in the 13th century. Paradoxically, it was the lovely Bièvre that was its undoing, attracting to its banks all the most polluting activities, in particular from the 17th century on, when these were expelled from the banks of the Seine in the heart of the city. Butchers were the first to settle here and dump their trash into the river, followed by tanners, curriers, cobblers, and later by dyers, weavers, laundresses and others, who transformed this happy watercourse, once frequented by diligent beavers (*bièvres*) into a dark, oozing river of hell – '*un fumier qui bouge*' ('oozing dung') according to Huysmans; '*cette salope de petite rivière*' ('this slut of a river'), according to Edmond de Goncourt. Even Rabelais had no kind words for the Bièvre and said that this 'Parisian Lady' was peed into by dogs, although a contemporary claimed that it was not the dogs but the students of the University who were actually paid to water her in this way. Up river, however, the waters maintained their purity and we know that Madame de Maintenon relished its crayfish.

Among the artisans who settled on its banks was the dyer Jehan de Gobelin, who may have come from Bruges, a city reputed for the expertise of its dyers, or from Reims as some historians are inclined to believe. He arrived at Faubourg Saint-Marcel in August 1443 and on the 23rd of that month rented a house on the banks of the river with the sign 'The Swan' affixed to it. Here he started what in the 17th century was to become the celebrated Gobelins manufactory, famous throughout the continent for its glorious tapestries. However, Jehan de Gobelin was no tapestry-maker but merely a dyer, which was why he had settled by the Bièvre, to make use of its waters. When he discovered a much-prized durable scarlet dye, jealous tongues accused him of having contracted a pact with the Devil. In fact, it was the salty quality of the river's water that helped him obtain this dye and the title of '*teinturier en écarlate*' ('scarlet dyer'). Jehan de Gobelin had 13 children, which was no special feat in those days, but it put him at the head of a large dynasty who lived on well into the second half of the 17th century. By then its members had gathered much wealth and had bartered their trade for financial or military careers, purchasing titles of nobility or buying high offices as magistrates. Having sold their property, they moved to the fashionable Marais, happy to leave behind the polluted Bièvre whose waters, into which the Gobelins workshops dipped, were as black as ink, according to the satirical poet Claude Le Petit, who wrote in 1668 that 'the black-skinned Devil, being too hot in Purgatory, comes to bathe here in the summer.' He also blamed the Gobelins for their share of responsibility in this ecological disaster:

> *C'est là le sieur Gobelin,*
> *Qu'il est sale et qu'il est vilain!*

There is master Gobelin,
How dirty and how ugly he is!

The last descendant of the dynasty, Antoine de Gobelin, became the Marquis de Brinvilliers, husband of the notorious mass poisoner, who, rather than providing her family with heirs, chose to eliminate its members, hoping to inherit the lot (see chapter on the 4th arr.).

When Antoine's ancestor Jehan had arrived here over two centuries earlier, the Flemish dyers were not the only foreign group living in Faubourg Saint-Marcel. The English too were present, as an occupying force in the aftermath of the Hundred Years War, and like the rest of the population liked to frequent its taverns. They preferred their own ale, however, and tried to introduce it among the natives, with apparently little success: the latter snubbed their barley-based drink and clung persistently to their own Dionysian customs and to their '*vinetum sancti Marcelli*'. They did, however, retain the name of the new beverage – 'good ale' – which, as true Frenchmen, they distorted into 'godale', and then again into '*godailler*' ('to booze'). Jehan de Gobelin, on the other hand, because of his Flemish origins, was accustomed to drinking beer and even opened a brewery on the banks of the river for the benefit of his employees, most of whom were fellow-countrymen from Flanders and enjoyed a hearty pint at the end of a day's work.

With so much wine and beer flowing about, the banks of the foul river attracted the most wretched riff-raff, who whiled away the hours in unsavoury dives along the river, drowning their misery in cheap alcohol, engaging in brawls and crime. It was among the embryonic working class of Faubourg Saint-Antoine (now in the 11th and 12th arrondissements) and among the rabble of the future 13th, 'more wicked, more inflammable and more disposed to mutiny than could be found anywhere else in Paris', according to Louis-Sébastien Mercier, that the French Revolution recruited its zealous hordes of angry followers. Restif de la Bretonne, a contemporary of Mercier, described how on the eve of 14 July the bandits from Faubourg Saint-Marcel passed by his house on their way to join those of Faubourg Saint-Antoine: '*Tout cela formait une tourbe formidable*' ('All this formed a formidable bog'). And it was the *Patriotes* of Faubourg Saint-Marcel who were the first to arrive at the Palais des Tuileries on 10 August 1792 and demand the abdication of the King.

It was here also that one of the most hideous episodes of the French Revolution took place, *le massacre de La Salpêtrière*, on the night of 3/4 September 1792. La Salpêtrière, originally a gunpowder factory (hence its name) set up conveniently opposite the King's Great Arsenal across the Seine, was converted at the time of Louis XIV into a sort of gigantic alms-house, into which were herded willy-nilly the tramps and vagabonds of Paris, its rascals and rogues, whores and cut-throats, charlatans and crooks – 40,000 in all out of a total population of 400,000! This initiative was intended to clear the streets of vice whilst providing shelter for this wretched portion of humanity. A royal edict of 27 April 1656 clearly stated the objective 'to put an end to beggary and idleness, as being the source of all disorder'. But the road to hell is paved with good intentions and what was meant as a charitable institution, where 'all the poor would be gathered on clean premises, so as to be tended to, be educated and be given an occupation', turned out to be a diabolical depot for the dregs of society, an infernal mosaic of human misery. The feeble-minded and the hardened whore, the offender and the outlaw, the outcasts and the homeless, the epileptic and the paralytic were penned up side by side in this purgatory, the men at Bicêtre, the women at La Salpêtrière. And despite the architectural care bestowed on the establishment by the greatest artists of the day – Le Vau, Le Muet, Libéral Bruant – who had at their disposal huge donations from Fouquet, Mazarin and Pompon de Bellièvre, and despite the efforts of its first chaplain and most charitable man in the kingdom, Saint Vincent de Paul, the institution suffered from horrendous overcrowding and appalling conditions.

These deteriorated dramatically after 1680, when, following a new royal edict, La Salpêtrière also became a jail for prostitutes arrested on the authority of a sealed letter from the King. Caught in the net on the streets of Paris, they were driven in carts through crowds of jeering Parisians to La Salpêtrière, where they were paired off with hardened convicts and shipped off to the New World to populate its newly conquered territories. The reign of absolutism had no concern for the suitability of the couples or for their uprootedness. Nor did it have much compassion for the mentally deranged, as the Duc de La Rochefoucauld reported after a visit to the place: 'Everything is in a state of neglect to a degree as inconceivable as it is distressing. All categories of madness are confounded; chained-up mad women (and there are many of them) are united with peaceful ones. The latter have to put up permanently with the horrific spectacle of the contortions and fury of their enraged inmates, which they accompany with perpetual screams, and never enjoy a moment of rest. . . Here there is no gentleness, no consolation, no remedy.' What the Duke had overlooked (or failed to mention) was that the building was also overrun by voracious rats.

On that night of 3/4 September 1792, the unbridled rabble of Faubourg Saint-Marcel, equipped with their notorious pikes, assaulted La Salpêtrière, initially with the generous intention of releasing the cruelly detained street-girls. However, with so much alcohol flowing in their veins, by the time they reached La Salpêtrière their brutish instincts got the better of them and the enterprise turned into an unutterable orgy of blood. Whereas 183 prostitutes were indeed released and hailed by the mob, 45 dishevelled, mentally-deranged women were dragged into the street and massacred in view of all. This prompted Madame Roland, hitherto a great supporter of the Revolution, to write in her *Memoirs* that the Revolution 'has been stained by villains and become hideous'.

With the coming of the Industrial Age the 13th arrondissement was predisposed to house the new workshops and factories of southern Paris. The rural stretches that had so far partly redeemed it and had made it congenial to Rousseau and Watteau were now choked by smoke and soot from chimney-stacks and packed with squalid hovels – 'a makeshift collection of planks held together by crudely cut cross-bars', as Victor Hugo wrote in *Les Misérables*. Households of a dozen people would cram into these damp shacks, a few of them often having to share one bed – when there was a bed. Usually the floor and a bit of straw would do. Cardboard replaced window panes, running water and toilets were unheard of – trash was simply thrown into the Bièvre, where it had accumulated for centuries, until the river was no more than an open-air sewer, spreading pestilence and epidemics, notably the cholera epidemics of 1832 and 1849 which hit the 13th arrondissement in particular. In 1905/6 the municipal authorities decided to cover over this health hazard, thus wiping the poor Bièvre off the face of Paris and out of the memory of future generations. Today one has to travel to Verrières-les-Buisson, south of Paris, to see the Bièvre flow in the open air.

Attempts to improve the environment of the 13th arrondissement and amend past errors, in the second half of the 20th century, have not turned out to be a success. Undoubtedly it was necessary to clear the area of its insalubrious streets, but the drab, unimaginative tenement houses that have replaced them are hardly more inviting, while the concrete high-rise buildings only mar the arrondissement further by jarring its skyline.

From the 1970s on, the 13th arrondissement has been showered with new projects, many of which have been completed and most of which give the impression of a replastering or patching-up job. In an effort to promote the arrondissement and give it a cultural dimension, a new branch of the university of Paris opened here, Paris I – Tolbiac, specialising in law and economics, but it too is just another vertical, unsightly construction. The 13th also takes pride in its Médiathèque – a book, record and video library, named after the late film director Jean-Pierre Melville, which opened in July 1989. Boasting 200,000 volumes on every imaginable field of knowledge, and every modern means of communication, it was meant to become a cultural magnet but, being situated in an unappealing neighbourhood, it draws few outsiders. The Grand Ecran on Place d'Italie is a multi-media hall with a three-dimensional giant cinema screen, the largest in the capital. Its deliberately contemporary structure boldly points to the sky, trying to look like some spacecraft. Whatever its architectural merits may be, it positively kills the general harmony of Place d'Italie, which still prevailed until a couple of decades ago; however humble, it was preferable to this high-faluting pretentiousness.

The Seine–Rive Gauche scheme is the largest urbanisation project of the century, involving a stretch of 2.7 km on an area of 137 hectares along the Seine, all the way from the Gare d'Austerlitz to the Paris ring road, the Boulevard Périphérique. It was elaborated during the optimistic decade of the 1980s with an initial budget of 22 billion francs and was meant to boost the economy of the arrondissement and contribute to the promotion of eastern Paris. However, with the economic recession of the 1990s, the authorities have become more cautious and building projects are not at the top of their agenda. The final destiny of Seine-Rive Gauche is yet to be determined, though its high-faluting proclaimed objective is 'to blend culture, finance and housing'.

President François Mitterrand also showed an interest in the development of Seine-Rive Gauche, making it the site of the controversial Bibliothèque de France, the last of his *grands projets*, which was scheduled to open along the Seine in spring 1995, at the close of his 14-year reign, but failed to meet the deadline. The new library, designed by Dominique Perrault, is situated on the site of the old freight railway station of Tolbiac,* an area roughly the size of Place de la Concorde, on which has been built a gigantic, cold and impersonal rectangle. Vast staircases lead to the entrance, reminiscent of those totalitarian regimes like to erect for their monuments. At its four corners four glass towers soar nearly 100 metres above the ground like four open books – a vertical structure which was intended to enhance the prestige of the rehabilitated east. Instead, it made yet another intrusion into the horizon and outraged the academic community, both at home and abroad, the prime customers of the library. Unimpressed by questionable architectural glamour, they have been more concerned about such practicalities as quick access to documents and, above all, about the storage in a glass tower of a national treasure which has been accumulated over 600 years. Some are sceptical about the suitability of a high-rise for the function of a library, others object to its being open to the general public and were particularly alarmed when President Mitterrand proclaimed in 1988, at the dawn of his second septennate, and on Bastille Day, that he wished the new library to be of 'a totally new type . . . and at the disposal of everyone.' The implications included robotisation, remote consultation and other futuristic technologies that would make it the library of the 21st century, equipped with 'an audiovisual tool that no other country in the world owns or can own'. The outcry in academic circles was followed by a furore in the media, who derided the project as a 'Disneyland of reading' and as 'the slaughterhouse of memory'. The authorities, notoriously one-track-minded and not easily swayed, remain impervious to the criticism and continue to pursue their course. Having marked out the 13th arrondissement to vie with Manhattan, vertical development must

* Quai François Mauriac

11

be the order of the day. After all, it was in the 13th arrondissement that the first Parisian skyscraper made its appearance. That was back in 1959 and it was 21 storeys high!

The new library was opened officially on 17 December 1996 by President Chirac. François Mitterrand was not to attend the inauguration, having passed away on 12 January. President Chirac, however, did not forget that the library had been Mitterrand's brain-child and re-named it on the occasion La Bibliothèque François Mitterrand.

WHERE TO WALK

FROM PLACE D'ITALIE TO THE CITE FLORALE

If one ventures into this land, it is out of curiosity; nothing calls you there, there isn't a single monument to see.

Louis-Sébastien Mercier, *Tableaux de Paris*

Although the above lines were written in the 18th century, they still largely apply today. If you are nonetheless driven by curiosity to discover an ordinary neighbourhood of Paris, avoid coming on a dull day when the area is downright lugubrious. The few astonishing pockets that redeem it – countrified remnants in the midst of urban disaster – are unimpressive without the helping hand of nature. Before making the journey, however, take into account that the Gobelins workshops can be visited on Tuesdays, Wednesdays, Thursdays 2–4 pm only,* while it is on Sunday mornings that Chinatown is at its most exciting and full of shoppers from the Far East Asian community.

PLACE D'ITALIE is a good starting-point. This is the hub of the arrondissement and can easily be reached by public transport. In ancient times this was the southern gateway of Paris that led to Rome and later to Italy. It is through this gateway that Napoleon entered Paris on 20 March 1815, after his successful escape from the island of Elba. At the time, open-air taverns (*guinguettes*) proliferated in the vicinity of its toll-gate, where Parisians would gather

* Guided tours only. Prior booking essential. Tel. 01 44 08 52 00.

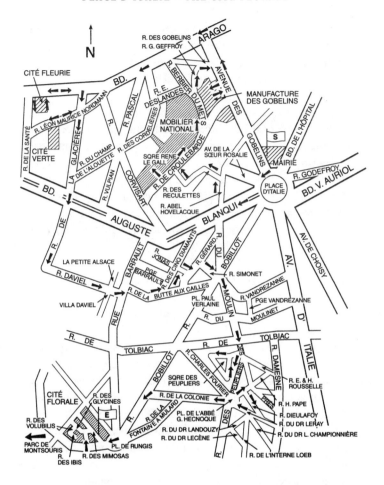

on Sundays and holidays to enjoy their tax-exempt wines. The gate was a symbol of oppression and in 1789, during the first revolutionary outbursts, the populace, goaded by the inflammatory oratory of the famous Mirabeau, came over to Place d'Italie and set fire to the gate.

To the north of Place d'Italie, between Boulevard de l'Hôpital and Avenue des Gobelins, stands the ostentatious **Mairie** of the 13th arrondissement, typical of the town halls built in the last century, and particularly festive-looking when decorated on special occasions such as Christmas time. Facing the Mairie across the Place is Kenzo Tange's cinematographic centre **Le Grand Ecran**, an obtrusive addition to a hitherto neighbourly spot. Inaugurated in 1991, it was meant to crown two decades of futuristic élan, when everything new in the 13th arrondissement pointed to or was named after the heavens and beyond, notably the unremarkable shopping centre adjoining it, Galaxie.

Running into the west side of Place d'Italie is the pleasant **AVENUE DE SOEUR ROSALIE**. Soeur Rosalie, real name Jeanne-Marie Rendue, deserves this smiling setting, for during the 19th century she was the only ray of hope in this dismal, Dickensian arrondissement, alleviating the pains of its ailing population, notably during the cholera epidemics of 1832 and 1849. During the 1848 Revolution, when violence took to the streets, she braved the infuriated rebels in an effort to appease them, at the risk of her own life.

The next artery, **BOULEVARD AUGUSTE-BLANQUI**, also affords a pleasant sight. Its picturesque kiosk, motley, cheerful flower-beds and *boules* players create a touch of small-town provincialism. A market is held along the Boulevard on Sunday, Tuesday and Friday mornings, adding extra colour to the place. Many of the vendors are North Africans, some are Far East Asians, both groups bearing witness to the ethnic evolution of French society. If you are interested in the sculptor Rodin, you may wish to walk down the Boulevard to no. 68, the site of his studio, where Camille Claudel used to visit him during their passionate love affair. It was located in a charming 18th-century *folie*, which had been built for one of the King's councillors, but has unfortunately been demolished, like the other *folies* that embellished these once bucolic parts.

Turn right into rue Abel Hovelacque and left into the dismal rue des Reculettes, whose winding course will take you to **RUE DE CROULEBARBE**, where you will turn right.

The windmill of the Croulebarbe family (whose picturesque name probably referred to the overblown beard of an ancestor) is mentioned way back in 1214 and appears on all the maps of pre-Revolution Paris. The street ran along the river Bièvre, an obvious location for the family's windmill, which disappeared only in 1840. By 1243 this prosperous family is known also to have owned a substantial, profitable vineyard and, by the following century, another property which was 'located along the road that leads from Saint-Marcel to Gentilly'. Nobody knows, though, how it came into the hands of the Order of Saint-Martin-des-Champs a few years later, all the stranger since their domain was situated at the other end of town. It still belonged to the Order at the time of Louis-Philippe, which explains why Fieschi, who, on 28 July 1835 had made an attempt on the latter's life on Boulevard du Temple (see 11th arr.), went into hiding here – he was the concierge of Saint-Martin!

In 1827 rue de Croulebarbe made the headlines when the goat girl of Ivry, Aimée Millot, was stabbed to death by the mentally unbalanced Honoré Ulbach in the middle of a thunderstorm – an appropriate setting for a melodrama. Aimée would come here every day with her goats and sit reading a book, looking lovely in her straw hat. Her murder aroused outraged compassion all over Paris: even the sensational arrival of the first giraffe in the Jardin des Plantes (see chapter on 5th arr.) – the first ever to tread French soil – was overshadowed by the crime. Ulbach was among the last convicts to be put to death on Place de Grève (now Hôtel-de-Ville), the traditional place of public executions in Paris up to the reign of Louis-Philippe. However, after the three-day riots of July 1830 that brought Louis-Philippe to the throne, the new King vowed never again to carry out executions on Place de Grève as a token of gratitude to the people of Paris, who had supported him heroically on that site.

Rue de Croulebarbe runs along **Square René Le Gall**. At the back of the garden a row of poplar trees denotes the subterranean course of the Bièvre. The street and the garden make for a peaceful, provincial atmosphere, a blessed retreat on a hot summer day, just off the busy main arteries of the arrondissement, a villagey atmosphere enhanced by the presence of the Basque restaurant Etchegorry, at no. 41, a well-known old-timer, and the provincial inn Chez Angèle, at no. 29. In the last century a countrified tavern stood here. It belonged to Madame Grégoire and was a favourite with the Romantic writers, especially Victor Hugo. At no. 33 stands Paris's first skyscraper, 21-storeys high. Square René Le Gall was opened in 1938 on land that used to belong to the Gobelins workshops, situated to the north-east, and was divided up as kitchen gardens among its craftsmen. It is now named after a member of the Resistance who was shot by the Germans.

RUE BERBIER-DU-METS branches off rue de Croulebarbe to the left and follows the meandering course of the Bièvre, running parallel to the curved back of the Gobelins annex, a building of reinforced concrete put up by Auguste Perret in 1935. A neat, modern building across the street, surrounded by a green stretch of lawn, houses the new Gobelins workshops, which face the north so as to enjoy a better quality of light. A pile of stones lying round in the garden by the street is all that remains of the exquisite 18th-century *folie* of Jean de Julienne, shamefully demolished recently for no good reason. Julienne's uncle was a famous dyer, Jean Gluck, who helped Julienne develop his workshop. The painter Watteau, a close friend of Julienne's, used the place as a base for his walks in the neighbouring countryside, a source of inspiration for his paintings.

Rue Gustave Geoffroy on your right will lead you to RUE DES GOBELINS. At no. 3bis a courtyard with an archway on its right leads to the site of the Hôtel Mascarini, the mansion of a wealthy financier in the 17th century, when members of society were attracted to these southern parts and their sunny stretches of neat vineyards. Only the orangery of the *hôtel* still stands, an early 18th-century addition. A more unexpected sight awaits you at nos 17 and 19 where, at the back of a drab courtyard, amidst a medley of shabby workshops and rickety offices, rises a genuine medieval manor, dilapidated and blackened by age, a stunning apparition from a fairytale book. This was the **Hôtel** or **Domaine de la Reine Blanche**, though no one knows for sure who the Queen was. It might have been Blanche de Castille, the mother of Saint Louis, but there are other candidates, for, up until the 16th century, when Catherine de Medici introduced black from Spain as the colour of mourning, it had been the custom for the widowed queens of France to wear white and several queens were known as Blanche. Be that as it may, in all likelihood the manor belonged to the royal family and was the site of the tragic scene of the *Bal des Ardents*, a fancy-dress ball held here on 28 January 1393. The feeble-minded Charles VI and five of his friends turned up dressed as savages. The Duc d'Orléans, purportedly curious to identify his brother the King, held a torch close

Hôtel de la Reine Blanche

to the faces of the 'savages' and (accidentally?) set their costumes aflame. Four of the unfortunate party perished in the fire, while one survived by jumping into a tub of water. The King was saved by the presence of mind of his aunt, the Duchesse de Berry, who rolled him in her coat, yet, while he did not lose his life, he lost the last remnants of his sanity after this traumatic experience. The mansion was promptly razed to the ground and for the next hundred years a market was held on its site every Monday as well as a fair twice a year. The present house was built some hundred years later. It is this house or the lovely one at no. 19, or both, that may correspond to '*La Follie-Goubelin*', mentioned by Rabelais in *Pantagruel*. Until recently this medieval manor, for so long forgotten, was visible only to those who cared to seek it out, but lately it has come to the notice of the municipal authorities, who would like to turn it into a cultural centre of some sort. We hope you will have seen it in its natural state, before this ill-judged design is carried out.

Turn right into **AVENUE DES GOBELINS**. The entrance to the **Gobelins workshops** is at no. 42. When Jehan de Gobelin settled in the house '*à l'enseigne du Cygne*' ('with the sign of The Swan'), little did he know that 500 years later his name would still be famous worldwide, but that it would be erroneously associated with the art of tapestry. His house was situated on the bank of the Bièvre, roughly where rue Berbier-du-Mets now meets Boulevard Arago. He may have come here knowing the secret the river held in its salty water, which would allow him to discover the scarlet dye that made his fortune.

It was under the new ownership of the Carraye family that tapestry was added to the activities of the establishment, especially from 1656, when the Dutchman Gluck took over with the help of Liansel. But the name Gobelin stuck. This was during the reign of Louis XIV, when every venture in the kingdom was to enhance the glory of the Sun King, and him alone, a policy supervised by his minister Colbert, who replaced Mazarin when he died in 1661. It is in this context that Colbert engineered the downfall of the King's treasurer, Nicolas Fouquet, that same year, whose magnificent palace of Vaux-le-Vicomte was perceived as a provocation, and who was sentenced to life imprisonment on charges of embezzlement. The following year Colbert bought up the Gobelins workshops for the King, too prestigious an establishment to remain in the hands of anyone else. From then on the workshops were known as Hôtel Royal des Gobelins. Louis XIV's grandfather, Henri IV, had already planned to set up tapestry workshops, as is testified by a royal edict dating from 1607, but his project never materialised, perhaps because of his premature death. He had even invited Franz Van der Planken and Marc de Comans from Antwerp to start up this craft in France. Nicolas Fouquet, however, had been bold enough to set up such workshops in Maincy, near Vaux-le-Vicomte, in 1658, having recruited craftsmen in Flanders. His Majesty must have eyed the workshops because in 1664 he had them merged by Colbert into those of the Gobelins.

This being the reign of absolutism, when all activities were concentrated and unified, the better to be controlled, the other tapestry workshops of the kingdom – Beauvais and La Savonnerie – were also moved to the banks of the Bièvre, where new buildings were erected to house them. Colbert also opened a school here, where all the future artisans of the Gobelins were trained or apprenticed. In 1667, cabinet-making was added to the activities of the Gobelins, which thus concentrated all the activities dedicated to the embellishment of the royal dwellings of France in '*La Manufacture royale des meubles de la Couronne ... à l'hôtel appelé des Gobelins', pour la gloire du roi*', as Colbert proclaimed. In 1667 too, a parliamentary ruling granted the Gobelins full monopoly over sales and all imports from abroad were banned. A director was appointed with sweeping powers to supervise the workshops' activities, the first of whom was the court painter, Charles Le Brun. He remained in office for nearly 30 years, with 250 craftsmen under his orders, tapestry-makers, painters, engravers, cabinet-makers, gold- and silversmiths. . . men, women and children, all living on the compound, so that their conduct could be controlled after working hours and moral disorder prevented. Sixty children went into a 10-year apprenticeship at the Gobelins before they qualified as tapestry-makers. The reign of absolutism was also a reign of prestige, and whereas Henri IV had been motivated by economics (hence the mulberry trees he had planted in the Tuileries gardens, in order to develop his own silk industry and dispense with imports from Milan), Louis XIV was driven by vanity and self-aggrandisement. He would come over in person to watch the progress of work. all of which was designed to ensure him glorious publicity. Thus, all the tapestries depicted either hunting scenes – the royal pastime *par excellence* – or the Sun King himself, sometimes in disguise. *L'Histoire du Roi* was the most prestigious series, to which Napoleon retaliated with *L'Histoire de l'Empereur*, commissioned from David.

With the death of Colbert in 1683 Charles Le Brun's career came to an end. Louvois, the King's new henchman, had his own protégé, the painter Mignard whom he wished to substitute for the ageing Le Brun (not that Mignard was much younger). Le Brun was aware of the manoeuvre and complained bitterly that he was no longer allowed to supervise the work at the Gobelins which was distributed and corrected by 'others', even in his presence, 'and I have been reduced to the rank of an ordinary workman.' Charles Le Brun was to die in 1690, a broken man. Things were never quite the same after his departure. Furthermore, with the resumption of wars, the state's finances were shaky and it was necessary to cut down costs. All the activities of the Gobelins ceased – a godsend for Faubourg Saint-Antoine where a golden age was now to commence. Tapestry-making, however, remained at the Gobelins, but that too was on the decline: whereas nearly 600 gold-embroidered tapestries were turned out during the 30 years of Le Brun's rule, fewer than 300 were made in the entire 18th century. With fewer orders coming from the royal court, it now became necessary to find new outlets abroad, which, rather belatedly, brought renown to the Gobelins outside France. The prestige of the Gobelins persisted through the generations and the Germans too commissioned works here when they occupied Paris during the last war. However, the workers put up patriotic resistance in their own way, slowing their activities to a near standstill and the Germans left before the orders had been completed.

During the French Revolution, the Gobelins workshops, the suppliers of luxury items to the privileged, aroused the wrath of the *sans-culottes* of Faubourg Saint-Marcel, who piled up all the tapestries at the foot of a tree of liberty they had erected in the courtyard and set fire to them. The furniture from the Gobelins was sent to the mint to retrieve its gold and silver. Nearly a century later, on 23 May 1871, the infuriated *Communards* also stormed this symbol of privilege and set fire to the workshops. Only the buildings along rue Berbier-du-Mets, the chapel, the entrance door and a few looms escaped the flames. The painter Courbet was called upon to restore the premises, and when a few months later activities resumed, the workshops were given the more appropriate name of Les Manufactures Nationales des Gobelins.

With the progress made in chemistry in the 19th century, 30,000 different shades could be obtained, which allowed for more variations and subtlety. On the other hand, the chemical dyes were less resistant to damage from light and air. Furthermore, the essence of the art of tapestry was now questioned. Charles Le Brun had argued that it should 'imitate the effect of oil painting', others that it was an art in its own right: 'To paint and to make tapestries are two absolutely separate things.' The issue was taken up again in the second half of the 19th century, and even more vigorously in the 20th: 'Tapestry is not a picture, big or small,' declared Le Corbusier. 'It must offer itself to the eye, level with the height of a man.' Jean Lurçat believed its role was to cover a bare wall which 'without this decoration would lack a *je-ne-sais-quoi* of the corporal, of the passionate, would, in sum, lack charm.' Lurçat, Le Corbusier, Matisse, Poliakoff and others tried their hand at tapestry, perpetuating an art which had survived from the Middle Ages, when the purpose of tapestry was to cover the bare walls of castles and help soften the atmosphere.

In 1990 the Gobelins workshops were to be transferred outside Paris as part of a nationwide policy of decentralisation, an arbitrary decision which was thwarted *in extremis* by the determined resistance of its workers and a general outcry. Admittedly, Paris plays an overbearing role culturally and economically, but moving the Gobelins out of their birthplace and natural environment would have been a historical outrage, particularly since these are the oldest workshops in France, the activities of which have never ceased since 1443, when a certain Jehan de Gobelin, '*teinturier en écarlate*' settled on the banks of the river Bièvre, in the house '*à l'enseigne du Cygne*'.

Turn left on Avenue des Gobelins and left once more into **BOULEVARD ARAGO**, a pleasant artery lined with shady chestnut trees. At no. 65 **La Cité Fleurie** is a stunning oasis, the jewel in the crown of the arrondissement, which narrowly escaped demolition thanks to the fighting spirit of its occupants and of neighbours. This artists' enclave was built in 1878, in the middle of what was then a wasteland, and was frequented at or just after the turn of the century by such artists as Rodin, Bourdelle, Maillol, Gauguin and Modigliani. Today's occupants may not have reached the same summits, but the place is delightful – a miniature village made up of 29 studios with their lovely little gardens, each the size of a pocket handkerchief.

Retrace your steps and turn right into rue de la Glacière and right again into **RUE LEON-MAURICE NORDMANN**. Behind a creaking old gate at no. 147 extends a leafy, picturesque alley, **La Cité Verte**, another artists' compound, where the bronze works of such artists as Lipchitz or Henry Moore were once cast by the sculptor Busato.

Back on rue de la Glacière, you can catch the no. 21 bus, heading south, and get off two stops later, at rue Daviel. Walk back on **RUE DAVIEL** across rue de la Glacière. You will come to two picturesque nooks: **La Petite Alsace** at no. 10, so called because of its half-timbered little houses with slanting tiled roofs, and **La Villa Daviel**, across the street, a humble working-class compound in the 19th century, now nestling charmingly in green vegetation in the midst of urban desolation.

Turn left into rue Barrault, then right into **RUE DE LA BUTTE-AUX-CAILLES**, which leads to the sleepy, little hill of the same name, once the home of quail and other species of fowl that people came to shoot here. On 21 November 1783, la Butte-aux-Cailles attracted widespread attention, when a gigantic, azure-coloured balloon appeared in the skies above, gloriously decorated with golden fleurs-de-lys and the signs of the Zodiac, leaving the inhabitants of Faubourg Saint-Marcel dumbfounded. Twenty minutes earlier members of the court and society, among them the Dauphin and Benjamin Franklin, had gathered at the Château de la Muette, on the western edge of Paris (now the 16th arrondissement), to watch the first manned balloon take off and soar into the sky, with Rozier de Pilâtre and the Marquis d'Arlandes aboard. When they landed, the delirious inhabitants of Saint-Marcel rushed at them and almost tore them apart in their enthusiasm! The two balloonists emerged unscathed in the end, although Rozier de Pilâtre's coat was torn beyond repair.

Turn left into **RUE DES CINQ DIAMANTS**, where you can get the feel of the neighbourhood. A young understated community of artists has taken up residence here, blending into the environment and preserving its character as best they can. To your left is the Passage Barrault, a narrow silent alley belonging to another age.

Turn right into rue Jonas and left into rue Gérard. You may

Rue des Cinq Diamants

wish to glance at a charming flowery house, draped with creepers, at nos 46–48, beyond rue Simonet.

Rue Simonet leads to the shady **PLACE PAUL VERLAINE**, a popular spot where the neighbourhood swimming pool, La Butte Aux Cailles, is situated. It is fed by the artesian well constructed by the physicist François Arago in 1865. The drilling was originally undertaken to increase the flow of the Bièvre and supply it with more water in case of drought. However, when drilling resumed 30 years later, a sheet of water of 28°C was reached providing an ideal temperature for bathing. The swimming pool was therefore built here in 1924 and is now a listed monument.

Continue into **RUE DU MOULIN DES PRES**, south of Place Paul Verlaine, once the old road that connected the windmill Le Moulin des Prés, and the village of Gentilly. Rue du Moulinet, running across rue du Moulin des Prés, refers to another of the area's windmills. Continue beyond rue de Tolbiac and turn right into **Square des Peupliers**, yet again a secret flowery enclave, so easily overlooked and therefore to be cherished. Back on rue du Moulin des Prés, continue diagonally right into rue des Peupliers then south to **PLACE DE L'ABBE GEORGES-HENOCQUE**, a shady, drowsy round-about, spared by modern times. Turn left into rue Henri Pape and walk along rue Dieulafoy and back again along rue du Docteur Leray, a countrified enclave of original architecture, displaying charming rows of houses crowned with steep slate roofs.

Back on Place de l'Abbé Georges-Henocque, take rue de la Colonie due west, then rue de Bobillot to your left to Place Rungis. A final remnant of a bucolic past – **La Cité Florale** – is tucked away west of Place Rungis, encompassed by rues Brillant-Savarin, Boussingault and Auguste Lançon. Here each tiny street bears, deservedly, the name of a flower – Iris, Volubilis (Morning Glory), Glycines (Wistaria), Mimosa – except for rue des Orchidées, which has been taken over by unsightly blocks of flats. La Cité Florale is within a few minutes' walk of the lovely Parc de Montsouris, but this is part of the story of the next arrondissement.

'CHINATOWN'

The Chinese neighbourhood of the 13th is basically a triangle, bounded by the Avenues de Choisy and Ivry and the Boulevard Masséna, lying to the south east of the arrondissement. It has therefore been dubbed le Triangle Jaune. This is by no means the Chinatown of San Francisco, nor even of New York, and only half its population is Asian. However, their presence becomes predominant on weekend mornings, when they do their weekly shopping.

Make your way from the junction of **AVENUES DE CHOISY** and **IVRY** into the latter and turn left into the **Olympiades** at no. 65, a pedestrian precinct of high-rise buildings, extending to rue de Tolbiac. You will notice the Oriental style of the roofs of the shops and restaurants and may understandably assume that they present an attempt to create local colour. Extraordinary as it may seem,

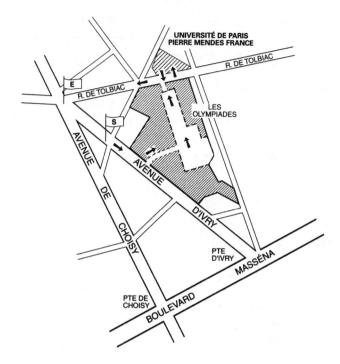

this exotic touch is purely coincidental, the complex having been completed in the early 1970s, before the arrival of the Asians, and was intended for French locals. This was when the 13th arrondissement, with an optimistic view to the future, was scattering high-rise complexes here and there, giving them such bombastic names as Olympiade, Galaxie and Super-Italie.

At no. 48 Avenue d'Ivry is the largest and most famous Asian supermarket, **Les Frères Tang**. The most prolific choice of exotic food in the capital is to be found here – from coconut milk to frozen eels, from canned bitter melons to a seemingly infinite variety of curry powders. Freshly arrived in France from Laos, the two brothers started their business in 1976 with one office and telephone. Today they are at the head of an empire that markets exotic food all over the Western world. Theirs is one of the more conspicuous success stories of the 13th arrondissement's Chinatown. There are other successful enterprises in the 13th arrondissement, such as *la tontine* – a family loan network which enables newcomers to have a start and makes local French people point an accusing finger at the invisible Chinese Mafia – but these operate behind closed doors, as do the numerous clandestine sweatshops that operate round the clock and are not accessible to the visitor.

Tang Frères supermarket has a car park for its customers, who come from all over the Paris area. Tucked away behind it is a Buddhist temple, from which emanates a sweet smell of incense. You are welcome to step inside, where you may find a serene worshipper, meditating or laying his offerings on one of the altars.

Quite a different atmosphere prevails opposite the Olympiade, on rue Tolbiac, where the **University of Paris I – Tolbiac** (specialising in law and economics) rises, a vertical structure of three superimposed glass blocks – rather an impersonal and uninviting environment for a place of learning. Like other recent buildings of the University of Paris, it does not contribute to creating a sense of community among its occupants, nor does it engender any respect for the premises. Shockingly ill-kept, they sadly demean the memory of the great statesman Pierre Mendès France, after whom the university has been named.

A meal in one of the Chinese restaurants is a self-evident conclusion to your visit. They are much cheaper than those of central Paris and the food can be just as good. What the atmosphere lacks in elegance, it gains in authenticity, often underlined by their gigantic dimensions (Chinatown Olympiades at 44 Avenue d'Ivry, for example, seats 600 and features an orchestra on Saturday nights).

LA SALPETRIERE

Lovers of 17th-century architecture may wish to visit La Salpêtrière, the largest hospital in Paris, sprawling on the north-eastern edge of the arrondissement. The main entrance is on **Square Marie-Curie**, on BOULEVARD DE L'HÔPITAL, adjacent to the Gare d'Austerlitz. Here stands a statue of Pinel, commemorating the 19th-century doctor who devoted his career to the relief of the mentally ill. The imposing façade of the institution ahead vividly recalls the façade of the Hôtel des Invalides, not surprisingly, since the two are roughly contemporary and were designed

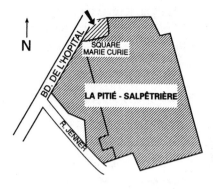

for a similar function, that is, to remove from the streets undesirable or cumbersome members of society and to intern them in a glorified setting as befitted the era of the Sun King. Homeless war veterans were shut up at the Invalides (1670) and all categories of paupers at the Hôpital Général (1657), which was made up of three sections, Bicêtre for males, La Pitié for boys and La Salpêtrière for women. Paris at the time numbered 400,000 inhabitants – 10 per cent of whom were homeless! As many as 10,000 were interned at La Salpêtrière alone, making it the largest hospice in the world!

Following the canons of the time, Louis Le Vau designed a compound in perfect geometric order around a square courtyard, La Cour Saint-Louis, endowing it with an austere façade in keeping with the nature of the institution. However, he was too busy with other ventures – the Louvre, Versailles, Vincennes – and had to pass on the torch to Duval and Le Muet, and it was Libéral Bruant, the architect of the Invalides, who was commissioned to build the institution's chapel in 1669 on the site of an earlier chapel dedicated to Saint Denis. At the entrance to the chapel is an elegant porch with three harmonious Ionic arcades, and a beautifully sculptured wooden portal, also dating from the 17th century. Inside the chapel a lantern-shaped dome surmounts a central octagonal rotunda where the high altar stands, the meeting-point of four austere equal-sized naves which make up the shape of a Greek cross. This design allowed the four groups of worshippers for whom the chapel was erected – men, women, boys, girls – to be seated apart yet close to the high altar – the demented, the feeble-minded, the homeless and the debauched – all of whom listened to the sermon and the Holy Scriptures read to them from the beautiful wrought-iron lectern that may still be seen at present. The chapel was in fact the keystone of the venture, which gave it moral and spiritual credibility, and it is not insignificant that the first chaplain of La Salpêtrière was no other than Saint Vincent de Paul, the most respected churchman of the 17th century, who had devoted his life to improving the lot of the poor and alleviating the pains of society's rejects (see also the 10th arr.).

Reality proved very different. La Cour Manon Lescaut, one of the hospital's courtyards, commemorates the tragic heroine of l'Abbé Prévost's novel who, like so many of her contemporaries, was locked up for debauchery in the prison section of La Salpêtrière before being deported to the 'islands'. Throughout the 18th century, La Salpêtrière remained the antechamber of deportation, helping France consolidate her grip on the newly acquired territories in Canada, Louisiana and the Caribbean Islands.

The mentally deranged had their own section in this purgatory, where they were chained to the cell walls, abandoned to their fate, bitten by rats, screaming out their agony. It was only in the early 19th century, at the instigation of Dr Pinel, that the approach to mental disease began to change. Friend of the *Encyclopédistes* and child of the 18th-century enlightenment, Dr Pinel did away with the chains, a revolutionary step and hitherto inconceivable. Pinel died in 1826 but he had shown the light to his followers and during the reign of Louis-Philippe the inmates' cells were also done away with – yet another revolution. In the second half of the 19th century, when Dr Charcot took over the department, La Salpêtrière became world famous as a psychiatric centre, and students came from all over Europe to listen to Charcot's lectures. Among them was a young student by the name of Sigmund Freud.

Today a cultural association, Les Amis de Saint-Louis, helps to promote the 17th-century chapel and bring it to the attention of the public by way of various activities. You may consider attending a chamber-music concert here on a Sunday afternoon.

THE 14TH ARRONDISSEMENT

MONTPARNASSE – a railway station, an unsightly high-rise, a sprawling stretch of drab, anarchical townplanning, whose undefined borders have enabled enterprising real-estate agents to extend its myth well into the 14th and even 15th arrondissements. The historical Montparnasse, however, the one where the myth was born, was no more than a street junction on the border of the 6th and the 14th arrondissements, the Carrefour Vavin, at Métro station Vavin, where the Boulevards du Montparnasse and Raspail meet.

In earlier times there was a mound of rubble on this site, the result of years of intensive extraction of stone from the area's quarries, with which a good part of Paris was built. Poetry-loving students liked to come here from the nearby Latin Quarter to recite their favourite poems or romp about. They nicknamed the mound *Mont Parnasse* in honour of the celebrated abode of the Muses in Greek mythology. In the early 18th century Louis XIV planned to complete the Grands Boulevards, the semicircular promenade that bordered Paris to the north, and extend it to the Left Bank, where it became known as the Boulevards du Midi (south). The scheme was only carried out in 1760, however, at which point the poetic mound was levelled and the muses forsaken for the next 150 years. During that period the area changed little. Because of their tutelage to Rome, the abbeys of Saint-Germain-des-Prés and Sainte-Geneviève had maintained their independence from the central royal authorities and prospered on their extensive fertile grounds south of the Seine. The city, therefore, developed to the north and it was only after its annexation to Paris in 1860 that the new 14th arrondissement began to take part, timidly, in the urban development of Paris.

The semi-rural atmosphere and the fresh air attracted artists, and Balzac, who lived on the site of the present no. 1 rue Cassini between 1829 and 1834, praised the quality of the area's cherries. Likewise, Chateaubriand stayed at no. 88 rue d'Enfer (now Avenue Denfert-Rochereau) in 1826, and described the house at length in his *Mémoires d'outre tombe*. The Passage des Arts, opened in 1839 at

Plaisance, and rue des Artistes, opened in 1853 near Parc de Mont-souris, also point to the early presence of artists in the 14th. Sculpture, a more prestigious form of art than painting in the 19th century, was particularly in demand when the fashionable cemetery of the south, le Cimetière du Montparnasse, was opened in 1824. Many sculptors, among them François Rude, Jean-Baptiste Carpeaux and Antoine Bourdelle, came to live here and flatter the vanity of their fellow mortals by providing them with flamboyant sepulchres.

The area was largely covered with cornfields, fruit orchards, vineyards and kitchen gardens. Before 1850 a few windmills still stood out against the horizon. Milk, butter, cheese and eggs could be bought directly at one of the local dairy farms. A local goatherd could even be seen milking his goats at his customers' doorsteps, while wine was bought in casks from the wine grower. This semi-rural life, with street vendors crying out their wares, colourful markets, a weekly bird-market at Place Denfert-Rochereau, annual fairs, street organs and street performers, was punctuated by the sound of church bells, for the better part of the neighbourhood was the property of religious orders whose beautiful grounds and the fragrance of their vegetation enhanced the appeal of the area to artists and writers.

The availability of vacant sites, where vehicles could be stored and horses stabled, also attracted the more pragmatically-minded transport companies. Trades and workshops connected with transportation sprang up and coachmen would be seen in the streets as often as nuns. However, the automobile soon rendered the horses superfluous. On 23 August 1902, the last horse-drawn omnibus was seen on the Champs-Elysées, plying between Porte Maillot and the Hôtel-de-Ville. Little by little the stables were vacated – a godsend for the artist community who promptly converted them into studios.

When, at the dawn of the 20th century, André Salmon and Paul Fort launched their literary magazine *Vers et Prose* and urged the world intelligentsia to join them in Montparnasse and turn it into an international centre of the arts, they were not particular about historical accuracy and set up their headquarters east of the original Montparnasse site, at La Closerie des Lilas, a café situated on the 6th-arrondissement side of the Observatoire crossroads.

Meanwhile, the 14th had entered the 20th century. The city was gnawing into the countryside, transforming it into a building-site. Bricklayers, plasterers and house painters filled the local bistrots and, together with the ever-growing influx of artists, added colour to the heterogeneous clientele. On 10 July 1913 the section of the Boulevard Raspail between rue de Vaugirard and Boulevard du Montparnasse was at long last completed and inaugurated by the President of the Republic, Raymond Poincaré, a workaholic who took the opportunity to express his disapproval of the slow progress of the roadworks. No sooner was it inaugurated than the wealthy Hélène, the Russian Baroness of Oettingen, and her half-brother, Serge Férat, moved to no. 278 Boulevard Raspail. These two lovers of the arts and supporters of the avant-garde literary review *Soirées de Paris*, threw open the doors of their new home to the neighbourhood's artists, whether *Fauves*, *Cubistes* or *Futuristes*, and lavished their Russian largesse on them. 'Most of those who have made or will make a name in painting, poetry, modern music, frequent this place,' commented Apollinaire. Among them were Picasso, Max Jacob, Archipenko, Zadkin, Modigliani and Kisling. When it was time to leave, the guests would retire to the new cafés on Carrefour Vavin and carry on their heated conversations into the early hours of the morning. After 150 years the Muses were back at Mont Parnasse.

All this happened in good time to accommodate the human tide that was streaming from far and near into this Promised Land of freedom of expression. No wonder so many of them were destitute Jews fleeing either persecution in Eastern Europe or the smothering restrictions of a fossilised ghetto life. And no wonder they took up residence in the cafés of Carrefour Vavin, where they found shelter, heating and electricity and a cup of *café crème* that could be bought on credit, or perhaps exchanged for a painting. Here they found a secure haven, surrounded by a cosmopolitan collection of outsiders like themselves and all of them too absorbed in artistic creation to bother about social or racial idiosyncrasies. Western Europeans – Germans, Scandinavians and English – mostly went unnoticed (though Zadkine did refer to the 'English Quarter'), except on the occasion of Mrs Pankhurst's visit to Montparnasse, when they gave the celebrated suffragette a rowdy welcome. There were also newcomers from Central and South America, even from Japan.

But predominantly they came from Eastern Europe – Russia, Poland, Lithuania, Romania – Jewish, more often than not. Those who would eventually 'make it' in Paris – Chagall, Soutine, Kisling or Zadkine, to name but a few – came to be known as *l'Ecole de Paris* – not a very appropriate name for a highly individualistic band of artists who shared a common destiny and a common lifestyle by force of circumstances, rather than a common concept or form of art. They were joined by their fellow-Jew Modigliani, an Italian, who, together with Picasso, Apollinaire and other friends from the artists' quarters of Bateau-Lavoir, had descended the slopes of Montmartre – by now too touristy and commercial for their taste – crossed the Seine and taken up residence in the 14th arrondissement, in search of authenticity. Max Jacob did not share their enthusiasm for the new mecca and scribbled on the wall of his Montmartre room '*ne pas aller à Montparnasse*'; he was nonetheless very often seen there in the company of friends, unable to resist the lure. As a newly-converted Roman Catholic, however, he would afterwards go to confession. Guillaume Apollinaire had no illusions about the durability of the area's atmosphere and predicted that the days of Montparnasse would be over 'when Thomas Cook comes along with his caravans'.

Russia's conspiring revolutionaries too set up their headquarters in the 14th arrondissement. They too needed cheap lodgings and there were plenty of small printing-houses around for their revolutionary press. Besides, nobody bothered them in the cafés of free-for-all Montparnasse. Trotsky was a regular at la Rotonde, across the Boulevard, in the 6th, where he struck up friendship with Diego Rivera, thanks to whom he moved to Mexico when exiled by Stalin. Rivera's gigantic murals in Mexico City, representing the Mexican people's fight for freedom, were tinged by their friendship. Lenin, however, was seen in the cafés less often than legend has it – he was too busy researching at the Bibliothèque Nationale and preparing the new destiny of his homeland to hang around in the cafés of Carrefour Vavin. His main distraction was a game of chess with his mother-in-law in the tiny two-room flat she shared with him and with his wife at 4 rue Marie-Rose, now a museum (by appointment only. Call 01 42 79 99 58)

World War I interrupted the show – there were no more gatherings in the home of Hélène d'Oettingen and Serge Férat and no more fancy-dress balls at Kees Van Dongen's place on Avenue Denfert-Rochereau. Fujita was no longer seen wearing his Greek-style, hand-woven tunic with which he hoped to conjure up images of ancient Greece, nor Max Jacob in his morning coat (a present from his tailor brother in Quimper), bowler hat and monocle. The café terraces were deserted.

Yet the war had begun in frenzied jubilation. Filled with patriotism, the entire population of the 14th arrondissement had streamed into the streets and the artists, in particular, had packed into Carrefour Vavin. The euphoria reached fever pitch on 2 August 1914, when the troops, glittering in their dashing uniforms and plumed helmets, and elated by the fulsomeness of their welcome, paraded through the Boulevard du Montparnasse, heading for the Gare de l'Est and a four-year inferno. Within a matter of days, the enthusiasm had abated and the people had trudged back home. Night after night the arrondissement was plunged into pitch darkness and eerie silence prevailed. Even rue de la Gaîté suspended its activities. This street, devoted, as its name suggests, to merry-making, had been the arrondissement's centre of entertainment since the beginning of the 19th century. Until World War I it was even known as rue de la Joie. There were expensive restaurants and cheap *guinguettes*; the flow of wine; the smell of mussels, potato chips and waffles, even the smell of cooking inside the theatres and music-halls, where the working-class spectators did their own cooking while waiting for the show to begin. This did not prevent the bourgeois from rubbing shoulders with them, especially at weekends, when everything was packed full.

This was also a street of vice. With the opening of the Gare du Montparnasse, many a wretched girl, driven out of Brittany by poverty, was beguiled into worse misery by such pimps as the main character of Charles-Louis Philippe's novel *Bubu de Montparnasse*. For the Montparnasse railway station was, and still is, the gateway to Brittany, hence the numerous fish restaurants and *crêperies* in the 14th arrondissement.

But now that war had broken out the music-halls and theatres had closed down and the streetwalkers slackened their pace. The streets were empty, the men had gone to the front. The international community of Montparnasse had embraced the French cause and was also drafted. The German colony had packed up and discreetly cleared out of the Dôme. Only vagabonds and unfit artists such as Soutine, wrecked by poverty, and Modigliani, ravaged by tuberculosis, alcohol and drugs, had remained behind, often ashamed to be seen in public. It soon became clear that the war was not going to be a walkover. By December rue de la Gaîté had settled down for a long conflict and decided it might just as well resume the revelling – a judicious decision for the soldiers on leave. Winters were harsh. The occupants of converted stables and other makeshift shacks suffered horrendously from the cold (–9°C in 1917). Old people and young children died of cold and hunger, among them Diego Rivera's son. Fujita's first wife, Fernande, remembered how she had burnt several of Modigliani's paintings in order to keep the fire going. On 23 March 1918 Big Bertha went into action. Between March and August her wayward shells hit Paris blindly, causing the deaths of 256 Parisians. The 14th arrondissement was her target several times, in particular on 11 April, when a shell hit the well-known maternity hospital Baudeloque on Boulevard du Port-Royal, killing 20 mothers, babies and midwives.

With peace restored the frantic show resumed with an explosion of activity never witnessed before. Montparnasse, heedless of darker days to come, entered those roaring years, that crazy decade of self-delusion, with a determination to have a wild time. Fernand Léger, a contemporary of that decade, perceived and grasped this state of mind: 'Man, exasperated, tense, immobilised for four years, can lift his head at last, open his eyes, relax, regain his taste for life. Wild, dancing, spending, frantic that he can now, at last, walk straight, shout, scream, waste.'

At night, while the genuine 14th frequented rue de la Gaîté and its traditional French places of pleasure, such as the Théâtre du Montparnasse and the Bobino music-hall, the sophisticated set vibrated to the sound of new rhythms – foxtrot, Charleston and later jazz. There were new establishments in the vicinity of Carrefour Vavin, but it was the Jockey, which opened in 1923 at the corner of rue de Chevreuse and Boulevard du Montparnasse (in the 6th arr.) that stole the show. There was nothing glamorous about its cramped premises, a Wild West saloon of sorts, with figures of cowboys and Redskins on the front, yet wealthy, trendy Right Bank bourgeois squeezed up against local bohemians in an attempt to dance to the music of an ex-cowboy pianist, two guitarists from Hawaii or simply a phonograph. There were no social barriers here and no affectation. Cocteau, Kisling, Pascin, Hemingway, Fitzgerald. . . all the celebrities of Montparnasse frequented the Jockey. Twice a night a bob-headed brunette, known as Kiki, would electrify the assembly with her black hose and garters, her stentorian, husky voice and her saucy songs.

Montparnasse even boasted the first institutionalised bordello on the Left Bank, the Sphinx on Boulevard Edgar-Quinet. In luxury it was a match for the Chabanais in the 2nd arrondissement, the mecca of the crowns of Europe and heads of state. The girls at the Sphinx were selected by the Madam, Marthe ('Martoune') Lemestre, at the Folies-Bergère and enjoyed excellent working conditions and social privileges, notably an annual three-week holiday on the French Riviera. For this was a progressive establishment with liberal views. Kisling came here to look for models and left his pictures on the walls, a gift to the place that had taken care of the *artistes* of Montparnasse. With its lavish setting, muted atmosphere, gorgeous girls and exquisite champagne, the Sphinx was so in vogue that during the 1937 World Fair it welcomed as many as 1,500 clients, among them quite a number of couples. However, in 1946 all the bordellos (*maisons closes*) of France were closed down by law.

La Coupole was to prove a less ephemeral enterprise. Its inauguration ceremony took place on 20 December 1927 amidst heavy drinking (the date of the 20th is said to have been chosen for the pun on *vingt* and *vin*, and because the figure 20, so they claimed, 'dispelled all melancholy'). The art critic André Warnod recalled how he had returned home on all fours to avoid tottering on the slippery ice. . . For some reason La Coupole was to overshadow the neighbouring cafés of Carrefour Vavin and has remained the tourists' mecca to this day. The founders of La Coupole, René Lafon and Ernest Fraux, started the new establishment as an act of revenge and defiance against the Dôme from where they had been fired. Determined to outdo their next-door rival by hook or by crook, they went all out to create something colossal. Supported by 32 columns 5 metres high, furnished with hundreds of metres of tables and benches, La Coupole employed 450 people – among them doormen in dashing garnet-coloured uniforms – and seated 600, which made it the largest eating-place in France. A huge restaurant with an open ceiling provided an extra attraction in warm weather and there was also a dance-hall with a full-size orchestra. The famous Art Deco glass cupola had nothing to do with the name, which was inspired by the neighbouring Dôme and Rotonde. The cupola was added only four years later and in any case soon disappeared behind plaster. Every 'Montparnos' frequented La Coupole – Picasso, Chagall, Soutine, Man Ray, Josephine Baker. . . to debate or meditate, and especially to see and to be seen in the most extravagant attire on this focal stage of the Crazy Years. Thus, no sooner had he arrived in Paris than Charlie Chaplin rushed over to La Coupole. And if Salvador Dali defined Montparnasse as 'the navel of the world', La Coupole was unquestionably the navel of Montparnasse. At present La Coupole is surmounted by a block of offices. The murals of Othon Friesz and Fernand Léger have been cleaned up and even the Art Deco *cupola* has been stripped of the plaster and revealed to view. It is now part of the Flo chain and serves the same mass-produced menus as its other sister *brasseries*. Although it is still packed out, the magic spell is broken and it is questionable whether an Orson Welles would still appreciate it. Today people go to La Coupole to eat, hundreds of mouths munching away in an eternal hubbub.

Some of the old-timers did not join in the festivities of the Twenties. Guillaume Apollinaire, who had recovered form his wounds at Verdun, succumbed instead to the Spanish influenza, together with 20 million other fellow Europeans. Ironically, he was buried on 11 November, while Paris was celebrating the Armistice. Modigliani passed away a year later, on 24 January 1920, followed by his companion Jeanne Hébuterne, who, in her sorrow, threw herself out of the window of their room while pregnant with their second child. Red Russians had also disappeared from the scene, having returned to their motherland to build a new society. Their place was taken by White Russians and another wave of Russian Jews. The German colony made a discreet comeback and resumed their seats at the Dôme as inconspicuously as they had vacated them four years earlier. The German art dealer Kahnweiler was also back, having spent the war in Switzerland, and tried to reassemble his old artists and to save from the wreckage whatever paintings he could. Once more foreigners from all corners of the world congregated in Montparnasse, and now there were many more of them. Exasperated at their presence, the artist Guy Arnoux stuck a French flag over the door of his studio on rue Huyghens and a plaque reading *Consulat de France*.

The lead role this time went to the United States of America, whose children strode in with flying colours. While Europe was in a shambles, the United States asserted itself as the predominant power of the world. Some of its wealthy nationals, such as the golden couple the Fitzgeralds, came over ready to paint the town red. However, the discerning pair chose to stay at the Ritz and came down to Montparnasse only for the fun. The less rich, such as Hemingway and Dos Passos, also had their fling. With the franc down and the dollar up they had never had it so good. Besides, there was no Prohibition in Paris!

This 'lost Generation', disorientated by an absurd war and a world that had lost its meaning, hoped to find solace in decadent Paris, away from the rigid code of behaviour of puritanical America. Nowhere could they find the same degree of freedom as in Montparnasse. Outside this unique pocket of bohemian extravagance, French social life was just as regimented – albeit by a somewhat different code of behaviour – but the expatriates knew and cared little about mainstream French life. Although France could boast as many as 80 feminist associations after the War, Victor Marguerite caused no small scandal when his novel *La Garçonne*, the story of a single mother of perfect moral integrity, was published in 1922 and he was stripped of his *Légion d'honneur*. America's Protestant expatriates did not see this side of France, and, like the Jamesian hero, Strather, a generation earlier, believed that in this sensual, Roman Catholic society they could give themselves over to pleasure with no sense of guilt or sin. Woman was instrumental in this quest, as expressed in Man Ray's photograph of the woman-cello, and Alice Prin, Man Ray's mistress and better known as Kiki, embodied this female ideal.

After running away from her bakery apprenticeship when she was only 14, she drifted into nude modelling (to the horror of her mother), alcohol and cocaine. One winter night during the War, shivering with cold and with nowhere to sleep, she fetched up with a girlfriend at the wretched artists' quarters of La Ruche, deep in the 15th arrondissement. Soutine offered them his hospitality at 2 am and virtually burnt every inflammable item in his possession to keep them warm. Ever since that day Kiki claimed to have had a crush on Soutine. Fujita experienced similar heroic generosity on the part of Fernande on his first visit to her, on a bitingly cold night during the War. In this case it was a genuine Louis XV chair, a gift from her father, that ended in the flames. Fujita was to marry the kind-hearted Fernande a couple of months later. When Kiki died at the age of 50, an alcoholic and a drug addict, abandoned by her former friends who had become rich and famous, Fujita was the only one to accompany her on her last journey to the poor people's cemetery of Thiais. Nonetheless, several wreaths were deposited on her grave, each bearing the name of one of Montparnasse's cafés – her 'family' paying her their last tribute.

In her heyday the fiery Kiki, everybody's model and at some time everybody's mistress, was the Queen of Montparnasse. She was that archetypal woman, sexually free, yet full of mystery, offering herself with childish ingenuousness, yet forever elusive. Man Ray won her heart while they were out at the pictures. A long-lasting love affair ensued, full of drama and volcanic passion – even pistol shots – as befitted Montparnasse. Man Ray immortalised her in *L'Etoile de Mer*, the first surrealist film, where she is seen with a rose between her teeth, and 300,000 copies have been made of the photograph taken from the film. Back in New York he had become acquainted with the Dadaists – Picabia and Marcel Duchamp – and he arrived in Montparnasse on 14 July 1921 to join their movement, the only American to do so. In their derisive, provocative, anarchical way, the Dadaists too were trying to cope with a shattered world. By adding a moustache to the delicate face of the Mona Lisa or exhibiting a toilet seat, or a urinal under the title *Fountain*, Marcel Duchamp wanted to shock the bourgeois and pull the rug from under the hordes of pretentious poseurs who purported to support the arts. Man Ray, once settled in Montparnasse, set out to photograph all its celebrities. In his tiny premises on rue Delambre, behind the Dôme – a single room which served as living quarters, studio and dark room – they posed for posterity and immortalised in black and white the golden days of Montparnasse – while Kiki, stretched on Man Ray's bed, waited for them to leave, impatient to be left alone with her lover.

Whereas pre-war days had been times of struggle and of genuine creativeness, post-war Montparnasse turned art and pleasure into an industry. In this the naive tourist was much to blame, raising the bids on questionable 'modern' art, and playing into the hands of shrewd profiteers. '. . . Butterflies from the world over . . . beating against its [Montparnasse] window panes in search of a flicker of genius', unaware that real genius had meanwhile migrated elsewhere – Picasso to the bourgeois rue de la Boétie in the 8th, Chagall to the residential Passy in the 16th, Fujita to a *hôtel particulier*. Matisse and Soutine had left Paris altogether and settled in the sunny south. . .

But another creative movement emerged in Montparnasse, bringing about a revolution in the arts. In 1924 André Breton, a close friend of Marcel Duchamp and a Dadaist himself, founded the Surrealist movement and produced its first official publication, *Littérature*, in collaboration with Philippe Soupault and Louis Aragon. The other members of the literary branch of the movement, among them Jacques Prévert and Robert Desnos, had their phalanstery at 54 rue du Château, a seedy, rundown part of the 14th, by then no longer the countrified neighbourhood where Le Douanier Rousseau, in order to make ends meet, taught *solfège* and drawing to the children of its concierges and shopkeepers. The premises themselves were actually comfortable and pleasant, almost elegant, thanks to the private income of one of the members, Marcel Duhamel. The surrealists spent their time here eating and drinking, reading and composing poetry, listening to jazz and making love. The girls were picked up among the admirers of the movement on the terraces of Montparnasse, but the scandalised, *petit bourgeois* neighbours earnestly believed that the place was a brothel.

Like their Dada predecessors, the Surrealists reacted to an ailing age. Max Ernst, Juan Mirò, Salvador Dali participated in the movement and, under the influence of Freud, tried to enter the realm of dreams and the unconscious. (Like Breton they wanted to find the beauty hidden beyond reality and to reconcile reality and dreams.) To achieve this they experimented with different odds and ends, substituting hair combs and bits of string and straw for paintbrushes. In between times they experimented in automatic writing which was supposed to replace conscious reflection even in one's sleep, and were amazed when the poet Robert Desnos would fail to be woken during those sessions. . . However, in 1945, when Desnos was lying on his deathbed, sapped by typhus in Theresienstad concentration camp, on the eve of its liberation by the Americans, he revealed that he had been cheating all along.

André Breton was notorious for his dogmatic politics and violent behaviour and became 'the terror of Montparnase'. He abhorred the place and generally stuck to his home on rue Fontaine in the 9th arrondissement, at the foot of Montmartre (although he did move to 33 rue Delambre in 1921, for a year). When the cabaret Le Maldoror opened on Boulevard Edgar-Quinet, using the title of Lautréamont's venerated work as its name, a sacrilege in the ghastly environment of Montparnasse, Breton felt himself justified in storming the cabaret with his disciples, who wrecked the premises before the police could be called. 'Anti'- everything and intolerant of anyone who did not fall into line with his own convictions, he did not hesitate to sabotage the work of his own friends, especially the painters, who, being less dogmatic and more independent-minded than the literary set, were more likely to be 'excommunicated' by him. Thus Juan Mirò and Max Ernst aroused his anger by doing the sets for Diaghilev's *Romeo and Juliet* – a capitalistic enterprise. Again he called on his followers to wreak havoc during the performance. The group was eventually expelled from the theatre and on their way out were successively punched, one by one, by Boris Koshno, Diaghilev's secretary. André Breton spent so much energy picking fights, falling out with friends and 'excommunicating' members from the movement that by the end of the decade the split was inevitable. In 1991, 87-year-old Naville, the last surviving Surrealist, recalled how back in 1928 Breton had called him 'a boa-constrictor' and 'an eminent reptile' because he did not share Breton's political views. The Chilean architect and painter Matta recalled having been excluded from the movement because of his love of mathematics, while Dali was excluded for having described Hitler as 'an erotic hermaphrodite'. . .

For the American colony, this fool's paradise was to end on 24 October 1929, when Wall Street crashed. Bank cheques could no longer be expected to arrive and US nationals had no alternative but to pack up and return home. The economic crisis in France did not start until 1932, and even though people could no longer afford the follies of the Twenties, the terraces of Carrefour Vavin remained crowded until the declaration of war on 3 September 1939. A new couple was emerging, at the Dôme this time, Jean-Paul Sartre and Simone de Beauvoir. In *La Force de l'Age* de Beauvoir wrote, referring to the Dôme, 'I have the sense of being part of a family and that protects me against depression.' Its three separate halls were now divided up among three different communities – Europeans, Americans and French. The terrace, however, was shared by *les Dômiens*, which included everyone. Among the Europeans the German community was pretty conspicuous. The German forces of occupation followed from 1940 on, and as a result Simone de Beauvoir left. With Sartre taken prisoner in Germany, she found she could no longer bear the place: 'The Dôme is noisy; lots of uniforms.' Besides, the Vavin Métro station closed down and remained so for the duration of the war. Moving a few stations further north on the Clignancourt-Orléans line, she landed with some friends at Place Saint-Germain-des-Prés and there inaugurated a new era. The days of Montparnasse were over.

History, however, never comes to a standstill and in the 1960s a different Montparnasse emerged further west. Practical-minded France, impatient to enjoy the new prosperity, was aware of the economic potential of the neighbourhood, thanks to its railway station that could link Paris with the south-west and open new horizons. Leaving nostalgia to sentimentalists, the authorities did away with the inadequate 19th-century provincial station that led nowhere except to Brittany, an economic backwater. A new station replaced it, turning Montparnasse into the gateway to the entire west and south-west and, beyond the national border, to Spain. Before long, bulldozers and drills started to extirpate seedy Montparnasse, levelling Henry Miller's *quartier louche*, working relentlessly and without respite, until 2 am sometimes, according to exhausted neighbours. Crumbling houses gave way to the third largest shopping centre in the capital, which has since cluttered the skyline and the neighbourhood. Since the motive was profit, environmental and aesthetic issues could not be taken into consideration.

Originally a beautiful spacious garden was planned above the station, but the addition of a large car park made this technically impracticable and some scanty vegetation is all that grows amidst this concrete jungle. However, the poetic name of the garden – Le Jardin de l'Atlantique (see also the 15th arr.) – has been preserved: Parisians have been trained in recent times to content themselves with symbolic names, surreal reminders of a lost countryside. Thus, the visitor to the Domaine de l'Océan has to summon up an ocean of imagination and goodwill in order to be spiritually transported to the shores of Brittany, Vendée or the Pays Basque and ignore the hideous high-rises all around.

Meanwhile the TGV train arrived here in 1990, necessitating a new station, the second one having become obsolete in turn. By 1995 it was used annually by over 50 million passengers. With Nantes at a mere two hours' distance from Montparnasse and Bordeaux only three, there was much business in prospect; building companies (unaware of the imminent recession) rubbed their hands, riding roughshod over the protestations of the local people and provided Montparnasse with 50,000 m² of office space. With a 21st-century major railway station slapped down in the neighbourhood, there was no way the village atmosphere of Montparnasse could be preserved. With all due respect to Henry Miller's affection for the old place, and particularly to the longer-standing residents who have been evicted from their homes, it must be admitted that many of these buildings were derelict beyond restoration. What is less forgivable is the fact that, for the umpteenth time, contemporary Paris has failed to ally technological progress with aesthetics and has permitted such an incoherent architectural mess to come into existence.

Fortunately, the 14th arrondissement extends way beyond the vicinity of the station and is, in fact, one of the more pleasant arrondissements to live in. With a combination of open-air markets, squares and gardens where old and young converge, it takes pride in its homely, unfussy atmosphere, prized by environmentalists and artists. Furthermore, the Cité Universitaire, the university's halls of residence at the southern edge of the arrondissement, and the proximity of the Latin Quarter to the north, account for the presence of students, academics, intellectuals and professionals. No wonder the 14th shelters a good number of associations concerned with social welfare, conservation and human rights, notably Amnesty International; and no wonder so many ex-students from the 1968 generation, known as *soixante-huitards*, came over to the 14th to start their new families.

Contemporary Montparnasse, a jumble of drab concrete, is of little interest to the pedestrian. Even Boulevard du Montparnasse, once the headquarters of the artist community, is now just an ordinary commercial artery. On the other hand, the out-of-the-way nooks where they lived and worked, away from the publicity and din of Carrefour Vavin, have largely been preserved and make for lovely strolls.

FROM 'CARREFOUR VAVIN' (PLACE PABLO-PICASSO) TO RUE DAGUERRE

Our first walk, in the north-western part of the arrondissement, starts at Carrefour Vavin, the cradle of Montparnasse, now renamed **PLACE PABLO-PICASSO**. Try to come here early on a sunny Saturday morning so as to include both the markets of Boulevard Edgar-Quinet and rue Daguerre in your outing, but first sit down for a hot *croissant beurre* and *café crème* breakfast on the sunny terrace of La Rotonde (in the 6th arr.), to soak up the subdued atmosphere of Paris as it awakes for yet another busy day. You can meanwhile recapture the feel of Montparnasse in its heyday, since all four strongholds of Carrefour Vavin are still there – **La Rotonde**, **Le Sélect** on your right (in the 6th), **Le Dôme** and **La Coupole** across the street (in the 14th). Of course today's Le Dôme – a good fish restaurant, with daily fresh supplies from Brittany – bears only a faint resemblance to the small establishment frequented by the expatriates in the 1920s, even less to the scruffy joint it was before World War I. Then it did not have a terrace, a point that was immaterial to its clientele of bricklayers and other workmen, who liked a game at the billiards table. The early artist community of Montparnasse had no use for terraces either – it was the heated

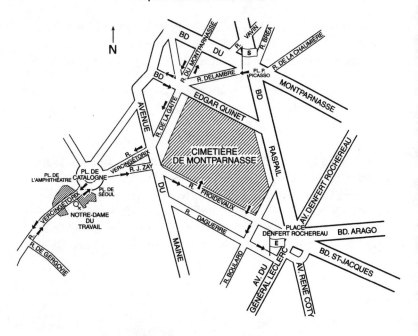

premises they were after and, having not a penny to their names, they often left unpaid bills or, like Kisling, bartered a painting for a drink. Only in 1923, when the Dôme was entirely renovated, was its celebrated terrace added, making it the most popular café in Montparnasse, albeit still primarily among those living on a shoestring, who could just about afford a *café crème* and a *sandwich*. The present upmarket Dôme has done away with its *tabac* and has shifted its main entrance from the side street, rue Delambre, to the Boulevard and has a lush display of oysters on the pavement. Inside, the Art Deco setting designed by Slavick creates a warm, comfortable atmosphere. The old photos of the Dôme's celebrated patrons that now decorate its walls are all that is left of its legendary past.

RUE DELAMBRE, where the entrance of the run-down Dôme stood, is our next destination. The modern Dôme has actually spilt into rue Delambre with its smart fish shop and an additional bistrot across the street. At one time or another, several artists lived in the street. Tsuguhara Fujita, newly married to Fernande Barrey, had his first studio at no. 5 where he installed a bathtub with hot running water and was taken for a tycoon (electricity was not in common use in Paris before 1920). Modigliani too owned a bath-tub, and his was made of zinc! Many models came over to Fujita to enjoy this luxury free of charge, among them liberated Kiki who, ignoring the neighbourhood's moral scruples, used to pose for him in the nude *and* in the courtyard.

Isadora Duncan stayed for a while at the apartment hotel at no. 9, next door to the Parnasse Bar at no. 9bis, which was packed at busy periods and remained open throughout the night. Opposite, at no. 10, the tiny Dingo Bar was the celebrated hang-out of expatriates and the place where Ernest Hemingway, still an unpublished writer, first met the already established Scott Fitzgerald in 1925. Jimmy Charter, the English barman and a former lightweight boxer, was largely responsible for the success of the establishment, as he knew how to look after his English-speaking customers and they followed him from bar to bar. When he decided to cross the street and work for the Parnasse Bar, it is claimed that the receipts of his new employers rose sixfold! Man Ray had his first studio at l'Hôtel des Ecoles at no. 15, now the well-known Lenox, to which he moved in 1921, when his friend the Dadaist Marcel Duchamp left for New York. This is where his career as a photographer began, and where James Joyce, Gertrude Stein, Jean Cocteau and the others filed in and posed for eternity in black and white.

But rue Delambre was also French, and specifically Breton, being so close to the Gare du Montparnasse that linked Paris and Brittany; and while the expatriates' presence was ephemeral, the Breton community has maintained its roots here for over a century. At no. 22, for example, is the Breton Mission where one can learn the Breton language and history, as well as dances and songs. One Sunday a month its members rally for the *fest-deiz* (feast of the day), asserting their ties with the beautiful western province. The Ti-Jos ('*Maison Joseph*' in Breton) restaurant and *crêperie*, at no. 30, has a pub in the basement, where they serve cider and beer. On Thursday nights Celtic music is also on the agenda, though usually Irish!

The presence of Bretons is even more conspicuous on **RUE DU MONTPARNASSE** to your right, which is lined with picturesque *crêperies*. The street also has a home for elderly artists, at no. 55/57. It is run by the city of Paris. Its residents are provided with studios

Rue du Montparnasse

and an art gallery where their works are exhibited alongside those of younger fellow-artists – a happy initiative, in the right place. At no. 42 **the Falstaff** has survived in the Breton heartland and has preserved its original oak panelling, a rare vestige of old Montparnasse, although today it is just an ordinary beer bar/restaurant. When 'Jimmy the Barman' left the Dingo Bar for the Falstaff in the late Twenties, his faithful Anglo-Saxon customers followed him, Hemingway and Fitzgerald in the lead. Jimmy was a good listener, had good tips on horse racing and knew how to smooth things out. When one night the six-foot Swede Jorgenson came over to the Falstaff to beat up writer and publisher Robert McAlmon with whom he had picked a quarrel at the Dingo the night before, it was Jimmy's soft talk that got the towering troublemaker to leave quietly. Both Jimmy and the customers liked the refined atmosphere, which contrasted with the other haunts where there was more fun and action, but where there was also more noise and drunkenness: not that one did not drink at the Falstaff, but here it was serious, heavy drinking. Jimmy ruled that every tenth drink would be on the house, which seemed to satisfy everyone. As before, he was responsible for the success of the Falstaff, while its two happy Belgian owners shared the receipts, and also the same mistress!

Retrace your steps and continue into **BOULEVARD EDGAR-QUINET** for a stroll through the colourful market stalls. Before World War I the market was a spectacle worthy of a medieval street scene or a René Clair movie: there were sword-swallowers, fire-eaters, dog-trainers, and carousels whirling to the music of a street organ. The cries of street vendors mingled with the tunes played by the band, and street singers would strike up a popular refrain and the crowds would join in. From time to time a drove of goats or donkeys passed by on its way to the Jardin du Luxembourg. The present market has enticing food displays and bright flowers, but it is somewhat pale in comparison with its former self.

The prestigious Sphinx, the only bordello on the Left Bank, was located at no. 31. Having been semi-rural at least until the Great War, the area lagged behind the Right Bank in matters of prostitution too, although the opening of the railway station of Montparnasse in 1840 secured a constant flow of girls from poverty-stricken Brittany, anxious to learn and ply the trade for a puny fee. But with the explosion of Montparnasse in the Twenties there was also demand for high-class, exclusive prostitution, supplied by the Sphinx. The opening of the Sphinx was marked with great pomp, invitations having been sent to all and sundry, singles and couples alike, and everyone was offered champagne as well as a guided tour of the chromium-plated, air-conditioned premises – a total novelty – and its magnificent Art Deco bar, a match for the hitherto unrivalled bar of La Coupole.

The **Cemetery of Montparnasse** extends south of Boulevard Edgar-Quinet, the site of the toll-wall and of the southern boundary of the capital in 1824, when the cemetary was opened. It was therefore known as le Cimetière du Sud. Cemeteries had been banned from Paris since the shutting down of the Cimetière des Innocents, on the fringe of Les Halles, in 1786, on the grounds that it presented a health hazard. Three new cemeteries replaced them outside the precincts of the capital in the early 19th century, Montmartre in the north, Le Père Lachaise in the east and Montparnasse in the south. The main entrance to the Cemetery of Montparnasse is at no. 3 Boulevard Edgar-Quinet but we shall enter it later from rue de Froidevaux. For the time being turn left into rue de la Gaîté (if you have walked all the way down the Boulevard, retrace your steps one block.)

RUE DE LA GAITE was a mere country lane in the 18th century. By 1804 it linked the toll barrier of Montparnasse and the village of Clamart. As at all the barriers in Paris, a cluster of *guinguettes* opened here providing locals with cheap, untaxed wine. Thus from the start, the street was singled out as a place of entertainment. There was plenty of demand for entertainment in a rural area which offered none. Indeed, no sooner was the street built, than it was lined with restaurants, cabarets and theatres at affordable prices. A popular refrain referred to

> . . . *un cabaret, barrière du Maine*
> *Au temps où le vin se vendait six sous. . .*

> . . . a cabaret at the Maine barrier
> In the days when wine was sold for six farthings. . .

And while the rest of the neighbourhood was plunged into darkness at night-time, rue de la Gaîté glittered with blazing street signs and crackled with the noise of the crowds. When in 1840 the railway station brought Brittany closer to Montparnasse, rue de la Gaîté was impregnated with the smell of oysters mingled with that of potato chips. The poor country girls of Brittany also made the journey and when they alighted at Gare du Montparnasse in their picturesque lacy costumes and tall headdresses, they too were lured by the attractions of rue de la Gaîté and soon the area was riddled with prostitution on a large scale.

Now that the pleasure business has taken over the street, sex on rue de la Gaîté is no longer spontaneous fun, the pulse of life which thrilled Henry Miller, but a profit-generating commodity, on display in sex-shops and peep-shows. In the 1980s as many as eleven sex-shops and three peep-shows were located in this relatively short street. Exasperated neighbours rallied to put an end to the crude destruction of their environment and succeeded in having the shop windows cleared, if nothing else. It is only for its exciting past that rue de la Gaîté is worth exploring today.

The restaurant Le Richefeu opened in 1802 at no. 1, a huge place which had three storeys, an additional terrace on top, and also a garden with a bower. Although the establishment catered to everyone, social segregation was practised: the higher one climbed up the building, the cheaper the fare and the worse the service. Thus serviettes were not provided beyond the first floor, and while dinner was served on the first, only cheese and chips were to be had on the terrace. Nobody seemed to mind, the place was packed and Monsieur Richefeu made a substantial fortune. At present the site is occupied by the inconspicuous Café de la Liberté, where Sartre liked to have his breakfast towards the end of his life, while tourists were still seeking him out at the Deux-Magots, in Saint-Germain-des-Prés.

A popular *café-brasserie* with six billiard tables stood at no. 6. In 1886 it became a *café-concert*, the Concert-Gangloff. After the Prussian War and the *Commune* of 1870–71, when Paris developed an unquenchable thirst for fun, the Third Republic, born out of the tragic bloodbath of the civil war of the *Commune*, provided fun in plenty, in a bid to secure its legitimacy. Places of entertainment sprang up throughout the city and competition was fierce. The Concert-Gangloff could not stand up to the celebrated Gaîté-Montparnasse just a few steps down the road, not even when experienced professionals took it over in 1896 under the name of Fantaisies-Montparnasse.

Turn right into **RUE DU MAINE**. Henry Miller lived on the corner house, at no. 1, in 1930, when he struck an advantageous deal with the Sphinx in which he would write the pamphlets for the house in return for 'a bottle of champagne and a free fuck in one of the Egyptian rooms'. Ahead is **Square Gaston-Baty**, where children play around a life-size statue of Soutine by Arbit Blatas. The sculptor has certainly captured the scowling face and inhibited posture of this tortured soul who liked to leave chunks of meat and bloody fowl on his canvases.

Retrace your steps and continue along rue de la Gaîté. During the Second Empire, a dance hall was located at no. 15. At that time regulations placed limits on entertainment so as not to undermine the theatre. Performers other than theatre actors were not allowed to disguise themselves, for example, nor to recite texts. At no. 17, **La Comédie Italienne** is decorated with characters from the *commedia dell'arte*. Its presence here brings a cheerful note to an otherwise unappetising street and even helps to sustain a glorious past, when the Italians were the only ones besides the official royal troupe allowed to tread the theatre boards of Paris.

Until recently the illustrious **Bobino** stood at no. 20; it began as a dance hall too, le Bal des Gigolettes, way back in 1800. When the old regulations were repealed, the new proprietor converted it into a theatre (in 1873) and named it Folies-Bobino after a member of the modest Théâtre du Luxembourg, which had opened during the Restoration near the Luxembourg Gardens. Pantomime, juggling, acrobatics and conjuring were the only forms of entertainment tolerated at the time and the regulations required that they be preceded by a an outdoor *parade*, a street performance involving farcical characters such as Palliaci and Harlequin (as on the Boulevard du Temple in the 11th arrondissement). The clown who played Palliaci in the *Parade* was nicknamed Bobino, and in 1830 the Théâtre du Luxembourg was renamed after him. It so happened that the theatre was demolished towards the end of the Second Empire, just before the new Bobino was built on rue de la Gaîté, but no connection between the two has been established.

The Folies-Bobino began unpromisingly, and only got worse when the obnoxious Richain took it over in 1894. Rude and miserly, he drove away both audience and performers. In 1896, the reporter of *l'Art Lyrique* related how his talented artists, disgusted at being maltreated, badly paid – if at all, and performing to 'widowed' seats, had quit. 'The great attraction is the *patron* of the establishment himself!' he added. 'This person, whose pretentiousness can only match his incompetence, seemed like a bear in a cage, threatening to bite everyone, but chickening out as soon as anyone approached to ask him why he was so insolent. This man of rare imbecility must have received plenty of "kicks up the arse" during his managerial and cabaret existence, as it is the only phrase he seems to know.'

In 1912 the Bobino opened a new chapter. Its new impresario, Montpreux, was a congenial person, the opposite of Richain, massive, red-faced and jovial. Everyone liked him. Spectators and critics came back to watch a programme drawn from the repertoire of classical theatre coupled with *café-concert* variety entertainment. Some excellent and renowned artists performed here, their names now forgotten, except for Mistinguett. However, according to one contemporary, the Bobino was an obsolete and shabby place – 'a sort of barn with paintings that had been washed out by the water of the sky'. Its seats were like armless, legless cripples and its curtain a rag that descended in front of its red-nosed audience, a common crowd by all accounts.

In any case, Montpreux had stepped in too late: for a while now the people of Paris had been under the spell of the cinema, still admittedly in its infancy and yet to become a talkie, but which already promised a thrilling, novel voyage into a land of dream-generating illusions, a means of transient yet total escape, of total disconnection from reality. One by one the glittering palaces of pleasure, the pride of the Belle Epoque, yielded to the inexorable advance of the *usines à rêves* ('dream factories'). Between 1910 and 1920 two thirds were turned into picture houses; those that, like the Bobino, put up a heroic resistance, obtained a lease of life until at best 1930, when the talkies finished them off.

The Bobino was fortunate to be bought up in 1926 by the giant Lutétia-Empire, which already owned as many as 15 picture houses in the city. The company decided to turn their new acquisition into a music hall and perpetuate old traditions. The Bobino was entirely renovated, sumptuously padded with red velvet and trimmed with gold. Huge mirrors multiplied the enchantment. However, the old structure was maintained and that was heart-warming. The new directors made sure that the quality of the show would equal that of the premises and hired the best artists such as Mayol, Yvette Guilbert, Damia . . . and also a young beginner by the name of Fernandel. All to no avail.

In the early 1930s, when the Bobino was about to surrender to the all-devouring cinema and to bear the inevitable prefix *Pathé*, the celebrated Goldin Mitty came to the rescue, putting on stage for the first time such performers as Charles Trenet, Tino Rossi and Edith Piaf, and turning it into one of the most reputable establishments of the capital. For the next few decades all the celebrities and stars of *la chanson française* would appear on its stage – Yves Montand, Jacques Brel, Léo Ferré, Mouloudji, Juliette Gréco, Les Compagnons de la Chanson, Barbara – and of course, Georges Brassens who made it his home. While the Olympia on the Grands Boulevards (see chapter on the 9th arrondissement) was associated with Right Bank entertainment, the Bobino was associated with Left Bank nonconformity, even though many artists, including Piaf, sang in both. It was here that she gave her last heart-rending performance, on 13 March 1963, six months before her death, aged only 48, wrecked by alcohol and drugs.

However, with the close of the 1960s, the last decade when French culture maintained its own identity, the great Left-Bank talents vanished, followed in 1971 by the unfortunate, sudden death of its brilliant impresario, Vitry. This time the enemy was perhaps even more implacable than the cinematography. A new tidal wave of world culture swept over Paris, carrying away the outdated *chanson française*. In 1984 the century-old Bobino was torn down and was replaced by a noisy disco-nightclub – the Wiz – where porn and violence were confused with modernity. But, strangely, the younger generation did not show up. So the premises were given their old name again and a practical new manager turned them into a multi-purpose establishment. At present the Bobino is once more the home of singers and other performers, but in a totally remodelled environment devoid of a soul. Was it necessary to do away with the old historical place? Those of us who had spent some of our best nights in Paris in the old Bobino have remained inconsolable to this day.

At no. 26 stands **La Gaîté-Montparnasse**, an elliptically-shaped structure, built with the stones retrieved from the temporary International Theatre of the 1867 Universal Exposition – a rare old shrine to have survived the last war as a *café-concert*, largely thanks to the revival of the music hall during the Occupation. It was regularly packed with happy, noisy, working-class people, who would do their cooking inside the hall and dine there during the long intervals. Shopkeepers with their wives and children occupied the stalls at 1 franc a seat; hatless milliners and workmen in canvas overalls would sit in the circle, the neighbourhood's rowdiest urchins and louts, in the gods, expressing their displeasure with

Théâtre Montparnasse

catcalls and whistles and by bombarding the stage with orange peels. Well-known figures could be seen in the audience too, enjoying the genuine atmosphere. François Coppée and Lenin were among them. The shows were of varied quality but some noteworthy artists performed here too, such as Mayol, Fréhel (the prewar equivalent of Piaf) and writer-performer Colette, freshly divorced from Willy. In 1945 a new era began on the Left Bank and the premises became home to an avant-garde theatre, which enjoyed the collaboration of Jacques Prévert, Harold Pinter and Roger Blin. The miracle is that somehow it has survived to this day.

Another shrine still stands across the street at no. 31, on the corner of rue Larochelle, the **Théâtre Montparnasse**, the earliest of Montparnasse's theatres. When it opened in 1772 it was called *La nouvelle troupe comique du Mont-Parnasse* and staged the usual repertoire derived from the *commedia dell'arte*. When a new owner took over in 1779, the troupe hoped for a better future but the *Comédiens-Français*, always lobbying against potential rivals, had the official inauguration cancelled. However, this being a suburban theatre, outside the city boundaries, the troupe was not actually banned.

In 1819 it was placed, like all the suburb theatres, under the authority of Pierre Seveste. Seveste, the grandson of the grave-digger who had buried Louis XVI after his execution (see chapter on the 8th arrondissement), knew where the King's remains had been laid and could help Louis XVIII to identify them. Louis XVIII, the late King's grateful brother, rewarded him for this with the unusual privilege of giving him authority over all the suburban theatres, a privilege which was handed down through the family. The quality of the show left a lot to be desired, but this did not bother the unsophisticated audience, who turned up with a cabbage stew, which they simmered over the stove before the show.

In 1888 the famous André Antoine took over the theatre every Friday, the closing day of his own Théâtre Libre in Montmartre, and catapulted it into the limelight, where it remained well into the 1950s. Gaston Baty, Louis Jouvet and Sacha Pitoëff were among its collaborators, and its productions of *Cyrano de Bergerac* and *La Dame de chez Maxime's* constituted historic landmarks on the Paris theatre scene.

The Casino-Montparnasse at no. 35/37 opened in 1911 only, but despite the growing competition of the film industry, it played to packed halls for about 15 years. Maurice Chevalier, Mistinguett and Damia all performed here till the 1930s, when, however, even Fréhel could no longer draw the public who was queuing up for the first talkies in front of the ever-growing number of cinemas. In 1933 it was converted into a cinema in its turn. The revival of the music hall during the last war restored it temporarily to its old vocation, which was sustained for a while after the war by a short-lived miracle – the success of Francis Lopez's operetta, *La Belle de Cadiz*, with Luis Mariano in the lead role. On the night of the première, 13 November 1945, the hitherto totally unknown young tenor from Bordeaux (who had also designed the costumes and the sets) received an ovation that verged on delirium. His suave voice, caressed and stirred the female members of the audience and swept them off their feet. Overnight he became the Parisian Valentino. As he soared to sudden, dizzying fame, he carried along with him both Francis Lopez and the theatre where the miracle had taken place. For two full years *La Belle de Cadiz* was performed to a packed theatre and extra chairs even had to be borrowed from neighbouring cafés. However, while Luis Mariano maintained his career to the last, the theatre could not repeat this feat. Today a characterless cinema complex stands here, bearing the functional name l'Espace Gaîté, in keeping with the neighbourhood's recent facelift.

Continue into RUE VERCINGETORIX, diagonally to the right. Nothing is left of the days when Gauguin lived on the second floor of no. 6 (1894) with his Indonesian mistress, Annah *la Javanaise*. He decorated his studio to look like a Polynesian cabin. On the glass entrance door he painted a palm tree with a Tahitian beauty underneath. Above the door he wrote: *Ici l'on aime*. . . Gauguin was at the peak of his fame, and was paid homage here by the likes of Edvard Munch and Strindberg. Even Degas deigned to come down from Montmartre to pay his respects, diluted, however, by scathing remarks about the futility of travelling in search of what can be found back home. In 1970 this historic landmark gave way to a Sheraton hotel (now Le Méridien). The glass entrance door with its soporific images of sunwashed islands had already been smashed accidentally in 1910, while it was being transported to the art dealer Paul Rosenberg, to whom the landlord was about to sell it.

It was not just no. 6 but the entire seedy neighbourhood that went – together with its share of drugs, admittedly – but also its population of modest, old-time locals (who are said, however, to have been rehoused in the area); it was replaced by yet another example of soulless townplanning.

You will now reach PLACE DE CATALOGNE, the work of the architect Ricardo Bofill. The place has been singled out as one of Paris's achievements of the last 20 years, and as such it was proudly shown to the Prince and Princess of Wales during their official visit to Paris in November 1988. If you see it floodlit at night, it certainly looks impressive, enhanced by the tilted round centrepiece with a sheet of water gliding over it and producing an enchanting shimmering effect. Not so during the day, when this jerry-built construction shows signs of premature old age. Rue Vercingétorix continues under an archway across the roundabout, which leads to the traffic-free Place de Séoul (also known as Colonnes) and Place de l'Amphithéâtre, respectively to your left and to your right. Place de Séoul is actually quite impressive when its curved glass façades catch the sun's rays or glitter in the night. The artistic intentions of Bofill cannot be underestimated; with a respectful nod to the Classical masters, he has integrated their heritage into our present age and his own personal style. However, despite the overall unity of the complex, it stands in a landscape of desolate cement, merely adding to the overall prevailing architectural mess.

Ahead is the solid, unpretentious church of **Notre-Dame-du-Travail**, looming out of the past, overlooking a newly laid-out garden and a fortress-like block of flats. As if in a desperate attempt to neutralise the disastrous effect, the bloc has been painted pink and an extensive strip of puny-looking trees and bushes has been planted in front of it – enough to make the artists' community of Montparnasse turn in their graves!

A red-roofed house has somehow survived left of the church, probably because it adjoins the church. In front of the house, an old shady tree and a few benches from another time have also been left in peace. The church itself is worth a visit – it has more to tell you about genuine Paris than many of the better known monuments and is a very original piece of architecture.

The opening of the railway station in 1840 and the annexation of the area to Paris in 1860 brought about a rapid growth of the population and the necessity to provide it with a new place of worship. The parish church built in 1848 on the neighbouring rue Texel proved too small. Even with its new extension in 1865, it could not contain the ceaseless flow of newcomers to this neighbourhood of Plaisance, which by then numbered 35,000 inhabitants. Needless to say, Plaisance was poor and Abbot Soulange-Bodin had his hands full trying to bring some light to the destitute, sickly and young who were left wandering about on the streets. The new church was therefore dedicated to Our Lady of Work, so as to restore dignity to the labours of man (and at the same time give credibility to the fight against idleness and crime). It was to be inaugurated in 1900, so as to coincide with the Universal Exposition, on whose building site many of Plaisance's inhabitants had been working. The Abbot thus wished to pay homage to the previous 1889 Fair, which celebrated man's faith in work and progress, as symbolised by the Eiffel Tower, and asked the architect Astruc to convey this spirit of modernity in the new church: 'The Church had to remind the worker of his factory so that he should feel at home, in his customary environment, surrounded by iron and wood, the materials that his hand transforms every day. . . But the House of God, if it reminded one of the factory and workshop where the workman laboured all his life, also had to be a feast for his eyes and a solace for his body . . . so that his eyes could bathe in the light and his lungs could breathe deeply the pure air.' Hence, the metal framework of the nave, made of 135 tonnes of iron and steel, a surprising sight as one walks in. These were salvaged from the gigantic Palais de l'Industrie which was built for the 1855 World Fair and replaced by the Grand and the Petit Palais for the 1900 Fair (see chapter on the 8th arr.). Abbot Soulange-Bodin also managed to salvage for his church a bell taken from the defeated Sebastopol by Napoléon III in 1854. Of late a local artist has decorated the walls with delicate painted flowers, which blend in beautifully with the metal framework, softening the atmosphere without spoiling its stark character. A few highly symbolic works of art are interspersed here and there, striking in their beauty or deeply felt emotions, notably a *Pietà*. The church also takes pride in its beautiful organ, which in 1985 replaced the old Cavaille-Coll. The new instrument allows for 150 combinations of sound and is enhanced by the excellent acoustics of the building.

Another survivor from the past is an antiquated *boulangerie* at no. 105 rue Vercingétorix, on the corner of rue Grégovie, Le Moulin de la Vierge (the Virgin's mill), dating from 1907. Candy-coloured angels float in a candy-blue sky of an optimistic ceiling, while traditional French bread and other appetising savories are on display in the window, side by side with American brownies.

Retrace your steps on rue Vercingétorix and turn diagonally right into rue Jean Zay, then right into **RUE FROIDEVAUX**. To any Parisian the rue Froidevaux is associated with the Cemetery of Montparnasse, the eternal home of many of France's intellectual and artistic elite, also celebrated by Georges Brassens in *La Ballade des Cimetières*.

Before it was confiscated during the French Revolution to be used for the burial of unclaimed bodies, the cemetery's grounds had belonged to the Christian Ordre de la Charité – their one-time windmill still stands within the cemetery's precincts (in the 9th

division), the only windmill to have survived in the 14th arrondissement. Its sails have long gone, but there is talk of fixing new ones. In
the early 17th century, when the rubble mound of Montparnasse
was still in existence, the jolly youths of the Latin Quarter who used
its lofty position to recite verse would wind up at the windmill to
feast on home-made *galettes* (pancakes), washed down by cheap
wine. The windmill was frequented by the students well after the
mound had been levelled and into the 18th century and it is claimed
that Voltaire was among the merry band. Voltaire was a student at
the Jesuit Collège de Clermont (now Lycée Louis-le-Grand), whose
hang-out was this mill, the Moliniste, whereas their opponents, the
Jansenists*, gathered at the Trois-Cornets mill, on the corner of the
present rue Raymond-Losserand and Avenue du Maine.

It was a business-minded miller who first had the idea of selling
galettes to his customers while they were waiting for their corn to
be ground, a gimmick that caught on throughout the Paris area. In
no time many of its windmills had taverns, the most famous being
the Moulin de la Galettte in Montmartre, immortalised by Renoir.
Now birds come in spring to nest in this ivy-covered vestige, while
dozens of cats roam here all year round.

As you wander through the cemetery (maps are available at the
entrance gate), you will come upon familiar names – Jean-Paul
Sartre and Simone de Beauvoir, of course, Tristan Tzara, Zadkine,
Soutine, Pascin – as well as their 19th-century elders, such as Sainte-
Beuve, Maupassant, Baudelaire. Baudelaire was deeply rooted in
Montparnasse. Convinced of the futility of travelling and of the
potentialities of an experience right at home, he announced his
intention to inscribe on the front of its station, ON NE PART PAS
('ONE DOES NOT DEPART'). Montparnasse brought him back into
its fold, although no tombstone bears his name: he lies next to his
mother and stepfather, Général Aupick, under the name of the latter who, even at present, when turned into a marble statue above the
grave, seems to overpower him. Renowned musicians lie here too –
César Franck, Camille Saint-Saëns and Clara Haskil among others.

Those who promoted the works of writers and artists also rest
here, publishers such as Messieurs Hachette and Larousse, Hetzel
who published Jules Verne, the famous art dealer Pierre Loeb,

* Followers of the Dutch theologian Cornelius Jansenius (1585–1638) who
believed in predestination and denied free will.

and also the promoter of the French language, Littré, who left a monumental dictionary. The sculptors who embellished the area and its cemetery are buried here too – Bourdelle, Rude, Houdon, Bartholdi, Brancusi – and Henri Laurens, who composed his own epitaph for his tomb by way of a statue entitled *l'Adieu!* An early Cubist work by Brancusi, *Le Baiser* (1910), stands here too, celebrating the final victory of love over death – which explains, perhaps, why it surmounts an unoccupied tomb.

The tomb of the Russian Alexandre Alekhine has occasionally drawn chess fans for a game in the shadow of the Grandmaster. The presence of Pierre Laval, the High Commissioner for Jewish Affairs under Vichy, who was executed during the Epuration, jars among these creative minds and may be seen as an insult to such occupiers as Robert Desnos who died in deportation in 1945. From his elevated position in the central roundabout, *Eternal Sleep*, frozen into the stone, watches over the past community of Montparnasse.

Back on rue Froidevaux, turn right into rue Boulard and left into **RUE DAGUERRE**, an exciting spot for lovers of lively village atmosphere: a colourful display of the bounties of France – her cheeses, meat, fish and bread, a riot of fruit and vegetables, enhanced in autumn by an extraordinary array of mushrooms and in spring by bunches of wild daffodils. Easygoing shoppers and packed crowds at the café tables that spill into the street are part of the show, enlivened by the cries of street vendors and occasionally by buskers, a vestige of happier days. At present a threat hangs over the scene, for rue Daguerre has been eyed by real-estate developers who have bought the old *lavoir* (wash-house), now the picturesque covered part of the market, in order to replace it with yet another modern block, complete with a car park which will of necessity wreck the pedestrian precinct. Many of the street's shops have meanwhile been franchised, which prompted neighbours in 1988 to found an association, *Les amis de la rue Daguerre*, to promote both the street and its varied population of craftsmen, shopkeepers, intellectuals, artists, young and old, all of whom have been honoured by the film director Agnès Varda, herself a long-time inhabitant of the street, in her film *Daguerréotypes*. Rue Daguerre is a perfect place to stop for lunch, before resuming your afternoon walk, preferably before 1 o'clock, when the market closes till 4 pm.

Le Lion de Belfort

FROM PLACE DENFERT-ROCHEREAU NORTH

This walk begins at **PLACE DENFERT-ROCHEREAU**, a star-shaped roundabout with seven broad arteries radiating from it, pleasantly surrounded by greenery and dominated by its famous lion, *le Lion de Belfort*, enthroned proudly on his elevated socle in the centre. The lion is a replica of the one standing in Belfort, which Bartholdi (better known for his Statue of Liberty) had moulded in homage to the heroic defence of that city during the Franco-Prussian war. The Avenue (running north) and Place Denfert-Rochereau bear the name of the Colonel who had led that resistance, a most convenient fluke, for the avenue was previously known as l'Avenue d'Enfer (Hell)! The Third Republic, then anxious to accommodate the Germans, arranged for the Lion to face west. When the Germans came back during the last war, they sent many neighbouring statues to the foundry (including the one

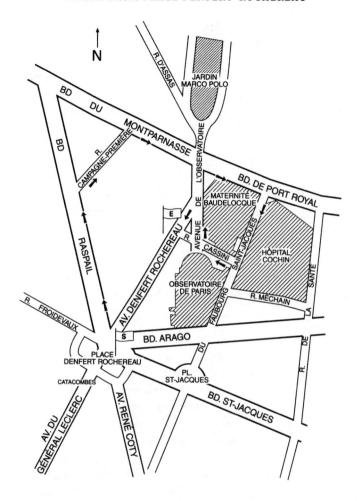

celebrating the Rights of Man), but the Lion was spared. It seems that the Germans, awed by the courage of the people of Belfort, preferred to let matters stand.

Avenue du Général-Leclerc, running south of the Place, commemorates the hero of the Liberation who, having reached the Porte d'Orléans on the southern boundary of the arrondissement, entered Paris on 25 August 1944 along its route. On either side of the Avenue stand Nicolas Ledoux's toll-gate pavilions, built to embellish the checkpoints of the toll walls where taxes were levied. Between 1786 and 1860 the walls ran along what were then the boundaries of Paris, in this area the present Boulevards Saint-Jacques, Raspail and Edgar-Quinet.

The pavilion at no. 1 Place Denfert-Rochereau, across the Avenue du Général Leclerc, now serves as entrance to the **Paris Catacombs** (open daily except Monday, 2–4 pm, Saturday and Sunday 9–11 am, 2–4 pm. Bring a light, and also warm clothes – temperature is at a constant 11°C/52°F).

The Paris Catacombs run 20 metres underground, a 1,500-metre-long maze of galleries padded neatly with the bones and skulls of six million anonymous Parisians, among them those of Danton and Robespierre. They were brought to these abandoned quarries towards the end of the 18th century from all the other burial grounds of Paris, predominantly from the Cimetière des Innocents near the market of Les Halles, which by that time had stretched beyond its capacity. According to medieval traditions, the living should look Death in the face, hence the implacable inscription at the gate:

> *Arrête! c'est ici l'empire de la mort!*
> Halt! here is the kingdom of death!

The builders of the Catacombs, with macabre nonchalance, used the tibia of the deceased to enhance the environment. A rotunda at the other end of the Catacombs has even been named *La Rotonde des Tibias*, itself a source of artistic inspiration to a later generation. Indeed, on 2 April 1897, at 2 am, a society concert was given here to an audience of a hundred appreciative connoisseurs. Eminent top-hatted artists, writers and journalists, as well as some elegant feather-hatted ladies gathered in this makeshift 'hall', renowned for its excellent acoustics. Both Chopin's 'Funeral March' and Beethoven's 'Funeral March' from the *Eroica* symphony were performed, overshadowed, however, by the 'Round of the Skeletons' from Saint-Saëns's *Danse Macabre* to which Cazalis contributed creepy lyrics depicting the white, cracking skeletons hovering about under their shrouds. Punctuated by the xylophone, the refrain went as follows:

> 'Zig, Zig and Zig,
> Everyone jigs about,'

News of the scandalous 'concert' spread throughout Paris in no time and the two guards who had been bribed (twenty farthings each) to allow this shockingly immoral happening to take place were fired at once (but were later re-employed).

In the more grave times of World War II, the Catacombs provided an excellent hiding-place for the Resistance.

BOULEVARD RASPAIL, north of Place Denfert-Rochereau, is our next destination. At no. 277 can be seen the magnificent grounds of a retirement home, of which more later. At no. 261, Jean Nouvel's glass tower houses the Fondation Cartier and is an open wound to all those who cherished the American Center of Paris that once stood on the site, a charmingly outdated house, built by the American Welles Bosworth in 1934, and serving the community with its wide range of cultural activities. By allowing it to be torn down – despite a lengthy battle to prevent this, supported by influential figures from the arts world – the authorities have taken another unforgivable step towards the obliteration of the intensely cultural past of the 14th arrondissement. In 1992 the red-roofed home of the American Center was replaced by a towering glass structure, the new home of the **Fondation Cartier** for the promotion of contemporary art. The lovely gardens of the old American Center are no longer used by the public and the historic 200-year-old cedar tree, believed to have been planted by Chateaubriand, now stands encased in a prison of glass. Meanwhile the new high-flying American Center at Bercy, for which this genuine place was sold, proved a financial fiasco and ended stillborn.

Turn right into rue CAMPAGNE-PREMIERE, once a stronghold of the artists' community of Montparnasse. In 1922, when Man Ray's new interest in photography required more space, he rented a studio at no. 31, a building decorated with impressive ceramics, which had won a prize in 1911. In December 1923 he moved from rue Delambre to the Istria Hotel at no 29, so as to live next door to his studio. He was followed by his close buddy Marcel Duchamp, who had returned from New York the same month, and by the latter's mistress, Thérèse Treize. Man Ray also moved in with his mistress, the celebrated Kiki, the 'Queen' of Montparnasse. From here they transported their passionate love affair to Carrefour Vavin and other Montparnasse haunts, demonstrating it Montparnasse-fashion with violent outbursts and gunshots in the air. Man Ray gave up both the studio and the hotel room in 1929, when he moved to rue du Val-de-Grâce in the 5th arrondissement.

The site of no. 17 was used by a riding school until 1914. There were plenty of horses in the area at the time, since this was the site picked for their depots by the Paris transport companies, all of which used horse-drawn vehicles. One such depot was situated on the vacant grounds of the northern side of the street.

A one-storeyed house stood until 1936 at no. 14, containing two shops and some wretched rooms in the attic. The shops – a bakery and a wine merchant – catered to the depot's coachmen, especially the wine shop! However, by 1925 a different clientele took over. One customer was the celebrated poetess Anna de Noailles, who liked to mingle with the community of Montparnasse and also to pose for Fujita. However, Fujita did not keep her as a model for she would not remain still. One of the attics was occupied by Verlaine who then let Rimbaud have it. He only stayed here for two months, a time punctuated, as usual, by fits of violence. The landlord, Verlaine, was no example of self-control either and in 1873 spent some time in prison for having injured Rimbaud! He made good use of that time, composing a very evocative verse on that seedy room:

> O chambre, as-tu gardé leurs spectres ridicules,
> O pleine de jour sale et de bruits d'araignées. . .

> Oh, room, have you kept their ridiculous spectres
> Oh, full of dirty light and of the noise of spiders. . .

A narrow entrance at no. 9, paved with bumpy cobblestones and lined with pot plants, leads to a courtyard with an unexpected fig tree. Built of materials salvaged from the 1889 Universal Exposition, the building was divided into more than 100 studios, responding to the needs of the neighbourhood in those days. Here only the song of birds interrupts the stillness, and the church bells chiming the quarters. Among its famous tenants were Rainer Maria Rilke, Rodin's then secretary, Modigliani, Whistler and Chirico, one of the early precursors of Surrealism. When Picasso and Apollinaire came over to his studio to look at his metaphysical paintings, they were overwhelmed.

Modigliani's *cantine* was just three houses down the street, at no. 3, a modest *crémerie* (dairy), bearing the sign Chez Rosalie, which also served as a restaurant, as was common in those days. The Italian Rosalie Tobia, Mère Rosalie to the community of Montparnasse, had begun as a model, one of the Italians picked up on the 'fair' held weekly on the corner of rue de la Grande-Chaumière and Boulevard du Montparnasse (see chapter on the 6th arr.). Posing as Venus for the highly regarded *Pompier** painter Bouguereau, she also agreed to work for such fringe characters as Whistler and Modigliani, portraying less pompous subjects and for a smaller fee... When cellulite got the better of her, she switched to the food business and played mother to the poverty-stricken artists whom she nourished with all her heart. On her tiny, dark premises below street-level, impregnated with the smell of onions and garlic, she offered a full, delicious Italian meal for the modest sum of 2 francs. Kisling, Soutine, Max Jacob, Salmon and Kiki too huddled on the backless benches on either side of the long wooden tables of the restaurant for a dish of pasta. Many ate on credit, others contented themselves with half portions or a filling minestrone. She was not interested in being paid with the 'dreadful' paintings of her protégés, as other café owners were, not even those by her fellow countryman Modigliani, the terror of the place, always drunk as a lord and creating havoc. When he refused to eat, she refused to serve him wine: 'A good-looking boy like you who does honour to our country!' When, eaten away by alcohol, he died on 24 January 1920 at the Hôpital Broussais-la Charité (on rue Didot, in the 14th arr.), the most famous artists and models of Montparnasse followed his hearse, which was overflowing with flowers, in a huge procession. At every street junction – all the way to the Père Lachaise cemetery in eastern Paris – a policeman was standing to attention in the shining uniform of the Republic. Thus in death did Modigliani wreak vengeance on the establishment.

Continue east along **BOULEVARD DU MONTPARNASSE** to its junction with Avenue de l'Observatoire. No trace is left of the Grande Chaumière, the open-air dance hall that was located on the site of this block between 1788 and 1853, embellished by clumps of shady trees and beautiful gardens, as famous as the Bal Mabile off the Champs-Elysées (Avenue Montaigne). It was started by an Englishman, Tickson, as a countrified place of entertainment, with

* Uncreative academic painters in the second half of the 19th century.

a few thatched huts scattered here and there, hence the name *chaumière*. Later a spacious, two-storeyed house replaced them, with magnificent gardens and grottos, unique in these parts. Students and *grisettes* used to come here, scorned by self-righteous Parisians, particularly when the polka was danced here for the first time in 1845. Worse was to come with the first performance of the daring *Robert Macaire*, an early version of the can-can, to be followed by the outrageous *chahut*. This time the police were sent over and had it banned at once! Ignoring the ban, Lola Montès came over with the celebrated clown Auriol to be swept onto the floor in a wild *chahut*.

Le **Bullier**, at the end of the block, is under the ownership of the historic Closerie des Lilas, across the Boulevard (see chapter on the 6th arrondissement), but has no past and cannot boast the same atmosphere. Its name, however, was borrowed from the historic Bullier, which was situated across the Avenue de l'Observatoire (in the 5th arrondissement), on the site of today's university sports centre, and was started by Monsieur Bullier. A modest establishment stood here at the time, where he planted lilac trees, after which the famous Closerie across the avenue was called. Students and *grisettes* came here too, as did Béranger, Henri Murger and Théodore de Banville, while the famous Mogador would dance under its bright, multi-coloured candelabra – the polka, the waltz, the mazurka – each vogue giving way to the next. During the Swinging Twenties, le Bal Bullier exploded with eccentricity, and when Kiki, the Queen of every ball, made an appearance here, practically in her most natural attire, everyone was thrilled. She was not the only one, for during the traditional orgiastic ball of the Beaux-Arts school, the celebrated *Quat-z-Arts*, a procession of students and models made their way from the Beaux-Art School on rue Bonaparte (in the 6th) to Avenue de l'Observatoire, similarly undressed and brandishing phallic symbols, wrecking café terraces, in other words, heralding in their own way the coming of the spring season.

The **Paris Observatory** stands at the southern edge of the Avenue de l'Observatoire, to your right, of which more later.

Continue into **BOULEVARD DU PORT-ROYAL**, across the avenue. At no. 123 the **Baudelocque** maternity hospital occupies the site of the Abbey of Port-Royal, the stronghold of Jansenism and, as such, the centre of religious and political controversy at the time of all-embracing absolutism under Louis XIV.

The original Port-Royal was situated in the Chevreuse Valley (near Saint-Rémy-lès-Chevreuse, within easy reach of Port-Royal RER station). Because it was situated in the heart of the country, it was known as Port-Royal-des-Champs. It was surrounded by forests rather than by fields, however, and these retained the humidity and rendered the environment insalubrious. It was therefore decided to transfer the female inmates to a new abbey on the edge of Paris, on the site of the Hôtel de Clagny, once the property of Pierre Lescot, the architect of the Hôtel Carnavalet and of the south western wing of the Louvre's Cour Carrée.

The Abbey in Chevreuse had been built at the dawn of the 13th century by the Order of Citeaux and adhered to its regulations for four centuries. But in 1609 its mother superior, Mère Angélique (real name Jacqueline-Marie Arnauld) set out to reform the Order, which substantially increased the number of new nuns. This was when she added the large red cross to the Order's white scapular as can be seen in Philippe de Champaigne's portrait of her, entitled *Port-Royal*, now hanging in the Louvre. It was the mother of Mère Angélique who financed the purchase of the Hôtel de Clagny, while the construction of the new convent was financed by several great families of the nobility such as the Guénégaud, the Sévigné, the Sablé and the Aumont. Angélique's mother, her six daughters and six nieces joined the Order and came to live here, while her eldest son and her youngest one (her twentieth child, the brilliant Antoine Arnauld) joined the community in Chevreuse. This had become a hothouse of intellectual celebrities (and as such even more dangerously influential), known as *les Solitaires de Port-Royal* or *les Messieurs de Port-Royal*.

It was at Port-Royal-des-Champs that Jansenism had first been introduced into France during the reign of Louis XIII by the Abbot of Saint-Cyran, the director of Angélique and her nuns. Although he was imprisoned by Richelieu, the architect of absolutism who had smothered all forms of religious dissension, the movement gained ground among such threatening circles as the Sorbonne and Parliament, the bourgeoisie and the parish priests. Absolutism was achieved under Louis XIV, but Richelieu had died without extirpating Jansenism from France. It is not insignificant that some of the defeated rebels of the *Fronde** found refuge at Port-Royal.

The doctrine of Jansenism had been elaborated by Cornelius Jansenius from his study of Augustine. Ruling out the importance of free will, he believed in predestination and in the need of God's grace in order to be saved, which would be bestowed only on the few. This was a pessimistically dangerous view to encourage among average mortals but it appealed to powerful intellects such as Pascal and Racine. Racine was educated by the 'solitary' gentlemen of Port-Royal-des-Champs as an adolescent, while 18-year-old Pascal reverted to them for a metaphysical answer to the enigma of man's dual nature, to the contradiction between mind and heart, in short, to the wretched condition of this *monstre incompréhensible*. It was at Port-Royal that he wrote his *Provinciales* in defence of Jansenism whilst launching an all-out, virulent attack on the casuistic Jesuits, a menace to Christian morals. He then undertook his much more ambitious work, an apologia for the Christian religion, fragments of which have come down to us as *Les Pensées*.

The Jesuits enjoyed the favour of the King, whose confessor, Père Lachaize, was appointed from among them. Under their pressure, Jansenism was branded a heresy and the premises in the now 14th arrondissement were closed down in 1688 which was felt as a tragedy by its inmates, but thanks to which the buildings have survived. Not so the Abbey. In 1705, at the urging of his new confessor Le Tellier, who had replaced the late, amiable Père Lachaize, alongside the Archbishop of Paris, de Noailles, and the head of police, d'Argenson, the King ordered the Abbey of Port-Royal to be cleared. Four years later, a company of 300 musketeers was sent over to demolish it and lay waste its cemetery. Relatives were, however, allowed to recover some of the remains including those of Racine, even though he had died in disgrace: these now lie at the church of Saint-Etienne-du-Mont in the Latin Quarter.

A new era began in 1715 under the Regent. The Jansenist parliament gained influence, which increased under Louis XV. In 1762 it was the turn of the Jesuit Company to be eradicated from the kingdom of France.

* The princely revolt against Louis XIV in August 1652.

The premises in the 14th arrondissement survived the Revolution and are today part of the hospital. To the left as one enters stands the 17th-century chapel where the remains of Mère Angélique have been buried since 1661 (under the floor of the choir). Behind it, above a flight of steps, a small door leads to a short corridor and to the 17th-century cloister, an exquisite haven of tranquillity.

The **Cochin** hospital, across rue du Faubourg Saint-Jacques, occupies the grounds of the Capucins' novitiate, whose head house was at Faubourg Saint-Honoré. It was Jean-François de Gondi, the future Archbishop of Paris, who in 1613 laid its cornerstone, boosting its economic development. Indeed, the novitiate was surrounded by sainfoin and alfalfa fields, vineyards and a wine press – a pretty sight.

Turn right into **RUE DU FAUBOURG SAINT-JACQUES**. The street meets the Boulevard Saint-Jacques at **PLACE SAINT-JACQUES**, a seedy spot bordered by taverns of ill repute in 1832, when the guillotine was moved here from Place de Grève (now Hôtel-de-Ville) so as to make public executions less conspicuous. For the same reason executions now took place in the very early hours of the morning – but the mob turned up anyway! In 1836 Thackeray came over to watch the execution of Fieschi who had made an attempt on the life of Louis-Philippe the previous July on Boulevard du Temple (see chapter on the 11th arr.). It was the day of Mardi Gras, and a tide of hideous, drunken, blood-thirsty revellers in their dishevelled disguise and smeared make-up was streaming in from as far away as the Champs-Elysées, across the Seine, then down rue d'Enfer (now Boulevard Saint-Michel and Avenue Denfert-Rochereau), to these remote parts, 'shrieking, jabbering, gesticulating, as the French will do . . . wishing to wind up the delights of their carnival by a *bonne-bouche* of a murder.' Their disappointment must have been great, as Fieschi's execution was delayed.

In 1938, at last, the guillotine was moved to the courtyard of the prison of La Santé, on the corner of Boulevard Arago and rue de la Santé. From then on it operated behind thick walls, concealed from the public eye.

Turn right into RUE CASSINI, an attractive, leafy street, home to several members of the intelligentsia at some time or another – Alain Fournier, the author of *Les Grand Maulnes*, lived at no. 2, the philosopher Alain at no. 6, the astronomer Camille Flammarion at no. 16, and Balzac, between 1829 and 1834, at nos 4 to 8 (then no. 1), occupied a three-room flat on the first floor. Deep in debt, Balzac often registered under false names, in this case the name of his sister, Madame Laure de Surville. Among his guests here were Madame de Berny, his mastermind and friend, who lived round the corner on rue d'Enfer (now Avenue Denfert-Rochereau) and George Sand whom he introduced here to the physicist Arago. It was here that he began his correspondence with Madame Hanska and wrote three of his masterpieces – *Le Père Goriot, Eugénie Grandet* and *La Peau de Chagrin*. He also left a written description of the area, as far as the Luxembourg Gardens, which, he said, was neither town nor country but an undefinable stretch, already studded with medical institutions and resounding ceaselessly with the chimes of church bells. *Boules* players were also part of the scene – '*braves gens qui continuent nos ancêtres*' ('honest folk who continue our ancestry'). Today's stroller will appreciate the early 20th-century architecture of the street, notably no. 3 with its concrete bas relief (1903), no. 3bis and its artist studios, nos 5 and 7 (1903–06) and a later house at no. 12 (1929).

Boules players

Ahead is the AVENUE DE L'OBSERVATOIRE. On your left, at no. 61, stands the **Observatoire** with its charmingly oversized dome. This lack of proportions would have been considered outrageous bad taste at the time of Louis XIV, when it was built, but the dome was not there at the time; the telescope was simply installed on the flat roof of the elegant building. In keeping with the aesthetic ideal of well-balanced order, the Observatoire was built on the axis of the centre of the Palais du Luxembourg, with the Avenue de l'Observatoire providing a splendid new vista.

The Observatory was founded in the first place to enhance the prestige of the kingdom. England had just founded its Royal Society and other European neighbours were following suit. After the intense scientific activities of the previous century, which both revolutionised man's fundamental grasp of the universe and left him dismayed, the secular authorities, having assimilated the new order, decided to pursue astronomical investigations. In France it was Colbert who incited Louis XIV to found the Académie Royale des Sciences. However, the promotion of science alone would not have sufficed to induce the prestige-oriented monarch to go to that trouble. It so happened that astronomy was fundamental to the determination of a ship's location at sea, an essential element in naval battles which could enhance his glory.

On 7 March 1667 the deed of purchase of a 2.5 hectare plot of land was signed by the King. This was an ideal spot from which to scrutinise the skies, outside the city boundary, where nothing but windmills and church towers obstructed the eye. The building was entrusted to Claude Perrault (the architect of the Louvre Colonnade and brother of Charles, the author of *Sleeping Beauty*).

Rue Cassini celebrates the dynasty of Italian astronomers who were invited to head the Observatoire, above all the earliest and greatest of them all, Jean-Dominique. Among other contributions to science, he drew a map of the moon and discovered the division (now named after him) that separates the rings of Saturn. Another 17th-century astronomer, Jean Picard, made the first accurate map of France, while the Dane Ole Christensen Roemer, during a visit to Paris, observed the eclipses of Jupiter from the roof of the Observatory and discovered that light travels at 300,000 km per second. Leverrier, director of the Observatory in 1846, discovered the planet Neptune by noticing the disturbances it provoked on

Uranus. He was also one of the founders of a scientifically based weather forecasting service in France. In 1854, when the renowned physicist Arago was director of the Observatory, a larger telescope with a diameter of 38 cm was installed, topped by the present dome for its protection. The telescope, still in situ, is used at times for preliminary observations but the skies of Paris have become too luminous and in-depth work has to be carried out further away. This, however, is still the centre for the study of the rotation of the earth and for the speaking clock, whose accuracy depends on astronomical factors. The Observatoire can be visited on the first Saturday of the month by prior arrangement, which requires a written application in a self-addressed stamped envelope and a two-month wait! You will be shown round by a professional astronomer. The lovely gardens, on the other hand, are open to the public in the afternoons: the entrance is on Boulevard Arago.

Continue along Avenue de l'Observatoire to its junction with **AVENUE DENFERT-ROCHEREAU** and cross over. To the left, at no. 68, the **Convent of the Visitation Order** nestles amidst age-old gardens, concealed behind a tall, thick wall. Founded in 1619 on rue Saint-Antoine, the community moved here only in 1841, where it also houses a faculty of comparative philosophy and a students' hall of residence. A few steps away is a wonderful arts and crafts shop selling monastic works from all over France (open from 1.45 to 7 pm, except Sundays) – liquors, crystallised fruit and fruit cake, china and ceramics, Provençal skirts, children's smocks and toddlers' rompers, hand-embroidered linen, ladies lingerie.

Nos 88 and 92 Avenue Denfert-Rochereau, respectively an institution for blind young women and an old-age home and hospital for priests, **La Maison Marie-Thérèse**, were originally one institution, the grounds of which extended all the way to Boulevard Raspail and included those of the American Center. It was started as a charity by the very pious Madame de Chateaubriand. Although she and her husband led quite separate lives he followed her in this enterprise, but money was short and it was only with the help of other philanthropists that little by little they could acquire the entire property. Most help came from Marie-Thérèse-Charlotte, the Duchesse d'Angoulême, the daughter of Louis XVI. The only royal to have survived imprisonment in the tower of the Temple, she came to be known as 'Mademoiselle du Temple'. The institution was to cater for upper-class patients who, through misfortune, had come down in the world. Many of them were priests. It was to be referred to as *infirmerie* rather than *hospice* so as not to humiliate its inmates, which speaks of the delicacy of Madame de Chateaubriand. The domain had a main building and a chapel, and next to them a little house surrounded by a garden, a farm and a farmyard, all of which was much to the liking of Chateaubriand, who stayed here with his wife periodically between 1826 and 1838. In his *Mémoires d'outre-tombe*, the better part of which he wrote in this place, he said, 'I find myself at once in a monastery, on a farm, in a fruit orchard and in a park. In the mornings I wake up to the sound of the angelus; I can see from my window a roadside crucifix . . . cows, hens, pigeons, bees; sisters of charity, convalescent women, old priests wander among the lilac trees, the azalea, the rhododendron. . .' It was also during his stay here that Chateaubriand was arrested for expressing his hostility to the new regime.

Financial difficulties were never overcome and although the conversion of the old farm into a chocolate factory did bring in a respectable income (the factory lasted until 1925!), the running costs of the establishment were too high and in 1838 the couple had to resign themselves to selling it to the Archbishop of Paris. Madame de Chateaubriand came back to die here in 1847, and was buried behind the high altar of the infirmary chapel. Chateaubriand was not to join her here upon his own death in 1848; he was buried in the chapel of the Missions Etrangères on rue du Bac (in the 7th arrondissement), where he was living at the time.

Because of the connection of the Royal Princess with the place, the chapel also contains some relics of her patron saint, Célestine, as well as some liturgical clothing embroidered by her mother, Marie-Antoinette. Chateaubriand's drawing-room still stands, now the vestibule of the chapel at no. 88, so do the four-storeyed infirmary and its chapel at no. 92 and the house facing the front, where he resided; but little is left of the gardens to which Chateaubriand had personally contributed: 'I planted there two cedars of Solomon and twenty three oak-trees of the Druids', he wrote in the *Mémoires*. Indifferent later generations allowed them to disappear, except for one surviving cedar, presently maltreated on Boulevard Raspail.

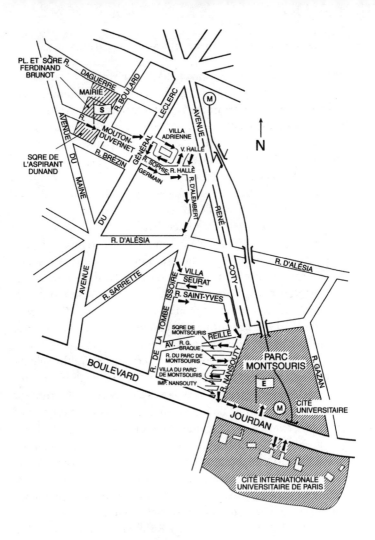

FROM PLACE FERDINAND-BRUNOT TO PARC DE MONTSOURIS

The last walk explores the south-eastern parts of the arrondissement, the richest in bucolic pleasures. We start from its administrative and social centre, **PLACE FERDINAND-BRUNOT** and
Square de l'Aspirant-Dunand, in the heart of the arrondissement,
opposite the imposing Second Empire Mairie. The court house,
the music and dance conservatoire, the swimming pool, open-air
market (Tuesday and Friday mornings) and an annual flea-market

held in spring, all congregate around this 'village green' where toddlers, retired old-timers and *boules* players spend timeless afternoons in a quintessentially '14th' atmosphere that is both Parisian and provincial.

Rue Mouton-Duvernet, running between the two squares, will take you to the **AVENUE DU GENERAL-LECLERC**. The porch at no. 19, across the avenue to the left, reads **Villa Adrienne** – a gateway to another world: an enclave of solid, sizeable provincial houses, brushed by the branches of venerable trees, is tucked away behind this porch, but a footstep away from the busiest street in the arrondissement! Each house bears the name of one of France's great writers or artists – Racine, Corneille, Molière, La Fontaine, Watteau, Delacroix, Poussin, Lully and Berlioz – as befits this culture-conscious arrondissement.

Back on the main street, the **Hospice de La Rochefoucauld** at no. 15 is a rare and beautiful example of the architecture of the last years of the *Ancien Régime*. It began as a philanthropic establishment for patients who had held respectable offices – churchmen, magistrates, officers – but had no private incomes, and bears the name of the Vicomtesse de la Rochefoucauld, although she had in fact donated only a small amount of money towards it. The real honour should have gone to the zealous Père Gérard, a member of the charitable Order of Saint-Jean-de-Dieu, but hers was an eminent family and a prestigious name. In the early 19th century it became a home for the aged as it still is today. The gardens, however, were drastically reduced with the advent of the railway track of the Ligne de Sceaux (now Ligne B of the RER) and the opening of the Avenue René Coty.

Retrace your steps and turn left into rue Sophie Germaine, then on to **RUE HALLÉ** with its enchanting crescent of quaint, heterogeneous houses, each with its miniature garden. Wander also into **Villa Hallé**, on the left, a secluded, narrow *cul-de-sac* overgrown with bushes and creepers and lined with rural-style houses. Rue Hallé has always been a favourite among the artist community. The war widow Mary Reynolds moved to no. 24 in 1920. A staunch supporter of the Surrealists, she became the mistress of Marcel Duchamp, who kept many of his belongings here. As well as her

Surrealist friends, the painters Georges Rouault and Fernand Léger used to visit here.

Turn right into rue d'Alembert and right again into **RUE DE LA TOMBE-ISSOIRE**. It runs into rue d'Alésia, a picturesque junction, thanks to the presence of the provincial-looking restaurant, Le Moniage Guillaume, displaying an old tiled roof and nestling behind a cluster of shady trees. The chanson de geste, *Le Moniage Guillaume*, relates the story of Guillaume d'Orange who came to the rescue of the besieged Parisians and slit the throat of the Saracen chef, the ferocious giant Isoré. According to oral traditions, his tomb, which was located around here, was 15 feet long. Historians disagree on the origin of the name La Tombe-Issoire, but one theory suggests that Issoire and Isoré are one and the same.

Continue along rue de la Tombe-Issoire and turn left into **Villa Seurat**, a leafy nook full of twittering birds and artists' studios, one of which was once occupied by Henry Miller, the most illustrious of his Parisian homes.

When Miller arrived in Paris in 1930, all he had was a toothbrush, razor, notebook and a pen, plus a walking stick from Mexico. And he did a lot of walking indeed, probably more than most of his fellow Americans. He met Anaïs Nin, the Hungarian photographer Brassaï and the American writer Michael Fraenkel, who offered to lodge him in his home on Villa Seurat. There Miller wrote the first pages of *Tropic of Cancer*, which in the novel becomes Villa Borghese, while his benefactor, Fraenkel, becomes Boris. Having spent time in Dijon and Clichy, Miller moved back to Villa Seurat in 1934, on the very day of publication of *Tropic of Cancer*. He settled at no. 18, this time as a full paying tenant. Among his neighbours were Soutine and Jean Lurçat, whose brother André had built nos 1, 3, 4, 8, 9 and 11 of the alley; but it was at his studio that people gathered – Blaise Cendrars, Anaïs Nin, Brassaï and Lawrence Durrell, who wrote of 'The heat and the fury of the days of the Villa Seurat. The good glasses of wine and the pleasant madness of typewriters.' Miller, Durrell and Anaïs Nin decided to start a publication. Their friend Alfred Perlès was chief editor of the *Booste*, published on behalf of the American Country Club. It now became *La Revue Officielle de la villa Seurat*, with Anaïs Nin as its society columnist, Durrell as the sports columnist and Henry Miller contributing a fashion column.

Discovering a new passion for astrology, Miller covered one of his studio walls with pictures from his astral theme and also scrutinised Jupiter – supposedly his lucky star – from the roof of his house. One night he was so absorbed in his observations that he went flying through the air, crashed through the skylight and landed two floors below. The fact that he escaped with minor cuts and bruises proved, so his astrologer friend Moricand said, that Jupiter was protecting him.

Miller loved the ugly, morbid rue de la Tombe-Issoire, which was falling into ruins in its pre-gentrification days, a street of fairy tales and perfect in its obsolescence. He wished it always to remain so and that none of its houses should be repainted. Modern-day Paris has paid little heed to his heart's desires and has gentrified all his favourite streets. Besides, World War II was to chase Miller away from Paris, first to stay with Lawrence Durrell in Greece, then back to the United States.

Continue along rue de la Tombe-Issoire, then left into rue Saint-Yves, which leads to Parc de Montsouris. Take **RUE NANSOUTY** along the western border of the gardens, the boundary of the most exquisite oasis in the arrondissement, where rows of quaint houses of eclectic styles nestle among a luscious vegetation of ivy, Virginia creepers and wistaria. Flower boxes add a cheerful note to the windows, while at night the light of the lampposts bathes the street in a romantic glow. Needless to say, the artist community spotted this nook. Georges Braque lived at no. 6 of the street that bears his name. Others contributed to it their architectural talent: Zielissky who built the house at no. 8 **rue Georges Braque** and Guggenbuhl who designed the one at no. 14 **Square de Montsouris**.

Continue along rue Nansouty and turn left into **BOULEVARD JOURDAIN**. At no. 19 is the main entrance to the **Cité Universitaire**, the oldest university campus in Paris, or, more accurately, its gigantic hall of residence since, although it has libraries, theatres and sports facilities, no teaching is offered here.

The Cité Universitaire was founded in 1920 by the French industrialist Emile Deutsch de La Meurthe, in memory of his wife. The idea of creating a students' village in the spirit of the medieval 'Collège des Nations', which clustered around the Sorbonne (rue des Anglais, rue d'Ecosse and rue des Irlandais in the Latin Quarter are reminiscent of them), had already been in the air towards the end of the 19th century, but it took the devastation left by World War I to promote the ideal of universal brotherhood and to accelerate the need for such a foundation. The League of Nations, for instance, was founded at that time. Conveniently, the demolition of Thiers's fortifications, which had proved useless in modern warfare, left some vacant space on the southern edge of the 14th. To this was added a section of the wasteland that encircled Paris beyond the walls – *la zone* – hitherto occupied by Russian and Spanish refugees, as well as gypsies and ragpickers and their medley of shacks, hovels and caravans. The foundation Emile et Louise Deutsch de La Meurthe – seven houses with picturesque, medieval, gabled roofs – was completed in 1925 and inaugurated ceremoniously on 9 July in the presence of the President of the Republic, Paul Doumergue.

Among the different buildings you will come to, the following are worth your attention: La Fondation Hellénique with its Ionic columns (built in 1932); La Maison Internationale (donated by J.D. Rockefeller Jr, in 1936); the Italian house, with a mural representing Saint Francis; La Maison de l'Asie du Sud-Est, easily identifiable by its lacquered furniture and potbellied Buddhas. The Institut d'Etudes Japonaises is topped by a pagoda-shaped roof and boasts two murals by Fujita, notably one representing the disembarkation of the Portuguese in Japan in 1542. Opposite is the pretty Swedish house, with its whitewashed walls and blue shutters. The Swiss house was built in 1932 by Le Corbusier, who also painted a fresco inside and designed the furniture. In 1959 he and Lucio Costa built La Maison du Brésil. The glass and metal building of La Fondation Avicenne was built by Claude Parent, and the Institut Néerlandais (1928–30) by Willem Marinus Dubok. Today 28 countries have houses here, providing lodgings to students of 122 different nationalities, a third of whom are French. Among its past residents some later attained worldwide fame – Jean-Paul Sartre and Raymond Barre of France, Senghor of Senegal, Habib Bourghiba of Tunisia, the Empress Farah Dibah, wife of the Shah of Iran, and Pierre Elliott Trudeau of Canada. Even the vegetation has been imported from the four corners of the earth – orange trees from Mexico, weeping willows from the Caucasus, fir trees from Canada and mulberry trees from China. During the summer holidays visitors can stay here at a very reasonable charge (tel 01 45 89 68 52).

Across the Boulevard Jourdain lies the **Parc de Montsouris**, the jewel in the crown. This is undoubtedly but a small-scale model of a London park, but its varied landscape provides a different enchantment at every bend, particularly in the early morning, before the arrival of the crowds, when it seems to belong to no one but yourself. In the afternoon it can be packed, noisy and dusty. The babble of children is often drowned out by the brass band. The musicians look good in their immaculate uniforms, but the effect is totally marred by the tinny sounds they produce, consistently out of tune. The audience, however, seems quite satisfied with the noise – they are after all getting a free concert. Then, every half hour on Wednesday, Saturday and Sunday afternoons, an old-fashioned bell summons the children to a magical performance of the modernised puppet theatre, which has recently replaced the traditional *Guignol*. The very young, however, do not notice any changes and they babble over with the same torrent of emotions as their parents did.

The restaurant next to the bandstand draws the better-off Parisians, who come from all over the city to enjoy the view and an open-air meal. Wedding receptions often take place here in summer, especially on Saturdays, the day chosen for most marriage ceremonies. Several brides can then be seen simultaneously in different parts of the park, their endless white skirts sweeping the rolling lawns, solemn grooms by their side, while a bunch of relatives surrounds them in their Sunday best, posing in front of some romantic statue for commemorative photos.

Parc de Montsouris was laid out by Napoléon III's landscape gardener Alphand on the site of four unused quarries. Work began in 1867, but it was an arduous task to transform this wasteland into magnificent gardens and took 11 years to complete (obviously the Prussian war and the *Commune* had also caused a delay). During the official inauguration ceremony, the guests discovered that the little artificial lake had dried up, owing to some technical fault. In his despair, the engineer who had conceived the lake committed suicide. The lake soon after filled with water and now hosts various colonies of wildlife and one pair of swans.

THE 15TH ARRONDISSEMENT

WHEN, in the late 1960s, a new class of young professionals was emerging from an ageing 19th-century France, they called the 15th arrondissement their own. Lying just across the river from the opulent 16th and blending into the no less prestigious 7th to its east, the 15th seemed a suitable address to these up-and-coming yuppies – not quite the best, yet close enough. The exorbitant prices of property in the 16th and 7th arrondissements were well beyond their means. And wouldn't they in any case have felt out of place among the old families secure in their social superiority? Here, in the 15th, ample space was available, precisely because of the economic and social changes taking place in France just then.

Previously a lower-class area, much of the land of the 15th had been occupied by hundreds of factories and workshops – including sulphurous gasworks and foul chemical industries, not to mention the malodorous slaughterhouse of Vaugirard. But now, with the new policy of economic restructuring and decentralisation, they were closing one by one – one out of three within 15 years! – to be replaced by as yet affordable blocks of flats and offices. Totalling an area of nearly 1,000 acres (350 hectares), this was the most gigantic clearance, the most spectacular and profitable real-estate transaction hitherto undertaken in the French capital. Thus the Vaugirard slaughterhouse was dismantled in 1979 and replaced by Parc Georges Brassens, which commemorates the self-effacing poet who had ended his life in one of the neighbouring side streets.

South-west of the Eiffel Tower, the heavy industries which had developed next to the harbour of Grenelle in the second half of the 19th century were replaced by Le Front de Seine, an unsightly complex of 18 high-rises begun in 1961, a time of poor architectural achievements, and constituting an eyesore on the riverside. In 1992 a new complex was inaugurated further down the Seine, on the western edge of the arrondissement, this time to replace the old Citroën car plant. But times have changed and in an environment-friendly age, much of the area was given over to a team of landscape gardeners, who laid out the spacious Parc André Citroën all the way down to the river, and were enthusiastically acclaimed by the media. Whether or not you like the contrived conception the French have of landscape gardening and the stylish constraints it imposes on nature, le Parc André Citroën is worth a visit, for it heralds the spirit of tomorrow's Paris, no less than the monuments erected in the last decade. Besides, Parisians love it.

With the dismantling of factories and workshops, half the working-class population of the arrondissement was moved out, much to the satisfaction of the gentrified newcomers, whose numbers more than compensated for this loss. With a total of 250,000 residents, the 15th is today the most heavily populated arrondissement, 20 per cent of whom are classified professionally as executives! Moreover, some of the younger natives of the 7th and the 16th have also moved here: even they can no longer keep up with the real-estate prices of their own territory. Crossing the river from the north and spilling over from the east, they have brought to the 15th a badly needed social aura, but they have not as yet been able to blot out entirely the proletarian stamp of its past. Short of wiping out the better part of the arrondissement, it would have been impossible to do so in such a short time. As it is, 40 per cent of its area has already been razed to the ground. Unfortunately, what has been erected in its stead often leaves much to be desired. . .

For although the 15th is prosperous, as many of its fashionable shops testify, it can hardly be called an attractive arrondissement. Humble dwellings and derelict constructions stand side by side with modern blocks of flats of variable quality and appeal, never attaining the magnificence of their wealthier neighbours (except at the eastern edge of the arrondissement, but then, this border strip is more of an extension of the 7th). Here and there some streets are lined with attractive, bourgeois, Haussmann-style, freestone buildings which were put up at the turn of the century, but these are not the rule. Devoid of beauty spots, of architectural harmony, and with no historical monuments to show for itself, the 15th is hardly a tourist Mecca. However, it can take pride in its world-famous Institut Pasteur where the fight against rabies continues, as well as research into other infectious diseases, notably AIDS, and which is also a centre for microbiological studies. Likewise, the 15th has a history of pioneering in aviation. It was on the site of today's heliport, at the south west edge of the arrondissement, which was incorporated into Paris only in 1925, that such aviators as Blériot, Roland Garros and the Voisin brothers experimented back in 1905. On 13 January 1908 Henri Farman was the first to complete a one-kilometre-long flight, after which le Terrain d'Issy, as it was then called, became the meeting place of the fashionable – men in chequered trousers and pointed shoes, with that extra touch of the light-coloured gaiters and the gloves; women in Liberty satins or embossed velvets. . . The following year, on 25 July, Blériot became the first man to fly over the English Channel, while in 1913 Roland Garros was the first to cross the Mediterranean.

If the 15th is no great draw for tourists, it is certainly a place of pilgrimage for mainstream France: year in, year out, following the cyclic rhythm of the calendar, multitudes of Frenchmen circle around Paris by way of its Boulevard Périphérique or the inner Boulevards des Maréchaux (also known as Extérieurs), heading, unflaggingly, bumper to bumper, towards the Porte de Versailles, at the southern edge of the arrondissement. After endless hassle and irritation, they swarm into the Palais des Expositions to visit one of its annual fairs or shows – le Salon de l'Auto, de l'Agriculture, du Prêt-à-porter – above all, La Foire de Paris, the major commercial event of France. With over a million visitors a year and a turnover of 130 million francs, with 3,500 exhibitors, from 75 different countries, this is a modern version of the Paris fairs held in medieval times. Every conceivable commodity is on display, from gardening utensils to jewellery, from the most exciting sports such as Benji, to traditional wines and gastronomy, from household goods and do-it-yourself components to international arts and crafts. Nor has entertainment been neglected – the medieval fire-eater, animal trainer and acrobat have been replaced by demonstrations of judo, karate, synchronised swimming and so on. This is also a major family outing, exhausting to parents and children alike, visited by people from all over the Paris area, the Ile-de-France, even the provinces, and, despite the hassle, they will be back next year.

Crowds also flock to the neighbouring Palais des Sports for the eternal Holiday on Ice or some other such popular entertainment, but, at least, with the brighter prospect of being comfortably seated.

No 36 rue des Morillons, next to Parc Georges Brassens, is another shrine to be visited by every Parisian at least once in a lifetime, not en masse, however, but individually. This is the Lost Property Office, to which the scatter-brained makes a private pilgrimage, despondent but with a secret glimmer of hope, hence the optimistic name of the place in French – *Objets Trouvés*. This was one of the last vestiges of pre-war France, where until very recently each of the 10,000 or so items that arrived here per month was sorted out manually and tied up with a string to which a handwritten label was attached – yellow labels for items lost on the Métro, green on buses, orange in airports and taxis, white in the street. Nothing seemed to have changed since the 1930s, when this department of the Préfecture de Police first established itself here. But the fantastic array of labelled keys is no longer on display. Computers have at last infiltrated these premises too, depriving Paris of its last outpost in the battle against modernity.

Those of you who are fond of statistics may like to know that nearly 150,000 items await their owners here, roughly 15,000 keys, closely followed in number by umbrellas. Some of the items vary with the season – sunglasses in summer, scarves and gloves (predominantly the right-hand glove, reputedly) in winter, school satchels in September and toys in December. The RATP, (the Paris transport authorities) are the main purveyors of the establishment – 40 per cent of items brought here were found on the public transport. Foreign passports are also handed in, as well as substantial sums of cash. After one year and one day unclaimed property is handed over to the finder who becomes its guardian, but who does not become its legal owner until 30 years have elapsed! If no such finder presents himself, unclaimed items are auctioned off.

The annual grape-picking ceremony at the resuscitated vineyard of the Clos des Morillons in the Parc Georges Brassens is a more joyous pilgrimage. It takes place on a Saturday in September or October. Some 600–700 kilos of grapes are picked that day, accompanied by folk dancing and music and much rejoicing as the harvest is loaded on to a brightly decked cart. The following summer, several hundreds of bottles of Clos des Morillons Pinot Noir – a fine vintage, according to connoisseurs – are sold for 50/60 Fr. each at 38 rue des Morillons. The proceeds go to charity.

The vineyard, with its 700 vines, was planted only in 1985, when the park was laid out. It was meant to rekindle old traditions, for before the Revolution, the vineyards of these sunny, southern slopes were the pride of the village of Vaugirard. Some malevolent tongues derided the quality of its wine, the sharpness of which 'would make a goat dance'. Sheer calumny, apparently, for it was even marketed abroad. Mention of its export to England goes back to 1453, when 'Jehan Legrand, husbandman, resident of Vaugirard, has received forty francs minted at Tours'. The English must have discovered the wine during the Hundred Years War that ended that year. Indeed, we know from the *Great Chronicles of France* that the English had occupied the undefended area stretching south of Paris, which included Vaugirard. An even earlier document, now kept at the National Archives, goes back to July 1230. This is a sales deed written on parchment, confirming that Milon Bergen and his wife Agnès sold one acre of vineyard to Etienne Poirier for the sum of 15 francs minted in Paris, paid in cash.

In 1717 as many as 27 of the 95 houses of Vaugirard were taverns, which meant they served wine. Parisians would come here on Sundays and holidays, especially after 1786, when the oppressive toll walls were built round Paris – in this arrondissement on the site of the Boulevards de Vaugirard, Pasteur, Garibaldi and Grenelle. Beyond the walls, wine escaped taxation and entertainment was cheap. Louis-Sébastien Mercier recorded that 'one drinks wine, one eats strawberries and peas. One dances to the sound of fiddles, musettes and oboes'. However, the prosperity did not last long – the profit-seeking winegrowers of Vaugirard replaced their wines with a new stock which yielded much more wine, but of poorer quality. The demanding consumers would have none of it and by 1810 there were no vineyards left in Vaugirard.

Before the 13th century Vaugirard, or Vauboitron as it was then called, was just a farm situated on the extensive domain of the powerful Abbey of Saint-Germain-des-Prés, along the ancient Roman road leading to Chartres and, beyond it, to the south-west. Today rue de Vaugirard (incidentally, the longest street in Paris) follows the same route. Like other areas of Paris its development in the 13th century was due to the religious orders. In 1256 Gérard de Moret, the Abbot of Saint-Germain, built a convalescent home and a chapel for his monks here, soon to be followed by a permanent establishment for the Benedictine Order, who set about clearing the land and planting vines and other crops. This was the nucleus of the village that was renamed Val Gérard after its founding father, eventually distorted to Vaugirard. Large herds of cattle grazed on its fertile land and the area became a major purveyor of meat to the city – hence the Vaugirard slaughterhouse.

No one knows why the village of Vaugirard was the object of ridicule. Even François I liked to make fun of its inhabitants and once signed his name as follows: 'François, first in name by the grace of God, King of France and Navarre, Marquis of Suresnes and Count of Vaugirard.' Burlesque literature in the 16th and the 17th centuries depicts it as a ridiculous village, focusing on its court clerk, a grotesque character who could not write while being watched. La Fontaine also mentions Vaugirard in one of his fables, '*Le singe et le dauphin*':

> . . . *de telles gens, il en est beaucoup*
> *Qui prennent Vaugirard pour Rome*
> *Et qui, caquetant au plus dru,*
> *Parlent de tout et n'ont rien vu.*

> . . . such people, there are plenty
> That take Vaugirard for Rome
> And who, prattling nineteen to the dozen,
> Talk of everything but have seen nothing.

A commentator on the fable wrote, 'Vaugirard: a very vulgar village on the outskirts of Paris' – a total misunderstanding, since La Fontaine simply meant a tiny village in contrast to the city of Rome. But prejudice dies hard. There was also the saying, 'I shall love you to folly' – a pun on *folie*, which also meant 'pleasure house' – 'and forsake you in Vaugirard', which was put in the mouths of cynical, fickle lovers, and points to the fact that some privileged people had country houses there. As a matter of fact, it was in one of the *folies* of Vaugirard that the painter Fragonard celebrated his wedding.

The presence of the privileged in the area was enhanced after Louis XIV had set up his court in Versailles in 1682. The quai de Chaillot and the Pont de Sèvres had not yet been built, and rue de Vaugirard, by then the busy high street of the village, became the major thoroughfare leading to the Court. Courtiers and powdered ladies in their stagecoaches could be seen rubbing shoulders with humble villagers in their carts, carrying wheat to the windmill (next to the present rue de Dantzig) or grapes to the wine press (on the unlikely site of today's Prisunic at 240 rue de Vaugirard).

Vaugirard and the neighbouring Grenelle were also a hunting ground for the nobility, who enjoyed exclusive hunting rights in pre-Revolutionary days. The commoners were obliged to tend the thickets where the game bred for the sole pleasure of the nobility, but woe betide a poacher caught killing a rabbit or a pigeon, an offence punishable by a fine or even imprisonment. This, though, was an improvement on the days of François I, when the first-time offender would be whipped until he bled, while a second offence would see him dispatched to the galleys! The hunting was an occasion for a display of magnificent attires, sumptuous embroidery, colourful feathers and great panache – all to the accompaniment of the tumult of the pack and the sound of the hunting horn. Both the Prince de Conti and the Prince de Condé came to hunt here – Conti from his residence at the Château d'Issy, Condé from the Château de Vanves (now Lycée Michelet).

The village of Grenelle too grew out of a religious domain, in this case the vast domain of the Abbey of Sainte-Geneviève in the Latin Quarter. It was given to the abbey in the early 6th century by the newly christened King Clovis in order to ensure its revenues. But while Vaugirard developed gradually, Grenelle sprang up overnight in the late 1820s in a hitherto uninhabited area. The alluvial plain of Grenelle, which stretched as far as Faubourg Saint-Germain in the 7th, was still submerged by the Seine in the 14th century. Its poor soil yielded little more than rye and alfalfa and did not attract settlers, but the plain contained the purest water and supplied the entire Left Bank. There were also quarries in Grenelle, although not to compete with those of Vaugirard, which provided the stone for the palaces of Tuileries and Luxembourg, the Invalides and the Ecole Militaire. The name Grenelle may have derived from *garanelle* (sand or sandy plain) or *garenne* (a rabbit warren) – much the same etymology, since sand is favourable to the development of warrens – which accounts for its success as a hunting-ground. The Château de Grenelle was the only dwelling here, the property of the illustrious Craon family. Next to it, the farm of Sainte-Geneviève, with its barns, courtyards, gardens and dovecote, was the property of the abbey and every Sunday and holiday a priest would come all the way from the Latin Quarter to celebrate mass in the chapel. Both farm and mansion overlooked the Place de Grenelle – now Dupleix – and were bought out at the time of Louis XV to allow the extension of the Ecole Militaire. The architect, Jean-Jacques Gabriel, used the Château as his headquarters between 1756 and 1764.

But France was heading for a period of turmoil and soon bucolic landscapes and Louis XV shepherdesses would be washed away by blood. On 29 January 1794 the Château became the Revolution's powder magazine. Paris had barely recovered from the bloodbath of the Terror when early in the morning of 31 August it was woken up by three terrific detonations. Gone was the Château de Grenelle. A pillar of black smoke coiled up, covering the cloudless, azure summer sky with a dark veil. Why and how the powder magazine had blown up was never found out.

The inhabitants of Vaugirard took an active part in the Revolution. In April 1789 they had gathered to designate their delegates to the General Assembly and written out their register of grievances, which was submitted to the Third State. In it they complained about the monks of Saint-Germain, the administrators of their village: 'big tithe-owners of the above-mentioned place, rendering no service, neither spiritual nor temporal'. As for the uninhabited plain of Grenelle, conveniently close to the Ecole Militaire, it came in handy for the setting up of a camp for three revolutionary battalions. Another camp was set up here during the *Directoire** to defend the new government if the need arose.

The plain also served as a field of summary executions until 1815. The condemned were lined up against the toll wall, just where the ticket office of Dupleix Métro station now stands. Among them were some émigrés who foolishly came back too soon, notably the widow of the Comte de Mesnard, who had been the mistress of George IV during her stay in England. Armand de Chateaubriand, the cousin of the famous writer, was another victim.

---

* French government between 27 October 1795 and 9 November 1799, when it was overthrown by General Bonaparte.

Grenelle retained its pastoral aspect until the 1820s, much to the satisfaction of Victor Hugo and his romantic friends – Mérimée, Delacroix, Vigny, Musset, Nerval – who would climb up the heights of Plaisance or Vaugirard to watch the sunset over the plain, the river and the hills of Passy and Auteuil beyond. It was those sunsets, transposed to Greece, that Victor Hugo described in his early poems *Les Orientales*, in 1829.

By then the plain had been acquired by the contractor Jean-Léonard Violet, and was undergoing major transformations. A few years earlier, Violet had already built up two new developments on the Right Bank – l'Europe and François I. Grenelle had the financial advantage of lying outside the toll walls, while the vicinity of the river offered further prospects for profit – a harbour for timber and other building material, a port and a toll bridge that would link it to Passy. Violet meant the new neighbourhood to be pleasant and even built himself a lovely house here. A 1300-seat theatre, le Théâtre de Grenelle, soon followed suit; it was hoped that this would enhance the prestige of the new borough, but it also aroused the jealousy of Vaugirard, whose local councillors voted against the installation of two street-lamps on the dark rue Mademoiselle which belonged to Vaugirard and led to the theatre, out of sheer spite. Violet named the borough Beau Grenelle, never doubting that before long it would become an insalubrious industrial area, for the very same reasons that had attracted him to it, namely, the availability of cheap land and the closeness of the river. He did not foresee that the port he built would start out as a financial fiasco owing to the opening up of the canals of Saint-Martin and Ourcq which linked Paris with the great industrial areas of the north-east, and also because of the huge investment it would take to improve the navigation on the Seine upstream and make it profitable. It was only when the City of Paris took these steps in the 1860s that the port of Grenelle became a profitable, even thriving enterprise.

The first enterprise in the 15th arrondissement was set up during the *Ancien Régime* at Javel, the plain along the river west of Grenelle, which also belonged to the Abbey of Sainte-Geneviève (*javelles* or *javeaux* in old French were unsteady islets created by river floods). There was a well-known windmill at Javel, Le Moulin de Javel, very popular among Parisians at the end of the 17th century, who would come over on Sundays to savour crayfish freshly caught in the Seine, washed down with wine from Vaugirard or Suresnes. Couples in illicit liaisons would come here to avoid preying eyes, as alluded to in a popular play, *Le Moulin de Javelle*, produced at the Théâtre Français on 6 July 1696. In 1777 the younger brother of Louis XVI, Le Comte d'Artois and future Charles X, bought up the place and built a chemical plant on the site. He was a prodigal young man, and although his brother the King provided him with an extremely generous allowance, he was always short of funds, which he hoped the factory would supply. He entrusted it to two chemists, Alban and Vallet, who invented on the premises the famous *eau de Javel*, cleaning liquid still commonly used in many French homes. The factory remained in operation for 112 years. A Citroën plant was opened on the site during the Great War, producing 50,000 shells per day. With peace restored, it was converted into a car plant and in 1919 the first standard Citroën was run on quai de Javel.

It was from 1830 on, during the reign of Louis-Philippe, that the industrialisation of the 15th arrondissement began, as indeed of all of France. It started modestly with chemical and metallurgical industries, building industries and textile mills, but it was only after 1860, when the area was incorporated into Paris – against the protests of its inhabitants – that the new arrondissement became heavily industrialised, in particular Grenelle (the 'Beau' had been realistically dropped) with its port, railway network, ironworks, boilerworks, rolling mills, rubber factories and glassworks, not to mention the putrid gasworks at La Motte Picquet. It was at Grenelle that the bridge of Arcole that links Notre-Dame and the Right Bank was built, as well as the bridges of the Lausanne-Fribourg railway line and, further afield, those of the Moscow-Novgorod line.

The technological and scientific progress of the latter part of the 19th century entailed the development of new industries, often related to construction. The two Universal Expositions of 1889 and 1900 on the nearby Champ-de-Mars gave them a further boost. Thus the general electricity and telephone companies were established in the 15th, as well as the lift company Edoux-Samain, which built the lifts of the Eiffel Tower, Armand Moisant, which built the Bazar de l'Hôtel de Ville and the Bon Marché, an industrial landscape which remained basically unchanged well into the 1960s, dominated by the Citroën plant with its 17,000-strong workforce. Citroën outstayed its welcome and moved out only in 1982, marking its departure with a procession of 41 of its models from 1919 to 1942, along the quai and up the Champs-Elysées. Even the Eiffel Tower was roped in to this big event, being temporarily decorated with the shining letters CITROEN.

Today office blocks have replaced chimney stacks, among them the 209-metre-high Tour Montparnasse, the tallest building in the capital. There was an outcry of protest when it was erected between 1969 and 1973, and an over-repeated joke, supposedly invented spontaneously out of the present circumstances, said that the Tour Montparnasse was the most beautiful spot in Paris because it was the only one from which it could not be seen! The joke had in fact already circulated in the late 1880s, when the Eiffel Tower was being erected. The tower was followed in 1990 by the new (and third) Montparnasse railway station, built to accommodate the South West TGV (high speed train) line to Spain, serving 59 million passengers a year and intended to become the largest railway station in France and the new centre of gravity of the arrondissement. As a concession to Parisians, who were totally disorientated in this surreal environment of concrete, a vast garden was laid out above the station, bearing the promising name of Le Jardin Atlantique. Vegetation from both sides of the Atlantic was planted as an extra gesture. However, it takes a lift and some corridors through one of the blocks on the Boulevard de Vaugirard to reach the garden and discover, to one's dismay, that it is literally hemmed in on all sides by fortress-like buildings, blotting out the horizon and fending off any hope of an Atlantic breeze.

The arty and bohemian crowd of pre-World War II Paris would have felt out of place in this Montparnasse of high-tech and real-estate speculation, which has shifted from the 6th and 14th to the 15th arrondissement. In those days the 15th served as living quarters on the periphery of Montparnasse for those too poor to live in the centre of action – the poorer they were, the further away they lived. The Cité Falguière on this side of the arrondissement offered shelter to the slightly better-off; the downright destitute lodged at La Ruche at Passage de Dantzig, on the edge of the horrific slum-belt of Paris known as *la zone* (see also chapters on the 14th and 19th arrs), and by the Vaugirard slaughterhouse.

La Ruche was the baby of the *pompier* sculptor Boucher, the darling of society though the son of poor farmers, who bought this piece of wasteland from the owner of the neighbouring bistrot, Le Dantzig, in order to house fellow artists. The *patron* of Le Dantzig was only too happy to be rid of it and sold it for a song. Slaughterhouse or no, the artist community was happy to have a roof over its head, all the more since Boucher planted the substantial plot of land with beautiful trees and in no time transformed it into a pastoral oasis. In order to extend the lodgings for future tenants, le Père Boucher, as he was fondly called, went over to the Champ-de-Mars and bought some vestiges of the pavilions of the 1900 World Fair, notably Eiffel's wine rotunda. This was common practice at the time and other artist quarters in Paris are still made up of such pavilions. Although he himself was the academic sculptor of the establishment, and no great artist, Boucher was fond of his anarchical, eccentric residents and overlooked their unpaid 50-franc rent bills. Few of the tenants were actually French, Fernand Léger being an exception. Most had escaped oppression and pogroms in eastern Europe – Lipchitz, Zadkine, Archipenko, Marc Chagall – a great majority of Jews, who, between the years 1905 and the outbreak of World War I, found at La Ruche the freedom necessary for creative minds and turned it into the birthplace of *l'Ecole de Paris*.

Even when La Ruche declined during the war, many Jewish artists went on living there, a fact that did not escape the vigilant eye of the Gestapo several decades later; Epstein and Granowski were rounded up from here, never to return.

Those were just drops in the ocean. The big round-up of Parisian Jews, La Grande Rafle, the one meant to cleanse the city of its Eastern European Jewry, sadly also took place in the 15th, in the Vélodrome d'Hiver on rue Nélaton, next to the Boulevard de Grenelle. In happier times Vél d'Hiv', as it was commonly called, had been used for sports and other miscellaneous events – boxing rounds starring such champions as Marcel Cerdan (also famously the lover of Edith Piaf), political meetings held by Maurice Thorez and Léon Blum, and a performance by the legendary tenor

Beniamino Gigli. Above all, it housed the famous six-day cycling races, which drew in 15,000 fervent spectators, who would camp round the clock in the velodrome for the entire duration of the race. But at dawn on 16 July 1942, a sordid page was to stain the history of France, when 13,152 Jews were snatched from their sleep by the French police to be sent to their deaths – a disappointing figure, considering that 28,000 arrests had been reckoned upon in the Paris area (the operation was originally intended for 14 July but, out of fear of public reaction, was deferred by two days). Adults without children were dispatched directly to the camp of Drancy, north of Paris, while those with children aged 2 to 16 – over 8,000 – were transported to Vél d'Hiv'. For two days convoys of Paris green buses, requisitioned for the occasion, plied the city with their load of victims, in broad daylight and in view of all, disgorging them in Vél d'Hiv. Here began a six-day inferno in suffocating heat up to 40°C, with no amenities, a foretaste of a long journey to come – children down with measles, pregnant women, hysterical mothers driven to acts of folly, shrieks of despair and nauseating smells of excrement that filled the entire neighbour-hood – all under the callous eye of the police. Occasionally a tear of sympathy was shed, or a helping hand proffered, but overall the police were 'obeying orders'.

Vél d'Hiv', like so much of the 15th arrondissement since, was demolished in 1958 and replaced by a block of flats. The Square de la Place du Martyr Juif was inaugurated along the quai de Grenelle to the left on 17 July 1994, endowed with a garden and a moving sculpture by Walter Spitzer. An annual ceremony now commem-orates the round-up of Vél d'Hiv, attended in 1995 by the newly elected President Chirac who, in a courageous speech, acknow-ledged for the first time in the name of officialdom France's responsibility in the crime. He also inaugurated a commemorative plaque, but despite its plea for remembrance, few people pass by it and fewer still notice it.

La Ruche too was meant for demolition in 1967, to be replaced by council flats, and only its artists' relentless determination, sup-ported by an anonymous gift from the United States in 1971, saved it. On the whole, the 15th is not the home of nostalgics but of go-getting, forward-looking, family-orientated Parisians, the pioneering territory of French yuppies (who have meanwhile spread elsewhere too), and as such takes pride in its quality of life. This is exemplified by the spectacular increase in its number of trees and gardens in the last 15 years: more than 3,400 trees and 27.5 hectares (68 acres) of new gardens, the most recent of which, the Parc André Citroën, endows the left bank of the Seine with a third esplanade, west of the Invalides and the Champ-de-Mars.

The shops and restaurants of the arrondissement also bear witness to its prosperity. Of course there are the traditional stalls on rue du Commerce and rue de Lourmel with their cascades of colourful, succulent fruit, their tantalising variety of cheeses and the rest – but it is the increasing number of luxury groceries and trendy caterers that is striking, along with the fact that practically all the big names in the capital have opened shops here – Hédiard, Dalloyau, Le Nôtre and Flo – as well as the fashionable baker Poilâne. Likewise, the pioneering *nouvelle cuisine* restaurant Pierre Vedel was set up in the 15th when this style of cooking became the rage. The health-conscious inhabitants of the 15th are also fortunate to have a large choice of fitness clubs, first and foremost Aquaboulevard, designed to meet the modern French craving for sunshine and tropical shores. The gigantic concrete and glass centre, which offers them plenty of exotic vegetation and blue waters (as well as shops and eating-places), is a temple of well-being. Here the cult of the human body is celebrated with all the customary rites of the modern age – jacuzzis, Turkish baths, biomarine treatments, saunas, sports and games. This dream-come-true attraction, however, is now in financial straits – once the novelty was over, and in view of the unavoidably exorbitant entrance fees, the crowds gradually dwindled.

With both feet planted firmly in the future, this arrondissement considers its children a top priority. Is it a coincidence that the late Françoise Dolto, the progressive psychoanalyst who believed in a child's right to happiness – a revolutionary idea in France – chose to open a family centre in the 15th? The Left Bank Bilingual School of Paris (French-English) also took up residence in the 15th, aware of the appeal of this facility to broad-minded, well-travelled people, determined to have their children learn English. Thus, although some of the inhabitants of the arrondissement prefer to withdraw into their national shell and support Le Pen's *Front*

National, the majority are preparing for tomorrow's Europe and embrace the international community. A considerable number of foreigners already work here for different companies, and the Japanese have established the Hôtel Nikko among the high-rises of the Front de Seine.

FROM MONTPARNASSE TO LA RUCHE

Although its own residents appreciate living in the 15th, with its ample amenities, the visitor is less likely to find charm in its cityscape of nondescript blocks of flats, some of them a downright eyesore. Indeed, you are not likely to come across a fellow sightseer on the streets of the 15th, nor to remember your excursion here as one of the highlights of your visit to Paris. Nevertheless, for the social observer of contemporary Paris the 15th may present special interest, as it was here that the transformation of the old Parisian way of life was largely enacted. Here Parisians first withdrew from the streets, relinquishing them to cars and to transients and shifting the action instead to isolated, standardised dwelling units. Here too anarchical concrete made its first appearance in the 1960s, since when it has spread like cancer into the rest of Paris.

However, there are still some pleasant streets and squares and hidden nooks which have survived discreetly in the shade of nondescript constructions; and the abundant food displays on some of the streets are always a heart-warming sight. So if you have time to spare and the sun is out, why not come and see how middle-class Parisians live today?

Starting on the corner of **AVENUE DU MAINE** and **BOULEVARD DU MONTPARNASSE**, at the north-eastern tip of the arrondissement, our itinerary includes the museum of the Institut Pasteur (open only 2–5.30 pm; closed weekends, holidays).

At 21 **Avenue du Maine**, nestling at the foot of the Montparnasse tower, is a lovely leafy alley, dipped in limes and crumbling under its rambling creepers – who knows for how long? Property developers rubbed their hands when the owner of the alley died, presuming,

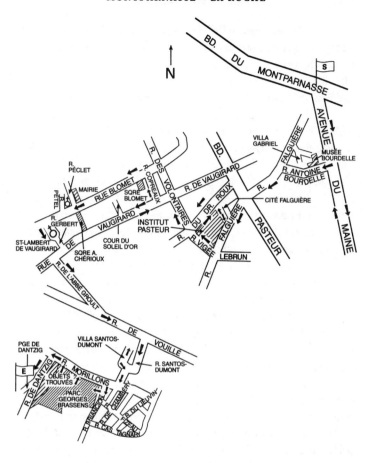

rightly, that owing to the exorbitant death duties levied in France the inheritors would not afford to keep the place. But they were thwarted when the City of Paris asserted its pre-emptive rights, for no better reason, however, than to carry out a real-estate operation of its own! As matters stand at present, the unfortunate historic alley, once frequented by Picasso, Braque, Modigliani, Soutine and Fernand Léger, and now one of the loveliest oases in the arron-dissement, may well be disfigured by the time you arrive.

Retrace your steps and take **RUE ANTOINE BOURDELLE** on your left. At no. 16, the one-time home of sculptor Antoine Bour-delle narrowly escaped demolition when it was turned into a museum, **Musée Bourdelle.** In 1929 the sculptor's widow, gener-ously backed by the art patron Ernest Cognacq, succeeded in buy-ing up the premises so as to preserve her husband's heritage and offer it to France; but the state simply rejected her donation! So did the City of Paris, which, however, revised its opinion 20 years later... Yet Bourdelle was one of France's major sculptors, quali-fied by Rodin as 'a scout of the future' (hence his contribution to the stunning avant-garde Théâtre des Champs-Elysées in the 8th arr.). Indeed, unlike academic sculptors and their moralising gran-diloquence and superfluous ornamentation (which Rodin had already dusted off and replaced with sensual energy) Bourdelle opted for a rigorous structure and a powerful rhythm, in keeping with his peasant origins. The artist's goal, he felt, was to capture the whole and recreate it – which set him miles ahead of the dogmatic approach of most of his contemporaries. No wonder his war mem-orial, which, rather than flatter heroic patriotism, expressed the terror and despair of the fighters, displeased the general public. The great philosopher Bergson admired his approach and his artistry: 'What strikes me as soon as I look at one of your works is that each part seems to contain the whole. Isn't that the mark of perfection?'

Antoine Bourdelle was also one of the prominent teachers at the celebrated Académie de la Grande Chaumière and left a deep impact on Montparnasse's artists, who, though freshly arrived from Eastern Europe, were labelled '*l'Ecole de Paris*', for lack of a better name. Some of them preferred to come and work here, in his studio, on what was then known as Impasse du Maine, notably Léon Indenbaum who described Bourdelle as 'a great master', 'a marvellous teacher'. Indenbaum was never so encouraged as when, one day, having examined his work, *Le Petit Pâtre*, the master turned to the class and said: 'Monsieur Indenbaum évolue' ('Monsieur Indenbaum is developing'). A happy atmosphere reigned in the studio, where the Russian students would sing songs of their homeland. Twice a week Bourdelle would come to check their progress and for a long while listen to the nostalgic melodies behind the door before entering.

Bourdelle settled down on these premises in 1884 upon his arrival in Paris when he was 23, and remained here for the rest of his life, until 1929. At first he worked and lived in the same studio, but gradually he acquired the neighbouring studios, where he installed his family whom he had brought from the countryside; this accounts for the heterogeneous character and miscellaneous layout of the museum. His apartment and his studio have been left as they were and are sheer delight, but the extension added in 1961 to mark the first centenary of his birth – a gigantic hall where some of his monumental sculptures are on display – is not an architectural success. Another extension was added behind the old studios by Christian Portzamparc (the talented architect of the Cité de la Musique at la Villette). Here are exhibited various studies, among them for the above-mentioned 1870 war memorial entitled *Montauban*. Other sculptures are scattered about in the attractive setting of the gardens, and it is mainly in the intimate and serenely charming back garden that you should seek them out.

When Bourdelle moved to Impasse du Maine in 1884, it was just a little alley with a couple of studios submerged in lush gardens. Beyond were cornfields and vineyards. After all only 24 years earlier the toll gate of Maine was still standing here, marking the boundary of Paris, a neighbourhood of pleasant *guinguettes* where Parisians came to relax on Sundays over a pint of cheap wine. Today Bourdelle's exquisitely outdated oasis is situated just next to the entrance to the tunnel of Avenue du Maine with its endless flow of zooming, whizzing traffic, an isolated survivor among the surreal concrete chaos of contemporary Montparnasse.

Continue along rue Antoine-Bourdelle and turn left into rue Falguière, which commemorates another prominent sculptor and teacher of Bourdelle. Cross the Boulevard Pasteur and continue to the second alley on your right – the celebrated **Cité Falguière**, the home of many an artist during the heyday of Montparnasse. Today it has little to show for itself but in the early days, when its houses were freshly painted pink, it looked pleasant enough to be known as La Villa Rose. Besides, living at the Cité Falguière was considered a social promotion in comparison with the remote artists' quarters at La Ruche. When the Hungarian sculptor Joseph Csaky (Szeged) left Budapest for Paris, he had not a penny to his name and had to make part of the journey on foot. Upon arrival at the Gare de l'Est he was fortunate enough to meet a kind-hearted stranger who saw him safely to Cité Falguière, his contact address where two of his friends were living: 'A pleasant, black-bearded gentleman, seeing I was lost, led me into a pit and paid for my ticket: for the first time I was taking the Métro. We got off at Pasteur station. My guide pointed out a sign: 'Cité Falguière.' Like everyone else, however, Csaky had first to content himself with La Ruche. Exceptionally, Soutine is believed to have started out here, in a corrugated iron hovel into which Modigliani crammed his volumes of poetry. All this is difficult to verify, since the artists kept moving about and settling in one another's lodgings. Lipchitz was definitely living at the Cité Falguière at the time and it seems that he introduced the two painters to each other. Between 1912 and 1913 Modigliani shared a house here with Fujita, Modigliani on the ground floor and Fujita above. This was a time of destitution, of unpaid bills, of migration from one address to the next. Modigliani, always penniless, ended up by being kicked out by the landlady, Madame Durchoux, a good lady who often turned a blind eye to the non-payment of rent, but whose patience, too, had its limits. Spending nights on the public benches of Paris, soaked in alcohol and drugs, was Modigliani's habit, but he needed a place to work, so he moved his belongings to another artists' refuge on 216 Boulevard Raspail in the 14th arrondissement (no longer in existence). It was at the Cité Falguière that the Romanian sculptor Brancusi initiated Modigliani in the art of sculpture. A generation earlier Bouillot had done the same for Gauguin. Bouillot was living at no. 4 and Gauguin came to see him from the corner house of 74 rue Falguière, his home between 1877 and 1880.

Continue along rue Falguière, turn right into rue Vigée-Lebrun and right again into **RUE DU DOCTEUR ROUX** for a visit to the museum of l'**Institut Pasteur** at no. 25.

Like Musée Bourdelle and other museums, this was the private home of Louis Pasteur, where he lived his last seven years. It had been allocated to him by the Institute, and was donated by his daughter after his death to be converted into a museum. When the museum was opened in 1935, it was arranged to look practically as it had at the time of Pasteur, and is therefore an invaluable sample of a typical late 19th-century bourgeois interior. Only the laundry room on the first floor was done away with and has been converted into a science hall (*salle scientifique*). On display are some of the items that accompanied Pasteur and his collaborators in their work, and this is a good place to begin your visit in order to retrace the development of his discoveries. Here you will see, for example, the first microscope he owned, when he was still a student. It had a magnification of 800 times – extraordinary for those days, though perhaps unimpressive in comparison with today's electronic lenses which enlarge an image one million times! Ironically, Pasteur never saw the viruses he was working on and it was only in 1962 that the rabies virus could be seen with the aid of a microscope. Also on display are two large cardboard models of crystals, cut out and glued together by Pasteur himself for the benefit of students who were sitting at the back of vast amphitheatres, so that they could follow his lectures on crystallography – evidence of Pasteur's qualities as a pedagogue. You can also see the utensils Pasteur used for his first pasteurisation and sterilisation experiments.

While Pasteur's notoriety is associated with his discovery of the vaccine against rabies in 1885, one must be aware that he was 63 at the time and that this was the result of his research in other fields that had begun in 1848. What the *salle scientifique* reveals is that, thanks to his systematically coherent and analytical mind, each discovery led to the next, each was a link in a chain that was broken only when he died in 1895. As he himself had said, 'Luck smiles on minds that are prepared.' Thus his discovery of fermentation, notably of wine and beer, led to his work on germs, then on animal diseases and finally human disease, which eventually led to his research on rabies.

His work on fermentation had major economic consequences. In 1857 the manufacturers of beetroot alcohol in the north of France, unable to account for the inconsistent quality of their product, turned to Pasteur, who had graduated from the prestigious Ecole Normale Supérieure, which was no small recommendation, and now held the chair of Chemistry at the University of Lille. In fact, Pasteur saw only what everyone else saw; it was his thought processes that were different. Thus in 1857 he determined that fermentation was caused by invisible organisms or germs called ferments and not by spontaneous generation, and deduced that by isolating and selecting the ferments one could obtain the desired quality of alcohol. Pasteur's sensational discovery secured the fortune of brewers, for which the grateful Dane Carlsberg paid him tribute by installing his bust on the brewery's façade in Copenhagen. This discovery led him to the conclusion that germs are to be found everywhere and that, since the theory of spontaneous generation was proved erroneous, they would have to be isolated if contagious diseases were to be fought successfully. From here it was but a short step to the development of pasteurisation – named after him – and sterilisation, processes that did not just contribute to the prosperity of some brewers but, for the first time in the history of mankind, towards the eradication of epidemics. Today l'Institut Pasteur is still one of only two establishments in France that prepares vaccines against various diseases. Following Pasteur's discoveries, victims of contagious disease no longer shared their room with other patients, let alone their bed, as had been the case for centuries.

But Pasteur was a doctor of science, not of medicine, and the medical community was as conservative as the rest of society. Outraged that an outsider should instruct them in conducting their profession, they mounted a fierce campaign against him and went on operating on patients in their morning coats and with unwashed hands. While doctors elsewhere in the Western world lost no time in acknowledging Pasteur's findings and applying them to their patients, it took French surgeons 20 years to accept the truth. How many lives would have been saved but for this blinkered attitude! Nobody, however, challenged him when he discovered the remedy for rabies in 1885, for it was incontrovertible that he had saved the life of a little boy bitten by a rabid dog. People streamed to Paris from all over Europe, even from as far as Russia, to be inoculated by Pasteur against rabies. By 1888 Pasteur had managed to persuade the international community to raise enough money for the founding of the Institut Pasteur to replace the laboratory of l'Ecole Normale Supérieure, which, he claimed, was no longer adequate for the advanced state of his research.

A part of the building was reserved for Pasteur's apartment, a grand bourgeois home by the standards of those days. It even had a bathroom and a bathtub with hot and cold running water – one of the first bathrooms in Paris and a real luxury in those days. The bathroom remains as it was, except that it is now also used as a wardrobe to store some of Pasteur's clothes and hats, along with his professorial gown, his insignia of the *Légion d'honneur* and his embroidered *Académicien*'s outfit, the celebrated *habit vert*. The other rooms are dark and stuffy, cluttered with austere family portraits in excessively elaborate gilt frames, (There are also some portraits painted by Pasteur himself, characterised by the same sharp observation that was so central to his scientific career). A suffocating atmosphere permeates the place, so foreign to the aesthetic canons of today. Paradoxically, it is a relief to visit Pasteur's crypt underneath, a glorious abode for his remains, bursting with luminous gilded mosaics.

As one of France's undoubted heroes, Pasteur was destined to be buried in the Panthéon but his wife changed her mind at the last minute and wished him to be buried in a crypt adjoining the Institut Pasteur. The inscriptions on the crypt commemorate Pasteur's ideals, which he shared with the Republic and its bourgeoisie, namely the love of science and art combined with patriotism and the Christian faith. The crypt itself is a reflection of the time, decorated in the Byzantine style, like the contemporary Basilica of the Sacré-Coeur. Pasteur's crypt is largely inspired by the mosaics in Ravenna, to which were added polychrome designs evoking Pasteur's discoveries. Pasteur's wife was laid here too in 1910, but his disciple and successor at the head of the Institute, Dr Roux, was not granted this honour and now rests in the garden. Thus, apart from Napoleon, Pasteur seems to be alone in having his own private crypt in Paris, and there isn't a village or town in France that does not boast a street or avenue that bears his name.

Today 2,600 people work in the institute, 1,100 of whom are scientists. Since it first opened, eight have been awarded the Nobel Prize. Every year 600 trainees from over 50 countries are welcomed to the Institut Pasteur, which, in its turn, is the living hub of a network of institutes in all parts of the world. In the last few years the Institute has been intensively committed to the fight against AIDS and its small hospital (100 beds) exclusively treats AIDS sufferers. Despite government subsidies, which total 40 per cent of the Institute's budget, most of the funds are raised by private donors, which enables the Institute to maintain its independence. The donors are not necessarily French; among them, for example, was the late Duchess of Windsor.

As you leave the Institute turn left on rue du Docteur Roux and right into rue des Volontaires, which will lead you to **RUE DE VAUGIRARD**, once the high street of the village of Vaugirard. Nothing is left of its rural past and the oldest vestige you can see – though perhaps not for long – is the 18th-century alley at no. 226 to your left, **La Cour du Soleil d'Or**, where the Auberge du Soleil d'Or was situated. On the night of 8 September 1796, 60 Jacobine conspirators gathered in this inn, where they had set up an arms and ammunition depot; hundreds more awaited instructions in other cabarets in the area. Their plan was to stir up the troops at Grenelle and overthrow the government, but the troops would not follow them and their conspiracy, known as the *Conjuration du Camp de Grenelle*, ended in bloodshed. Some of them managed to flee through a narrow passage leading to the present rue Blomet, but 132 were arrested, 31 of whom were shot on the plain of Grenelle and many others deported. Incidentally, five years earlier another abortive conspiracy had been fomented at the Soleil d'Or, organised by Citizen Thévenot (but the great Condé was behind it), in the hope of exterminating all the members of the Jacobine Club and bringing Louis XVI back to the throne. The Mayor of Vaugirard got wind of the conspiracy and had Citizen Thévenot arrested.

Those who were lucky enough to escape after the 1792 conspiracy did so by way of the narrow alley, la Cour du Soleil d'Or, precisely the spot that a committee of conservationists have been trying to save, advocating the preservation of the site on historically valid grounds, all the more justifiable since the 15th arrondissement has little history to show for itself. Today the Cour du Soleil d'Or is a dead-end alley, so you will have to retrace your steps on rue de Vaugirard to join rue Blomet.

Turn left on rue Copreaux and left again on **RUE BLOMET**, a typical nondescript street, yet another stronghold of Montparnasse in its heyday. No. 33 was the site of the celebrated Bal Nègre to which everyone swarmed in the 1920s. Originally this was just an ordinary neighbourhood café. At weekends, however, its back room became the dance floor of the area's West Indian community, who exploded to the rhythm of beguine, their own variety of jazz, swaying to exhaustion to the wonderful sound of a clarinet in an atmosphere hanging heavy with the smell of rum. From time to time they gave the floor to outdated folk groups in their traditional garb who would sing sentimental songs from the colonies. Needless to say, at a time when jazz and all things black were the 'in' thing, and the accordion and the *bal-musette* had been ousted, this exotic, colourful place could not long escape the attention of Robert Desnos, who was living just a couple of houses away. He soon stirred up his Surrealist friends who, together with the rest of Montparnasse, invaded the place and called it their own. By the same token they of course destroyed its atmosphere. Once the painters of *l'Ecole de Paris*, Jean Cocteau, and the American expatriates had moved in, the genuine Antillais no longer felt at home and deserted the place. The crowd of the Roaring Twenties did not stay for long and Le Bal Nègre was once more just an ordinary neighbourhood café. The Antillais, however, never came back. The present owner has tried to revive it by adjusting to new trends. It is now called the St Louis Blues and serves a potpourri of Manhattan cocktails, Tex-Mex cuisine and Auvergnat- or Périgord-style salads.

Just a few steps up the street, at no. 45, is **Square Blomet**, a neat garden surrounded by surreal-looking highrises. It is situated on the site of one of the two phalansteries of the Surrealists, the other being on rue du Château in the 14th arrondissement (see that chapter). The artists here were less fanatical about ideological and political issues than their literary counterparts in the 14th arrondissement, and also less violent. The first to arrive was Juan Mirò, who made himself an impeccably neat nest inside a dilapidated house that threatened to collapse, but which was not devoid of pastoral charm, shaded by the overhanging branches of the neighbours' trees. In early spring he even benefited from their purple, fragrant lilac blossoms. André Masson, on the other hand, lived here with his wife and little daughter in appalling poverty and amid a barely conceivable clutter. Among their friends who stayed at or frequented the place were Robert Desnos, Michel Leiris, Alberto Giacometti and Jacques Prévert. Despite its historical interest, the house was probably beyond repair and was torn down, but at least one had the good idea to replace it with a garden. It would have also been a good idea to fix a plaque at the entrance as a tribute to its former tenants, and another one next to Mirò's sculpture, *l'Oiseau Lunaire*, inside the garden, which was offered to the City of Paris by the artist, and of which no mention is made.

Most of the houses along rue Blomet are of little interest but no. 48 across the street is a rustic old building, a welcome survivor. Keep on walking as far as **SQUARE ADOLPHE-CHERIOUX**, on your left, and the traffic-free **RUE PECLET** with the imposing **Mairie** on your right. Built for the better-off few at a time when the 15th arrondissement was essentially proletarian, it is a pleasant spot, which has not been wrecked by concrete and has preserved an architectural unity. Continue along rue Blomet to rue Pétel, the next street to your right. A turn-of-the-century *boulangerie* stands on its corner, from which emanates a wonderful smell of fresh bread. On the right-hand side of rue Pétel is a tiny Russian Orthodox church, resplendent with icons and, if you hit it at the right time, with melodious services.

Back on rue Blomet, as you reach **RUE GERBERT** on the left, you will notice two attractive, solid bourgeois buildings, another indication that this was where the more affluent people lived, around the **church of Saint-Lambert**. It was built during the Second Empire to satisfy the needs of the growing population of Vaugirard. The church has no great artistic merit, but at least its simple austerity does not interfere with the surroundings, which have preserved their old-fashioned provincial character. As you skirt it to reach the entrance, which faces east according to tradition, you will come to the continuation of rue Gerbert, which will take you back to rue de Vaugirard; there turn right, then left, into rue de l'Abbé Groult.

Continue along the latter and on to rue de Vouillé. Turn right into **RUE SANTOS-DUMONT**, a haven of pastoral serenity, especially as you penetrate the U-shaped alley of **Villa Santos-Dumont**, whose Art Deco houses are surrounded by tree branches and creepers and are animated by a lively chorus of birds. In these discreet, hidden parts poet and singer Georges Brassens spent the last decade of his life, at no. 42 rue Santos-Dumont. Ever since his arrival in Paris in 1939 from his native southern Sète, his Parisian territory had always been the 14th arrondissement, where he had first boarded with his maternal aunt, Antoinette, at 173 rue d'Alésia. In 1944, when he needed safer shelter so as not to be sent a second time to Germany on an STO (Service du Travail Obligatoire) mission, his aunt sent him to her friend Jeanne, who lived in a wretched hovel with no gas, no electricity and no running water, at no. 9 Impasse Florimont, an 'appendix' of rue d'Alésia. Here she shared a humble existence and a heart of gold with her husband Marcel and with a wide spectrum of animals, both four-footed and feathered. It was to Marcel, who had hidden him from the Gestapo and offered him a roof, that Brassens dedicated his famous *Chanson pour l'Auvergnat*:

> *Elle est à toi cette chanson*
> *Toi l'Auvergnat qui sans façon*
> *M'as donné quatre bouts de bois*
> *Quand dans ma vie il faisait froid. . .*

> This song is for you
> The Auvergnat who without ado
> Gave me four bits of wood
> When my life was bitter cold.

And it was to Jeanne's duck, whom the threesome had not the heart to drop into the cooking pot, that Brassens dedicated his exquisite *La Cane de Jeanne*, when the bird eventually died a natural death:

> *La cane*
> *De Jeanne*
> *Est morte au gui l'an neuf,*
> *Elle avait fait, la veille,*
> *merveille!*
> *Un oeuf!*

> Jeanne's duck
> Has died
> She died on New Year's Day
> And had made on the Eve,
> How marvellous!
> An egg!

Even when Brassens was financially secure, he would not betray his benefactors and the woman who had mothered him in Paris. For over 35 years he went on sharing their humble roof and fare. But after Marcel's death in 1965, when Jeanne, already in her seventies, and knowing herself equally doomed, married briefly a 37-year-old

Parc Georges-Brassens

fellow, Brassens decided to move out. Jeanne had only a few months left and Brassens, after a short stay in a huge block of flats in the 14th arrondissement (so unlike him), moved to the quiet rue Santos-Dumont. His life-long companion, whom he had met after the war, the Eastern European Joha Heyman – Püppchen, to him – was always hidden from the public eye, but always present by his side.

Leave rue Santos-Dumont on its southern side. Turn right into rue des Morillons on the northern boundary of a network of narrow, sunny alleys, bordered on the west by rue Brancion. It was opened in the middle of the 19th century by the developer Chauvelot, and was named le **Village de l'Avenir**. Its street names and the obelisk that once stood there commemorated the victories of the Italian campaigns and was a popular attraction for a Sunday stroll. If you come here in fine weather, when the enclave is bathed in sunshine, you will appreciate why it was propitious for vine-growing. Early 18th-century archives record that its vineyard, le Clos des Morillons, bore black grapes. North of rue des Morillons, on the other hand, the land was taken over by quarries, all the way to rue de la Convention, the stone of which was used for the building of the Ecole Militaire.

Turn left into **RUE BRANCION**. At no. 15 still stands boxing champion Jean Walczak's café, looking as it must have done some 40 or 50 years ago, the kind of place Georges Brassens found congenial. Old pictures, yellowed with age, and autographed by such notables as Marcel Thil, Maurice Holtzen and Marcel Cerdan, line the walls and until recently friends of the *patron* gathered here on Sunday afternoons for a game of *belote* (a card game).

Cross over and walk into the **Parc Georges Brassens**, lying on the site of the old slaughterhouse of Vaugirard, which used to supply the entire Left Bank. Some vestiges of it remain, notably two sculptures of cattle by Auguste Cain surmounting the main gate of the gardens on rue des Morillons, as well as Baltard's characteristic iron pavilions, which now house a secondhand book market at weekends. The books are well worth browsing through, provided you know French. There is also a herb garden whose exquisite fragrance will keep your mind off the ugly high-rises that obstruct the horizon to the south. A vineyard of 700 vines recalls the old vineyard of Vaugirard, highlighted by a grape-picking ceremony on a Saturday in either September or October, depending on the year (to be checked at the Mairie).

Exit through **RUE DES MORILLONS**, turn left and walk past the red brick offices of the Objets Trouvés (lost property). Turn left into rue de Dantzig and diagonally right into **PASSAGE DE DANTZIG**, the last destination on this itinerary. Tucked away in these remote parts – even more remote in the early years of the century – nestling among venerable trees, is the celebrated **La Ruche**, standing behind an imposing gate – a moving sight, so impregnated is La Ruche with the history of many of this century's great artists. Chagall, Zadkine, Soutine, Archipenko, Kisling, Lipchitz, Fernand Léger and many others, all lived here at the outset of their careers.

However, this was hardly a paradise – most of the artists ran away from here as soon as they could afford to! When he washed up here in the autumn of 1910, Zadkine commented, 'To tell the truth, it was a sinister Brie cheese.' He went on, 'A pile of stones, a jumble of chairs and other broken furniture, leaning in their misery against the walls of this mortuary institution.' How could it have been otherwise? To start with, La Ruche rose in the middle of a desolate plain – *la zone* – where 'vegetation was rare and shade was totally unknown', and where a well-structured society of rag-pickers ('*zonards*') held sway. Even worse, La Ruche had been erected just next to the slaughterhouse! 'Two, three o'clock in the morning. The sky is blue. Dawn is rising. Over there, further away, the cattle were being slaughtered, the cows were bellowing, and I painted them. I can still hear their screams in the night as their heads were being cut off,' wrote Chagall in his autobiography. On the other hand, the rent was only 37 francs a term and unpaid rents were overlooked by the kindly Boucher. He also overlooked, without batting an eyelid, the arrival of new tenants who moved in secretly in the middle of the night, such as Soutine, a total stranger whom he bumped into the following morning, and whom he greeted naturally, as if he had always been there. It is true that Soutine had got lost on the way and might otherwise have turned up earlier. Still, Boucher never checked his identity, which was all to the good, since Soutine had no identity papers and was not to have any for the next seven years.

More than a landlord Alfred Boucher was a philanthropist who had founded La Ruche as a calling and a mission to help out needy artists. In 1900, while roaming around this section of the *zone*, he stepped into a rickety wineshop and struck a deal with its owner to the satisfaction of both sides: 5,000 francs for 5,000-square metres: the wine merchant got some money for his worthless land and Boucher got some land to lodge his future protégés. The Universal Exposition having just closed down, Boucher, like many other Parisians, went over to the fair grounds to see what could be picked up among its abandoned structures and came back with the booty of Gustave Eiffel's octagonal wine pavilion and the impressive iron gate of the Palais de la Femme. He then set out to turn his piece of wasteland into a pleasant oasis by planting trees and bright flowers along neatly raked paths. The place was named La Ruche (beehive), both to symbolise the dynamic tenants he meant to house here and because of the honeycomb shape of the studios, imposed by the octagonal shape of the pavilion. Other buildings were added behind this main rotunda and were occupied by the better-off tenants, the most attractive and comfortable of them being '*le coin des Princes*', next to which Boucher had built himself a house too. Chagall confirmed this hierarchy: 'I lived in the Rotunda, where the proletarians and the poorest lived. The stone buildings were occupied by the

La Ruche

better-off. The rich went to Montparnasse.' If you felt weary by the time you came here, you can imagine what it must have been like for those artists who could not afford a Métro ticket, when they wanted to socialise or find shelter from their freezing studios in the cafés of Carrefour Vavin (see chapter on the 14th arr.). You will understand why they left for Montparnasse as soon as they could, even though the hovels of Montparnasse did not necessarily offer more comfort, nor were they necessarily any cleaner.

Alfred Boucher was no great sculptor but his academic works pleased officialdom, whom he served sincerely and for which he was rewarded amply. It was while riding in the barouche the Queen of Romania had offered him for the marble sculpture he had made of her that Boucher first discovered Vaugirard and the Passage de Dantzig. Boucher wallowed in his success, and was overjoyed when he was awarded the Cross of the *Légion d'honneur*, hesitating whether to wear it on the left- or right-hand side of his chest, and finally opting for the proud centre. But he never forgot or disowned his humble origins and wished from the bottom of his heart to help his tenants whose talents he acknowledged to be greater than his own. To help them sell their works, he opened an exhibition gallery in the Rotunda, and in order to offer them entertainment, he opened a 300-seat theatre where, incidentally, Louis Jouvet made his debut when he was still a student in pharmacology. Admission fees were optional, which was not enough of an incentive to fill the theatre, despite its undeniable quality. Its remote location was too much of a deterrent and it had to close down after six months.

When the band of Eastern Europeans invaded the premises in the second decade of the century, bringing along both anarchical ideas and an anarchical lifestyle, the benevolent Père Boucher simply referred to himself as 'the hen that hatched duck eggs'; but he never complained and never stopped protecting his community. On one occasion, when the Fine Arts Under-Secretary of State, Dujardin-Beaumetz, came to visit the place, a couple of intoxicated residents were hopping about on the lawn in the nude. The outraged minister inquired what that was, to which Boucher replied, 'Two happy men!'.

But World War I brought an end to the bliss. With no further formality, Chagall closed his rickety door with a wire and left for Russia. Of course, he never retrieved his works which he had left all over his wretched studio. It is very unlikely that they were stolen by the refugees from the north of France who occupied the premises for the duration of the war and who were certainly unaware of their value. It seems that at least some of the canvases were used to cover the chicken coops: on a visit to the States years later, Chagall recognised his painting *Les Amoureux*, which he had left lying on his table, stained with chicken droppings that never came off.

Others must have served as fuel during the bitter winter nights of 1917 or earlier.

World War II brought calamity on a much greater scale, when Granowski and Epstein were dug out here by the Gestapo and their French collaborators and were carried off as sacrificial quarry together with one hundred other artists of Montparnasse. Neither of them was to return. This time it was not the refugees that invaded the deserted La Ruche but the butchers of the nearby slaughterhouse, one of whom bullied Picasso's sensitive nephew Juan Fin, who arrived here in 1946. But the artists returned little by little – Reyberolle, Simone Dat, Tisserand, Yankel, Ben Dov, Polak, and younger ones such as Bernard Buffet – and life returned to normal.

In 1967, the heirs of Alfred Boucher were planning to sell La Ruche to the French council housing authorities (HLM – Habitation à Loyer Modéré). André Malraux moved into action to thwart this death threat. President Pompidou bought a bronze by Arp to raise some money and the sale of Degas's *Groupe de Danseuses* fetched some more. But an additional one million francs were still needed. Rescue came from the United States, the accursed Uncle Sam who is always denounced for killing French culture, but who more than once has saved it from destruction.

There are now only 23 honeycombs in the Rotunda, instead of the 80 original ones. Like the rest of the 15th arrondissement, La Ruche has been upgraded, its studios enlarged and equipped with modern amenities. Today's tenants are carefully selected and do not sneak in late at night. They also must be registered with Social Security. Nostalgic sentimentalists will regret the passing of that anarchical spontaneity, but the residents of those days, who had to live among piles of rubbish and rats, could not wait to get away. Apollinaire, invited over by Chagall, walked in cautiously, 'worried that the entire building might collapse suddenly and carry him off in its ruins.' They would have certainly appreciated today's central heating; Chagall would have loved to see his studio doubled in area, and all the residents, including Père Boucher, would have taken pride in the beautiful oak staircase that graces the entrance hall of the Rotunda.

THE 16TH ARRONDISSEMENT

> Paris is the capital of France and the 16th arrondissement is
> the capital of Paris.
>
> Victor Hugo

FEW Parisians would agree with the comment of Victor Hugo,
himself a resident of the arrondissement: to most Parisians *Le
seizième* – the mere sound of which evokes opulence and privilege –
is a soulless, boring residential area. True, much of it has gradually
been taken over by embassies, banks, multinational companies,
Arabian sheikhs, 'show-biz' stars and many *parvenus*. In this age of
easy money, it comes as no surprise to learn that dubious deals are
contracted on the sumptuous Avenue Foch and its environs and
that drugs and high-class prostitution lurk about in the neighbourhood too. As a result, the Avenue Foch, once the home of
Fernandel, Marcel Pagnol and Maurice Chevalier, has lost some of
its aura and now ranks only third in the property market, behind
the Avenues Gabriel and Raphaël. However, it is largely thanks to
the above-mentioned establishments and residents that some of
France's architectural heritage here has escaped demolition, since
only they can afford to settle in the area's *hôtels particuliers*. Many
Parisians scoff at the 'pointed' accent of the inhabitants of the 16th
and their 'British' air. They ignore its bustling neighbourhoods, its
exceedingly interesting Art Nouveau and Art Deco architecture
and its score of museums. They also look down on the area's
nouveaux riches, who can boast neither pedigree nor education,
whereas, in point of fact, both blue blood and culture have been
entrenched here for centuries.

Like all the outlying parts of Paris, this was a rural area before the
Revolution, whose country folk clustered around the villages of
Auteuil and Passy and the borough of Chaillot, cultivating small
market gardens. Vineyards climbed up the sunny hillside, sloping
down towards the Seine (hence rue des Vignes and rue Vineuse),
whilst windmills stood up against the horizon of the plain of Passy
(hence rue de la Tour, which commemorates an old windmill and

was known in the 18th century as rue du Moulin-de-la-Tour). But the area also had a forest and mineral water, which were to attract the upper classes and royalty to these western parts well before their move to Versailles.

The prehistoric forest of Rouvray (*rouvre* means 'common oak'), which in the days of Gaul stretched all the way to Rouen, was largely cut down over the centuries for its excellent wood. Parts of it, however, were preserved by the kings of France as a hunting-ground for their favourite pastime. Charles X, the last of the Bourbon kings, still hunted deer here in the last century. Today's forests of Saint-Germain-en-Laye and Marly, the woods of Meudon and Chaville, as well as the traffic-criss-crossed Bois de Boulogne, are all remnants of that thick, ancient forest.

The kings erected splendid hunting lodges befitting their rank, which often also served as love nests, notably François I, who built a hunting lodge in the Bois de Boulogne on his return from his Spanish captivity. To protect his privacy, he forbade his courtiers to settle in the vicinity, but they, resentful at not being able to spy on his amorous activities, retaliated by naming it le Château de Madrid, a reminder of the King's humiliating defeat to Charles V of Spain and his captivity in Madrid. Here Henri II set up Diane de Poitiers and Henri IV installed Gabrielle, and also, it is rumoured, a pretty young nun from the Abbey of Longchamp. He later gave it as a farewell gift to Queen Margot, overjoyed at being able to sever their marriage bonds. The mansion was bought for a song during the Revolution by a certain Monsieur Leroy (!) and was demolished soon after.

Le Château de la Muette was also a royal hunting lodge. Its name may have derived from *meute* (pack) or *mue* (meaning the casting of the horns and, by extension, the place where the stag's horns are kept). Originally built by Charles IX, it was totally re-modelled as a palace by Philippe Delorme for Charles IX's sister, Marguerite de Valois (the future Queen Margot). Later it was in the hands of the Duchesse de Berry, the daughter of the Regent and granddaughter-in-law of Louis XIV, who hosted glamorous receptions here, notably one in honour of Peter the Great of Russia. Knowing her days to be numbered, she was determined to enjoy them to the full by indulging in revelry and debauchery. Malevolent tongues, however, claimed that it was precisely her life of dissipation that was the cause of her premature death, at the age of 24.

The young Louis XV stayed there next. He would later have it entirely rebuilt by Gabriel for his consecutive mistresses, la Duchesse de Châteauroux and Madame de Pompadour. Marie-Antoinette followed suit upon her arrival in France awaiting her marriage to the future Louis XVI. After her marriage she liked to escape from the tedious formalities of Versailles to La Muette and to the neighbouring pleasure gardens of Ranelagh.

On 21 November 1783 at 1.54 pm, an astonished assembly of distinguished gentlemen, among them the Dauphin and Benjamin Franklin, his guest of honour, watched the first manned balloon take off from the Château de la Muette with the physicist Pilâtre de Rozier and the Marquis d'Arlandes aboard. The Duc d'Orléans pursued the balloon on horseback as far as he could. After twenty minutes the balloon, an apparition of azure decorated in gold, landed on the Buttes-aux-Cailles (now in the 13th arrondissement) to be greeted by a frenzied crowd who ripped off Rozier's clothes as souvenirs. Pilâtre de Rozier was sadly to die some time later while trying to cross the English Channel in the same manner.

The Château de la Muette was considerably damaged during the Revolution but remained in use until the 1920s. Its owners at the time, the heirs of the famous piano-maker, Sébastien Erard, unable to meet its exorbitant maintenance costs or find a buyer, had to pull it down. The estate was eventually bought by Henry de Rothschild who built a new house on the site, now the seat of the Organization for Economic Cooperation and Development (OECD).

Chaillot too had royal connections. Catherine de Medici liked to stop at a *pavillon* on the hill of Chaillot, on the way from her residence at Saint-Germain-en-Laye to Paris. Eventually she had it enlarged and embellished. In 1654 Henrietta Maria of France, the daughter of Henri IV and the widow of Charles I of England, purchased it and converted it into a convent for the Order of the Visitation, an elegant order of ladies of quality, where she herself and other princesses would go into retreat. It was here that Bossuet delivered his famous *Oraison funèbre* (funeral oration) for her in the presence of the entire court. In 1721, the notorious bandit Cartouche penetrated into the convent's chapel with designs other than spiritual but, awed by the majesty of the place, he left empty-handed. However, it seems that virtuous conduct was not always strictly observed here – in 1800 a 300-metre tunnel was discovered under the section of the toll walls that ran here, through which brandy had been smuggled into the convent!

A little further down the slope was the Couvent des Minimes, a men's institution whose members were known as wine growers and followed the example of Saint Francis of Assisi, leading a life of humility (hence their name) and strict restrictions. To prevent unnecessary temptation, a double wall separated their institution from the female one. A third religious institution was situated in the Bois de Boulogne, the Abbey of Longchamp, which too catered for ladies of high rank. Many a princess took the veil, not always willingly, in the magnificent Gothic abbey lying on the banks of the Seine.

Founded by Saint Isabelle, the sister of Saint Louis, the abbey enjoyed such prestige that Pope Leo X honoured it with a visit in 1521 and named it after its founder, 'Isabelle the Blessed'. Saint Vincent de Paul, who was born some fifty years later, found less sanctity in the place and complained about the nocturnal encounters between nuns and outsiders, often friars and even confessors. Some parlours, he said, were equipped, contrary to regulations, with grilles or windows 'which present imminent dangers to virgins consecrated to Jesus Christ'. By the time of Louis XV, the elegant ceremonies of Holy Week had become a veritable extravaganza, when all the upper set paraded here in their plush attire, celebrated actresses competing with ladies of fashion, young beauties with their wealthier elders. Men as well as women would ruin themselves in order to outshine their fellow beings on the promenade of Longchamp. On one occasion an Englishman turned up in a silver coach studded with precious stones!

The abbey was gone with the Revolution but the upper set have continued to parade in their best attire, congregating around the racetracks that were set up in the 19th century, a natural substitute for the house of God in a hunting area where horses were in plenty, and at a time of frenzied Anglomania. Today they attend the flat races of Longchamp and the obstacle races of Auteuil, especially on the occasion of the Prix Diane-Hermès at Longchamp, and the Steeplechase at Auteuil, which both take place in June.

Nature also endowed these parts with mineral spring water, as can be seen from the street names rue des Eaux, rue de la Source, rue de la Cure, rue La Fontaine (originally named after a fountain in Auteuil, and not after the famous fable writer who had, indeed, sojourned in Auteuil). Louis XIII came to Auteuil already as a child, as reported in the diary of his famous physician, Androuet, and Richelieu even built himself a country home in Auteuil: le Château du Coq, so called after its weathercock. It was later used as a love nest by Louis XV who came here under the transparent guise of Le Baron de Gonesse. The entire literary set of 17th-century France found peace and quiet in Auteuil too – Molière, Racine, La Fontaine, La Bruyère, among others; above all Boileau, who spent more than 20 years in a humble one-storeyed house on the site of the present 26 rue Boileau, away from the city hubbub, which he vividly described in *Les Embarras de Paris*.

It was the waters of Passy, however, rather than those of Auteuil, that turned the neighbourhood into a fashionable spa, with the additional attraction of being so close to Paris. Discovered in the middle of the 17th century by the Abbot Ragois, Madame de Maintenon's confessor, they were immediately praised by the Paris Faculty of Medicine, and in the 18th century taking the waters in Passy, conveniently located between Paris and Versailles, became a favourite pastime. All the nobs of society gathered in Passy, especially at the Château de Passy, the home of Farmer General (tax collector) le Riche de la Popelinière, a lover of the arts who entertained such literary and artistic figures as Diderot, Rousseau, Marivaux, La Tour, Chardin and Rameau, as well as most foreign ambassadors, the Scottish philosopher David Hume and the English historian Edward Gibbon.

The gatherings in the home of Madame Helvétius in Auteuil were more intellectual, bringing together the greatest minds of the Age of Enlightenment – Diderot, d'Alembert, André Chénier, d'Holbach and Turgot. They called their circle *La société d'Auteuil*, while their admired hostess was known as *Notre-Dame-d'Auteuil*. Many of them ended on the scaffold, the Revolution not being particular about the victims' ideological loyalties, but Madame Helvétius managed to save her neck. The Americans John Adams and Thomas Jefferson were also guests at her home, not to mention Benjamin Franklin, France's darling and Madame Helvétius's close friend. Turgot described him as the great citizen of the world, '*qui arrache la foudre au ciel et le sceptre aux tyrans*' ('who snatches the lightning from the heavens and the sceptres from the hands of tyrants) – the tyrant in this case being George III of England. The reference to the lightning was a tribute to Franklin's invention of the lightning conductor. As a matter of fact, it was in the 16th arrondissement, on the site of 62 rue Raynouard, that he carried out his first experiments.

Writers and artists continued living in the 16th after the Revolution. Musée Balzac on rue Raynouard is located in one of the novelist's homes. He moved there in 1841 as 'Monsieur de Brugnol', a name borrowed with minor alterations from his housekeeper Louise Breugiol, to elude his creditors. The house had a second entrance on rue du Roc (now rue Berton), enabling him to slip away should his creditors find his whereabouts after all. Rue Berton is the continuation of Avenue Marcel Proust, a reminder of another novelist who was born in the arrondissement and lived here his last few years, under duress, his uncle's centrally located flat on Boulevard Haussmann having been put up for sale. Proust had hoped his move to 44 rue Hamelin in the remote 16th would be temporary, but he was too ill to make another move.

In 1885 the Goncourts started a literary salon, *Le Grenier*, at 67 Boulevard de Montmorency, where some of the most prominent writers of the time met – Zola, Maupassant, Théophile Gautier, Daudet and others and where they set up the Académie Goncourt, of which more later.

Cultural brilliance continued after World War I, when a scintillating circle gathered around the Princesse de Polignac, née Winnaretta Singer. The door to her music room on Avenue Henri Martin was open as much to promising talents as to wealth and lineage. Eric Satie was received with open arms when he arrived every week, always in his pince-nez, always carrying an umbrella, always in the same dusty or drenched shabby suit, having walked 11 km (7 miles) from his grotty lodgings in Arcueil, south of Paris, to the sumptuous mansion on Avenue Henri Martin. Chanel was not allowed in, however. When asked why she never invited Chanel, Winnaretta answered, 'I never entertain my tradespeople.' This was probably just a sally of envious spite – after all, Winnaretta herself was the daughter of the Singer sewing-machine manufacturer and was titled only through marriage, while Chanel's *salon* was frequented by the same musicians as her own, notably Ravel, Stravinsky, Cole Porter, the *Groupe de Six* and Jean Cocteau.

Many writers had their homes in the 16th – Feydeau at 60 Avenue Foch, Mauriac at 38 rue Théophile Gautier, James Joyce at no. 34 rue des Vignes, André Gide on Villa de Montmorency and Victor Hugo at 24 of the avenue that now bears his name. On 27 February 1881 an immense crowd gathered in front of his house to celebrate his eightieth birthday throwing flowers to the writer who thanked them from his balcony.

The annexation of the 16th arrondissement to the city in 1860 inevitably led to its urbanisation. Dramatic changes occurred once Haussmann sliced it lengthwise, by way of rue Michel-Ange and Avenues Mozart and Paul Doumer. Likewise, with the opening of the circular railway around Paris, la Petite Ceinture, the Bois de Boulogne was severed from the city, and although Napoléon III had it landscaped with winding alleys, lakes and waterfall, the density of traffic passing through it was from the start too high. At the time this was largely compensated for by the ravishing spectacle of carriages parading along the Allée des Acacias carrying such celebrated demi-mondaines as Hortense Schneider, Pomaré, Cora Pearl and the famous actress Rachel, who was called to order for riding in a carriage too similar to the one used by the Empress!

Today the beautiful people have retreated to private corners of the Bois such as the Racing Club, or walk their dogs before the crowds arrive. At weekends parking space is as hard to come by as it is in town, while at night this is, as one journalist has put it, 'the largest open-air brothel in the world'. Some lovely pockets subsist nonetheless, often on its fringe, notably the magnificent Parc de Bagatelle. The earlier mansion by the same name (trifle!) was razed to the ground in 1777 by the Comte d'Artois, Louis XVI's brother and future Charles X, who, before leaving for Fontainebleau at the beginning of the autumn for the hunting season, as was the custom of the court, bet his sister-in-law, Marie-Antoinette, that a new *pied-à-terre* would replace it, amid entirely renovated grounds, by the time they returned to the city at the end of October for the Toussaint. It took the feverish labour of 800 workmen and 63 ceaseless working days to win the bet, the result of which is an exquisite English park laid out by Thomas Blaikie and a gem of a house built by Béllanger, renamed La Folie d'Artois. After the 1830 Revolution the estate became the property of Lord Hertford. Queen Victoria came here during her visit to Paris in 1855, while Sir Richard Wallace, who had graced Paris with his fountains, died here in 1890.

The recent urbanisation of the arrondissement, combined with its prosperity, provided Hector Guimard, the Art Nouveau pioneer, with much available space for his creative mind. What better source of inspiration than the leafy environment of the 16th for his revolutionary concept that art should follow the flowing, curved lines of nature? Other radical architects, Rob Mallet-Stevens and Le Corbusier in particular, took a different line in the 1920–30s, preferring the geometric style of Art Deco.

While these pioneers contributed to the architectural rejuvenation of the arrondissement, immigrants also added new blood to the old community, which is of greater variety than its stereotyped reputation might suggest. This is the largest arrondissement, over 4,000 acres with 180,000 residents; the more modest households are found in the south, the old aristocracy around la Muette. The moneyed middle class can be found in different areas. The presence of Iberian nationals who have gone into domestic service is particularly noticeable during holidays, when their employers vacate the city – an old tradition going back to the days when those who could not afford to go away would leave the shutters closed to keep up appearances. Meanwhile, the international set of overnight multimillionaires have taken up residence around Avenue Foch, equipping their homes with Turkish baths, tropical jungles and Byzantine halls. For the quintessentially Parisian actress Arletty – Garance for those who remember her in *Les Enfants du Paradis* – living in the 16th meant more modestly 'the joy of having the Seine at one's feet'.

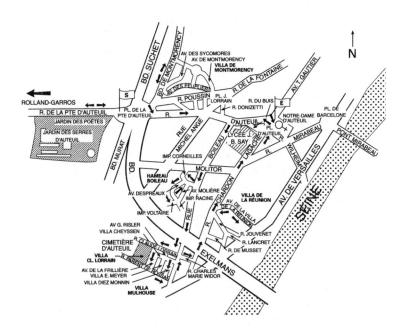

AROUND AUTEUIL

The old village of Auteuil is best visited on a Wednesday morning, when the open-air market on Place Jean Lorrain adds to its local colour. The village had its heyday in the late 17th and 18th centuries, when it lay on the route between Paris and Versailles (hence the Avenue de Versailles). As one Parisian pointed out at the time, whereas the Pont-Neuf was the busiest thoroughfare in Paris, this was the busiest road in all of France.

Back in the Middle Ages, the wine of Auteuil had gained a reputation that spread beyond the borders of France. A Danish bishop by the name of Roschild thanked the canons of Notre-Dame for the excellent quality wine from Auteuil they had sent him as a gift: 'Vino optimo Altolil'. At the time of Pierre Abélard, students came to Auteuil to drink its wine and every 22 January – the holy day of Saint Vincent, patron of the vineyards – was celebrated here with much rejoicing. But later the wines of Passy and Chaillot began to compete with it, eventually bringing about its decline.

Auteuil remained a pleasing rural area into the 20th century, at the beginning of which a goat boy could still be seen here with his flute, milking the goats at the customers' doorsteps. Maurice, the son of Edmond Rostand, loved Auteuil 'because it is already Paris without quite being so yet'. Even today some old-timers speak of 'going to Paris' (*aller à Paris*) – after all, Auteuil, like the rest of the 16th, was not incorporated into the city until 1860. Ten years later it was still a remote neighbourhood, where Proust's mother found shelter and quiet during the Prussian War and the *Commune* that followed, away from the famine and bloodshed of Paris. She moved to her uncle's house at 96 rue La Fontaine where she gave birth to the boy Marcel on 10 July 1871.

Start out from LA PLACE DE LA PORTE D'AUTEUIL on the edge of the Bois de Boulogne, pleasantly enhanced by a pretty 'châlet' restaurant and an air of well-being. The **Roland-Garros Tennis Stadium**, where the French Open takes place, is a short walk away in the direction of the Bois, to the west. Two lovely gardens are also situated in that direction – **Le Jardin des Serres d'Auteuil** and **Le Jardin des Poètes**, where Homer is honoured with an oak tree and Dante with a laurel bush.

Retrace your steps and turn left into BOULEVARD DE MONT-MORENCY, which runs between la Petite Ceinture, the old railway that circles Paris, and the **Villa de Montmorency**, a ravishing oasis which opens on to no. 93 (The main entrance is at 12 rue Poussin, unfortunately barred to outsiders by a female *Gardien-Chef*, as she is officially described in bold characters on her little hut by the entrance barrier). The enclave was built on the site of the gardens of the Château de Boufflers, its alleys following the same lay-out as those of the old park. The Château itself stood on the site of 60 rue d'Auteuil. The park was landscaped by an English gardener and enchanted visitors, among them Marie-Antoinette, and on the day of the execution of Louis XVI, his brother, the Comte de Provence and future Louis XVIII, even came to plant a poplar tree here. Horace Walpole, on the other hand, found 'the lawn bearable but of a green hardly likely to impress an English gentleman', although he did admire the view. Walpole complained in general about the way the French clipped trees to look like broomsticks!

The Comtesse de Boufflers was the mistress of the Prince de Conti, the Grand Prior of the Temple, where he held a brilliant *salon*. (see chapter on the 3rd arr.). She can be seen among society in Ollivier's celebrated engraving of little Wolfgang Amadeus Mozart playing the harpsichord before the Prince. She was reputed to be of small virtue, and malevolent tongues even claimed that she was visited by night by the notorious bandit Cartouche. Rousseau described her as being 'cosmopolitan in the lower half of her body'. She retired to Auteuil in 1776, upon the Prince's death, together with her stepdaughter Amélie, the two being known as the Dames de Boufflers. Here she maintained the traditions of the Temple with her brilliant *soupers*, which were held three times a week and to each of which she invited 15 illustrious figures – Rameau, Boucher, Madame de Staël, Turgot and Walpole among them.

The two ladies escaped the Revolution with less than a year's detention, but they were ruined financially and had to let the estate. Their tenant was that crafty dodger Talleyrand, the only prominent figure who managed to wriggle his way through the successive regimes of those troubled times and die of old age in 1838 – a *tour de force!* Napoleon was not fooled by him, however, and qualified him as '*de la merde dans un bas de soie*' ('shit in a silk stocking'). The last landlady of the estate was the Duchesse de Montmorency, from whom the Pereire brothers bought it in 1852 to make way for the adjacent circular railway (see chapter on the 17th arr.).

No. 67 Boulevard de Montmorency, an elegant yet at present shabby-looking house, dozing in the sun under a blanket of Virginia creeper, was the home of the Goncourt brothers, 'Le Grenier Goncourt' (the 'Goncourt Attic'), to which they transferred from rue Saint-Georges (in the 9th arr.) their collection of earthenware, bronzes, Far Eastern items and china, drawings and bibelots – an extraordinary jumble. This also became the seat of the Goncourt Academy, founded by Edmond de Goncourt to provide a pension for ten writers who became members of the Academy and were to award a yearly prize of 5,000 francs for a work of fiction written by a talented young author. Among the first to be awarded the prize, still during Edmond's lifetime, were Alphonse Daudet and Huysmans. Daudet's son Léon became a member of the Academy in 1900, replacing his late father.

Retrace your steps to Place de la Porte d'Auteuil and turn left into RUE D'AUTEUIL, once the village high street, still leading to the 'village square' – la Place d'Auteuil – and its church. The Château du Coq, built by Richelieu in the early 17th century, was situated between nos 63 and 73, a simple country residence or hunting lodge before Louis XV turned it into a magnificent mansion some hundred years later. Its botanical gardens extended beyond the present Avenue Murat, part of which now make up the Jardin des Serres d'Auteuil.

The house next door, now no. 59, was the home of Madame Helvétius who bought the property from the painter Quentin La Tour in 1772. The place was already a stronghold of society at the time of La Tour – Rousseau, Diderot, D'Alembert, Sophie Arnould, Fontenelle, Buffon, le Maréchal de Saxe, all came here to have their portraits painted by La Tour. So did the philosopher Helvétius, whose literary *salon* on rue Sainte-Anne (now in the 2nd arrondissement) was one of the enlightened centres of Paris. It was to this house that his grieving widow retired after his death, where, following in his footsteps, she perpetuated the *salon* tradition. Talleyrand, however, was unimpressed and observed sarcastically, 'Everyone hastened to display his wit, nobody considered gathering any'.

Madame Helvétius, although no longer in the prime of life – she was 53 when she moved to Auteuil – was admired and courted by her guests. Both the minister Turgot and Benjamin Franklin wished to marry her but she remained faithful to the memory of her husband. She was, nonetheless, most affected by Turgot's death and Benjamin Franklin's return to America and felt their absence very keenly. On one occasion Fontenelle, a very close friend who often stayed for the night, and by then in his nineties, met her unexpectedly in the morning, when she was still barely dressed. 'Oh Madam!' said the old man, 'if only I were 80!' John Adams's wife had a different view. In one of her letters, the puritanical New Englander wrote how disgusted she was with the lack of propriety of Madame Helvétius – by then 60 years old – and with the liberties she took with Benjamin Franklin. Voltaire, another of her admirers, once said, 'There are in

Paris a great number of small coteries presided over by a woman whose spirit dawns as her beauty declines.' She certainly proved him right a couple of years after the Revolution, when Napoleon paid her a visit and expressed his surprise at the modest extent of her property. To which the lady replied, 'General, if only one knew how much bliss can be contained in a few acres of land, one would reflect less about conquering the world.'

In 1870, these few acres of bliss became the scene of a crime of major political consequences. The house was occupied at the time by Prince Pierre Bonaparte, Napoleon III's cousin. On 10 January 1870, following a political argument between Pierre Bonaparte and the journalist Victor Noir, the prince pulled out a pistol and shot the journalist dead. Over 200,000 opponents to the regime took to the streets. A massive demonstration on the Champs-Elysées took place during the funeral and was violently repressed by the police, who arrested the charismatic Henri Rochefort, one of the opposition's leaders and chief editor of *La Marseillaise*. Prince Pierre Bonaparte himself was politely acquitted on 26 March, which did not boost the popularity of the regime.

Ahead is **PLACE JEAN LORRAIN**, previously known as Place de la Fontaine after its former fountain, which was renowned for the quality of its water – Louis XV would drink no other during his stay at the Château du Coq. If you have come here on Wednesday morning, you will savour the colourful atmosphere of the open-air market. At all times you will enjoy the Wallace Fountain standing gracefully among shady trees.

Continue along rue d'Auteuil. At no. 43/47 stood the magnificent Hôtel Antier, also known as the Hôtel des Demoiselles de Verrières. Today the building on the site belongs to a French oil company – La Française des Pétroles – who bought it from the Rothschilds in 1954. The only way to peep in is through the barrier at 3 rue Michel-Ange – the inflexible doorkeeper is unlikely to let you in without written permission.

Mademoiselle Antier, highly acclaimed as an interpreter of Lully's operas, came from Lyons. A determined, cynical social climber, she made use of her successive or simultaneous lovers (such as the Farmer General Le Riche de la Poplinière and the Prince de Carigan) to carry out her designs. Both court and town society were invited here to her dazzling balls, notably to those held successively in 1744 in honour of the convalescent Louis XV.

The mansion later belonged to the two gorgeous Verrières sisters, Marie and Geneviève, whose father, an ordinary café owner by the name of Rainteau, capitalised on his daughters' beauty by offering them up to the renowned Maréchal de Saxe, thus securing their social ascent. They became actresses – the traditional springboard into the world – and a theatre holding 400 seats was built in the back garden, where naughty and otherwise banned plays, unfit for the eyes of the common people, were staged for the privileged few. Marie, the brighter of the two, had several children by her different lovers. One of them was the daughter of the Maréchal de Saxe, Marie-Aurore, who was adopted by Louis XVI's mother and was later married to an illegitimate son of Louis XV. Being of poor health, he died without consummating their marriage. Marie-Aurore then married Dupin de Francueil, a handsome man by whom she had a son – Maurice Dupin, who became the father of George Sand! The American reader might like to know that both John Adams and his son John Quincy were guests at the Hôtel de Verrières.

At no. 40 rue d'Auteuil stood until recently a restaurant called l'Auberge du Mouton Blanc, a name perpetuated since the time of Molière, when he came here with his friends – Racine, La Fontaine, Lully, among others. Molière may have had a place on the corner of the present rue Théophile Gautier, where his friends may have gathered too – no one knows for sure. These were happy days, according to Madame de Sévigné, who also took part occasionally in the *soupers d'Auteuil* and wrote of the Auberge du Mouton Blanc, '*Combien gaies ces diableries*' ('how jolly those devilments'). One time, however, when everyone had had too much to drink – except Molière, who was unwell and had stuck to milk – they went on philosophising into the night and got on to the subject of man's wretched condition. They ended up utterly depressed and decided to walk to the Seine and drown themselves in unison. Molière, the only sober member of the group, managed to persuade them to postpone their act until the following morning, arguing that such a noble deed should be carried out in broad daylight. The next morning they revised their plans, as Molière had anticipated, sparing France the loss of some of her great thinkers and creators. The story was reported by Louis Racine, the playwright's son. In 1991 Le Batifol, yet another all-devouring chain of restaurants, which had already made a clean sweep of the Jockey, the landmark of Montparnasse's nightlife, spread its tentacles to Auteuil. The mural from 1900, which until then had decorated the wall to the left of the entrance, has also – alas – disappeared. Inspired by an old engraving, it depicted Molière at the Auberge du Mouton Blanc, reading from *Le Misanthrope* to his circle of friends.

Cross over. The **Lycée Jean-Baptiste Say**, stands at the back of a courtyard on the charmingly villagey corner of 11bis rue d'Auteuil and rue du Buis, displaying beautiful 18th-century Palladian architecture.

Retrace your steps and turn into **RUE BOILEAU** on your left. In prehistoric times the Seine flowed here, which accounts for the shells and crocodile teeth unearthed during archaeological digs in 1838. Closer to our era, rue Boileau was one of the three streets of the old village (together with the present rues d'Auteuil and La Fontaine) and was known as rue des Garennes. It led to the gallows of Auteuil which stood close to the present Porte de Saint-Cloud. At no. 16 stands an attractive 19th-century building, then used as a rest-house, les Bains d'Auteuil, frequented by such prominent members of society as Prince Napoléon, Jean-Baptiste Carpeaux, Adolphe Thiers, Alexandre Dumas, Victor Hugo and Alphonse Daudet.

A block of flats now stands at no. 26. In the 17th century the site belonged to Boileau, the author of *L'art poétique*, after whom the street is named. Boileau bought the place in 1685, a much larger property at the time, which expanded even further over the generations. He seems to have spent here the happiest years of his life, albeit in poor health, 'as happy as a king in his solitude, or rather in his hostelry at Auteuil,' according to Racine. He spent much time playing skittles with his friends and was quite vain about his skill at the game. Apart from his wife and Racine, his close friend who dropped in regularly, his companions in residence were his gardener Antoine Riqué and his wife Babet. Boileau clearly held Antoine in great respect, as the following verse shows:

> *Antoine gouverneur de mon jardin d'Auteuil*
> *Qui dirige chez moi l'if et le chèvrefeuille*
> *Et sur mes espaliers industrieux génie*
> *Sait si bien exercer l'art de la Quintinie.*

Antoine, ruler of my garden at Auteuil
Who commands at my place the yew and the honeysuckle
And on my espalier this industrious genius
practices so well the art of La Quintinie*.

Boileau also kept an old horse, an ass and a cat. However, by 1700 he rarely came here, grieved by the death of Racine the previous year; he sold the property in 1709 and died in Paris two years later. When the Regent's physician Claude Dehaies Gendron came to live here some time later, his friend Voltaire visited him and was appalled by this 'most unsightly shady dive'. He nevertheless lauded it as the seat of Parnassus, so great was his respect for Boileau.

At no. 38 is the entrance to another ravishing and serene leafy nook, **le Hameau Boileau,** to which you will find the gate unlocked, if you avoid coming at weekends or in August. Most of its houses date from 1825–30, but even the modern blocks of flats are unobtrusive.

Turn right into **RUE CLAUDE LORRAIN** and left into the countrified **Avenue Georges Risel** at no. 25, part of an enclave known as **La Villa de Mulhouse.** It is so narrow it will not take a car. **Avenue de la Frillière** beyond it opens into the tiny **Villa Lorrain,** dipped in flowers and the twitter of birds. At no. 57bis rue Claude Lorrain ahead is the new **cemetery of Auteuil,** which in 1793 replaced the old cemetery on the present Place d'Auteuil, for lack of space. Here lie the cartoonist Gavarni, the composer Gounod, the sculptor Carpeaux and the composer and conductor

le Hameau Boileau

* Jean de la Quintinie, 1626–1688, famous agronomist from Charente

Musard, a star in his day who made Paris dance to his newly invented *quadrille*. Madame Helvétius is also buried here, and so is
the heart of her 'spiritual' son, the celebrated Dr Cabanis, next to
his wife, Charlotte de Grouchy.

Retrace your steps and continue along rue Charles Marie-Widor,
then turn left into **RUE CHARDON-LAGACHE**. No. 47 opens
into the **Villa de la Réunion**, where Gavarni spent his last years and
where Carpeaux had his studio. At no. 41 stands l'Hôtel Jassédé,
erected by Hector Guimard in 1893 and decorated with ceramics by
Emile Muller.

Rue Chardon-Lagache was named after the philanthropists
Pierre-Alfred Chardon and his wife (née Lagache) who founded a
home at no. 1, exclusively for destitute old people. Another such
home, Sainte-Périne, stands at no. 17 and both occupy the beautiful
grounds of the former domain of the Génovéfain Order. The Rossini Foundation, a separate section of the institution at the corner of
rues Wilhem and Mirabeau, was bequeathed by the composer
Rossini for destitute or incurably ill French and Italian singers.

Continue along rue Chardon-Lagache to **PLACE D'AUTEUIL**
and its church, **l'eglise d'Auteuil**, once the focal point of the village.
Rising in its centre is the mausoleum to the memory of the
Chancelier d'Aguesseau and his wife, which was erected by order of
Louis XV. Despite a short period of disgrace for having opposed the
financial reform introduced at the time of the Regency by the
Scotsman Law* (and rightly, as it turned out), he was one of the
most honoured figures of the reign of Louis XV, and it seems that he
lived for many years in the splendid *hôtel* that now houses the Lycée
Jean-Baptiste Say. The monument marks the site of the old village
churchyard, next to the parish church. It was the priest of Auteuil
who had interceded with Louis XIV on behalf of Molière's wife to
allow her husband to have a Christian burial at Saint-Eustache (see
chapters on the 1st and 2nd arr.). The first church of Auteuil dated
from the 11th century, but the present one, the work of Vaudremer,
was built only in 1877. Some old houses still stand around Place
d'Auteuil, helping to re-create the old village atmosphere.

* Controller general of the finances who founded a banking system to eradicate
the exorbitant national debt, but which ended in bankruptcy owing to frantic
speculation.

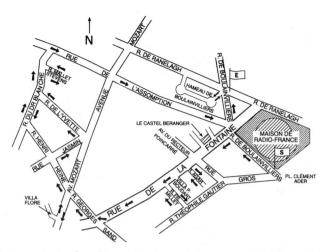

Between Auteuil and Passy further north was an unbuilt stretch of land which was developed only after the area was annexed to Paris. Around the turn of the century it provided space for Hector Guimard and others in his wake to explore a new style of architecture known as Art Nouveau, disparagingly dubbed *style nouille* by Paul Morand because of the spaghetti-shaped lines that characterise it. It was rather the curving forms of nature that Hector Guimard had in mind, to which bear witness his soft green entrances to the Métro stations. However, a generation later architects substituted geometric rigour for his natural profusion and invented Art Deco. Discovering the Art Nouveau and Art Deco heritage in the neighbourhood will be the main focus of the following walk.

Start at **PLACE CLEMENT ADER** next to the **Maison de Radio France,** home of French National Radio, which also boasts a good concert hall. Walk into **RUE DE BOULAINVILLIERS** along its western side. An elegant house used to stand at no. 15, surrounded by a pretty garden, which served as a detention centre for the deserters of the Garde Nationale between 1864 and 1870. It was nicknamed l'Hôtel des Haricots (beans) because of the unimaginative menu it served to its inmates, many of whom were great celebrities such as Alfred de Musset, Théophile Gautier, Gavarni, Daumier, Balzac and Baudelaire, who spent their time covering the walls with witty graffiti and cartoons. An earlier institution was founded during the Revolution, on the premises of the Collège Montaigne in the 5th arrondissement, likewise nicknamed Collège des Haricots – its menu must have been just as unimaginative!

Turn left into **RUE LA FONTAINE**, where, at no. 14, stands one of Guimard's best-known buildings in Paris, **le Castel Béranger**, built between 1894 and 1898. The artist's manipulation of the Gothic style is spectacular (notice the gargoyles and the blend of animal and vegetal forms, notably on the fountain in the courtyard). Needless to say, the average mortal was bewildered by his architecture and the building was nicknamed Castel Dérangé ('deranged'). Notwithstanding, the City of Paris awarded the façade first prize, which boosted Guimard's career overnight. The entrance hall, beyond the fabulous wrought-iron gate, is stunning with its blend of brick and glass and its Gothic staircase. All being well, you will be able to walk in during week days, although certainly not at weekends.

 A later compound was erected across the street in 1911, between **RUES GROS** and **AGAR**. Note the attractive plaque carved in the stone in memory of the actress Agar, who lived in Auteuil between 1870 and 1880 and after whom the street is named. The spectacular balconies on the 6th floor run throughout the street where everything bears Guimard's stamp.

Continue along rue la Fontaine and turn left into **RUE FRANCOIS-MILLET**. At no. 11 is another block of flats built by Guimard in 1910. Notice on the right corner the pretty garden and church, now part of an orphanage, reminiscent of a pastoral past. Back on rue La Fontaine, at no. 60 stands a *hôtel* built by Guimard in 1912 for a friend.

Turn right into rue Georges Sand and left into **AVENUE MOZART**. At no. 122 is the **Hôtel Guimard**, built by the artist for himself and for his wife, the American painter Adeline Oppenheim, between 1909 and 1912. He set up his agency on the ground floor, a studio for his wife in the attic, while the couple's apartment was situated on the main floor. Because the house was built for his own use, Guimard could follow his aspirations, and he abolished all right angles. Thus the living and dining rooms are oval in shape. The façade overlooking the side alley, Villa Flore, on your right, looks almost human! How different from the building opposite, an Art Deco construction dating from the 1920s.

Retrace your steps and turn left into RUE HENRI-HEINE. At the corner of RUE JASMIN is a much later work by Guimard, built in 1925/6. Turn right into rue Jasmin, a pleasant street with the tiny Cour and Square Jasmin running into it.

Turn left into rue de l'Yvette and left into RUE DU DOCTEUR BLANCHE. At no. 51 is Le Corbusier's foundation, located in the Cubist white villas of Raoul La Roche and Albert Jeanneret (1923) at the back of a dark, leafy alley. You can see on display in one of the windows his celebrated deckchair, which began its long career on this site. The library, which is open to the public, contains practically all the research work of Le Corbusier.

Retrace your steps and continue to no. 9 rue du Docteur Blanche which opens into RUE MALLET-STEVENS, another lovely nook, built in the 1920s by Robert Mallet-Stevens for himself and for his friends (Mallet-Stevens lived at no. 12, where he died in 1945), in a style of exemplary purity of line, surrounded by a countrified environment. Mallet-Stevens was a great socialiser and invited Tout-Paris to the inauguration of the alley in 1927.

Continue along rue du Docteur Blanche and turn right into rue de l'Assomption, which commemorates a magnificent convent that once stood here in exquisite rolling grounds. Walk downhill in the direction of La Maison de Radio France and turn left into rue de boulainvilliers and left again into the Hameau de Boulainvilliers, a tiny remnant of the 8-hectare grounds of the Château de Passy. (The Consulate of the Philippines is now located here, enabling you to walk in during opening hours).

First mentioned as the castle of Passy in 1381, the *château* itself was situated halfway up the present steep rue de Boulainvilliers. It was in the 18th century, when it was the property of the Farmer General Le Riche de la Popelinière, that it became a social centre of dazzling glitter, described by Farrère in *Le Dernier Dieu.*, long out of print. 'The authentic *folie* of a French Duke, an accomplice and companion of the Regent. Violins must have made a frenzy of sound but little by little, they fell silent.' Indeed, the best orchestra in Paris used to play here, conducted from the harpsichord by no less a musician than Rameau. However, La Popelinière also took under his wing some beautiful sinners, which is why his home

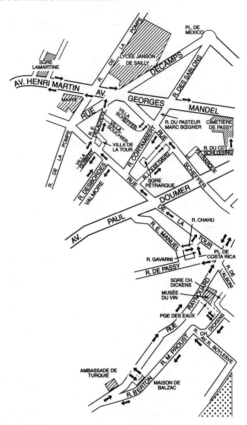

came to be known as *Le Temple des Muses et des Plaisirs*, although, in view of the diversity of guests who frequented the place, some preferred to call it the *ménagerie*. La Popelinière may have been a cuckold himself, for when a month after his death at the age of 70 his widow of 23 gave birth to a boy, it was rumoured that the father was Louis XV, although he was given the name of Alexandre-Louis-Gabriel La Riche de la Popelinière.

The resplendent gardens, landscaped by Le Nôtre, were devastated by the English in 1815, and the house itself was demolished in 1826. All that is now left is the name of the last owner and a pretty nook, immortalised by the now-forgotten Farrère: 'the silent oasis continued to be at that time – but for a few more years only – a haven for great dreamers, the last of their race . . . where Claude Debussy had just died.'

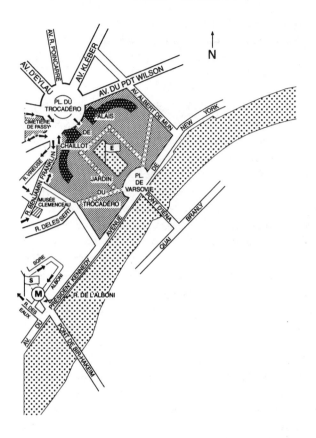

THROUGH PASSY TO CHAILLOT

This walk takes you from Passy to Chaillot in the northern part of
the arrondissement. Passy was first mentioned in the 13th century
as Passius. It was mentioned again at the time of Philippe Le Bel,
who allowed local peasants to kill the rabbits that were ravaging
their fields, a great privilege when one remembers the fate met with
by the peasants of Grenelle, across the Seine, for interfering with
the lord's game (see chapter on the 15th arr.).

An exciting way of reaching Passy is by Métro from the 15th
arrondissement, south of the Seine. The brief train ride between
Bir-Hakeim and Passy offers a spectacular view of the river and the

Eiffel Tower, and **Passy Métro station** is full of charm, set among greenery on a steep slope rolling down to the Seine. A couple of paths once ran down the hillside, used by the inhabitants of Passy to lead the cattle to the river.

A long flight of steps on your left will lead you up to **Square Alboni**, a serene nook whose silence is broken only by the arrival and departure of trains and by the song of birds.

The Italian soprano Marietta Alboni was one of Paris's idols in the 19th century. Her performances at the Théâtre des Italiens regularly brought the house down and fetched her a small fortune of 3,000 francs per night! Alboni was also known for her generosity and her gracious contributions to social welfare. Residing in these countrified parts, she decided to finance the square and the street that runs out of it, in return for which both have been given her name. They were laid out in 1894, the year of her death, and in good time for the 1900 World Fair. The square's opulent blocks of flats were originally used as hotels to accommodate well-to-do visitors to the fair. By 1925 the entire neighbourhood had swapped its greenery for constructions referred to by the writer Julien Green as 'Babylonian buildings' and 'fortresses of boredom'. There is worse to come: as you turn right into rue des Eaux beyond **RUE CHARLES DICKENS**, you will notice on your left a steep, crevasse-like passage with a long flight of steps, a dark ravine of concrete, the continuation of rue des Eaux, so remote from the days of the fashionable spa of Passy after which it is named.

To its right stands an attractive neo-Louis XVI house dating from the early 19th century, where **Le Musée du Vin** occupies a vast 14th-century vaulted cellar. It is also known as **Le Caveau des Echansons**. This was once part of the domain of the Minimes, whose wine-growing monks kept their wine in these vaults. Here you can see historical scenes animated by wax dolls showing, for example, Napoleon tasting a Bourgogne and Balzac walking down the stairs in his white dressing-gown to escape his creditors' bailiffs in his nearby home on rue Raynouard, as well as a display of various items connected with wine. The *bonshommes* cultivated their vineyards roughly on the site of the present rue Vineuse and their claret was so praised that Louis XIII came over to drink it after the hunt. **Square Charles Dickens**, next to the museum, is a charming nook, whose pretty houses climb on either side of a flight of steps. Pretty pots of geraniums against bare paving add a bright, somewhat Provençal touch.

Turn right into Avenue René Boylesve and left into Avenue Marcel Proust which continues into the astonishing **RUE BERTON**, a narrow, silent alley, steeped in lush greenery and miraculously overlooked by the forces of urbanisation. It even boasts the boundary stone that marked the border between Auteuil and Passy in 1731. The garden of **Musée Balzac** rolls down to no. 24, but the main entrance is at 47 rue Raynouard to your right, the oldest road in Passy, going back to Gallo-Roman days. The museum is located in a charming, rustic house standing in a lovely, tree-planted garden, displaying green shutters, a match for any pretty house in the heart of rural France.

Balzac's mistress, the Polish countess Madame Hanska, was of a different mind and found the house appalling, likening it to a *guinguette*. Balzac had more serious preoccupations at the time: he had moved to this hiding-place in 1840 to escape his creditors and their bailiffs, of which he had informed Madame Hanska in a letter dated 16 November: 'From the moment you receive this letter, write to me at the following address: Monsieur de Brugnol, rue Basse (now Raynouard) in Passy-lès (near) -Paris. I am well hidden here for a while.' Thanks to the vigilant housekeeper, Madame Louise Breugiol, Balzac escaped the bailiffs. Nobody was admitted without the password – 'The plum season has arrived' – followed, on the first landing, for extra safety, by 'I am bringing lace from Bruges'. Through his correspondence with Madame Hanska we also have a clear idea of Balzac's timetable: 'Working, dear Countess, is to get up every night at 12 and write till 8, to breakfast in a quarter of an hour, work till 5, dine, go to sleep and start all over the following day.' Indeed, his output during his seven-year stay here was staggering and included such masterpieces as *Le Cousin Pons, Les Illusions Perdues* and *La Cousine Bette*. No wonder he needed his notorious coffee-pot, which never left his desk and sustained him throughout. It can still be seen in the museum, alongside a wide spectrum of possessions that accompanied the author during his prolific career.

As you visit the museum or stroll in the gardens, you will enjoy,

Rue Berton

like Balzac, a view overlooking the **Hôtel de Lamballe**, tucked away among the trees. An aristocratic domain was already in existence here in 1400, and over the centuries it belonged successively to various members of prominent families – the Fusée in the 16th century, Claude Chahu, the Lord of Passy, in the 17th century, the Duchesse de Lauzan in the early 18th century, when the most dazzling receptions took place here, notably the one she lavished in honour of the Duchesse de Bourbon. The main façade at the time overlooked the Seine. The elegant staircase had a double ramp leading to the gardens and there were three tiered terraces going down to the river. On ball nights, the palace would glitter above the water with a myriad of candles.

At the time of the Revolution, the landlady of the mansion was the Princesse de Lamballe, the widow of the debauched son of the Duc de Penthièvres. It was her misfortune to be a member of the spoilt aristocracy at the wrong time, and worse, Marie-Antoinette's closest friend. For this sin she was dragged out of the prison of La Force in the Marais on 3 September 1792 and massacred by the savage mob on the corner of rues du Roi-de-Sicile and Malher; after which her head was impaled and carried by the gloating crowds to the Temple, to be exhibited in front of the window of Marie-Antoinette's cell. Her mansion was sequestrated and, having changed hands and functions, went into decline and lost the better part of its grounds. Balzac is said to have nurtured hopes of moving here one day – he too preferred grandeur to picturesque rusticity. Instead it became a mental home run by the illustrious Dr Blanche who moved here from Montmartre (See chapter on the 18th arr.).

When Blanche's son inherited the institution in 1852, he turned it into a retirement home for members of the intelligentsia. Among its inmates were Gérard de Nerval, who wrote here drafts of two of his major works *Sylvie* and *Aurélia*, Gounod and Maupassant, who died here in July 1893. The place closed down soon after, Emile Blanche himself having died the following month. At the turn of the century both the Hôtel de Lamballe and Balzac's hiding-place belonged to the Comte de Limur. The hôtel was sold to the state and given to the Turkish Embassy in 1922, in return for the mansion in Istanbul offered by the new Turkish Republic to France, but Balzac's home was turned into a museum by the Comtesse de Limur, who gathered an invaluable library and a wealth of documents which she bequeathed to the City of Paris, a contribution which helped to preserve the building in an area where developers and speculators are constantly on the look-out. The story goes that one developer made the extravagant suggestion to the museum's curator of reconstructing the house on the roof of the new block he proposed to put up in its stead!

As you leave the museum turn left on **RUE RAYNOUARD**. The street had several residents of note such as the singer Fodor at no.

38, the *chansonnier* Béranger at no. 42 and Benjamin Franklin, who lived across the street from the museum, on the site of the present nos 64–70, in a handsome house surrounded by pleasant grounds and shady trees, part of the estate of the Duc de Valentinois. It was on the adjacent site of no. 62 that he experimented on and eventually installed his first lightning conductor.

Benjamin Franklin had come to Paris in 1776 as the spokesman of the budding American Republic and to plead for the support of Louis XV against the English, their common foe. America was indeed on the map and Franklin was the pet of the capital. Twice a week he would walk out of his house in his modest brown garb, carrying his white walking stick, and head down to Auteuil along the rue Basse (now rues Raynouard and La Fontaine) to visit the widowed Madame Helvétius. Totally infatuated with her, he asked her to marry him, but she wished to remain faithful to her late husband's memory and declined. When Franklin left France in 1785, by then an ailing man who had to be carried to Le Havre in the Queen's litter, he had on him some mineral waters from Auteuil as a souvenir. Madame Helvétius was much grieved by his departure, and her sorrow was compounded when her other faithful friend, Turgot, died shortly after.

Retrace your steps across the street. At no. 51–55 is a well-known building of reinforced concrete, the work of Auguste Perret, who lived here from 1932 until his death in 1954. In the 19th century the Hôtel Delessert stood at no. 19. The Delesserts were a Protestant banking family who had come from Geneva, to which they had escaped from Lyons at the time of Louis XIV, when the Protestants were being persecuted. Their property extended all the way down to the Seine and had once been the home of Le Ragois, the chaplain of Madame de Maintenon and promoter of the spa of Passy. It was in these grounds that in 1720 he discovered three springs of ferruginous water, which he began to exploit in 1725. Enjoying the support of the medicine faculty, which proclaimed Passy's water to be the best in France, Le Ragois's enterprise became an immense success, the more so as it was so close to the capital and on the way to Versailles. Women came to find a cure for sterility, and everyone else came for the pure air, the fun and simply to keep up with the trends. The 18th-century counterparts of today's joggers were just as committed to their own exercises, which followed a morning glass of water and consisted of five regular walking steps alternating with a pirouette. As usual, the *chansonniers* observed it all with their sardonic cynicism; in one song, after fruitless endeavours to find a cure for her ills, a young female patient

> through the rescue of Cupid recovered.
> This is by no means a marvel;
> in Passy, it is said, such things do happen.

In 1752 a certain Le Veillard took over the resort and added a games room, a theatre, a puppet theatre and ballrooms. But in 1785 Benjamin Franklin took Le Veillard with him to America, thus turning on the trickle of the brain-draining that later became a flood – after which Passy began to decline as a spa. The final blow came in 1865, when it was decided to distribute the water. . . free of charge! As if by magic, the waters of Passy lost their virtues and high society migrated elsewhere to seek cures for its troubles.

Benjamin Delessert bought the property in 1800, and incorporated to it the springs in 1803. He had meanwhile invented a method of extracting beet sugar, and during Napoleon's Continental ban on Britain (1801) he erected on his property the first beet sugar refinery in France (on the site of the convent of the Minimes by the Seine, now 14/16 quai de Passy). This was a major economic and political event which allowed France to dispense with imported cane sugar. Napoleon was thrilled with Delessert's invention and when visiting the refinery, took off the *croix d'honneur* from his own chest and pinned it on to Delessert's, at the same time bestowing on him the title of 'Baron'. Delessert proceeded to construct a suspension bridge connecting the refinery and his mansion, which contributed to the development of engineering, and the physicist Arago sent his students of the Ecole Polytechnique to view and study the bridge. A cotton mill soon followed. A man of vision, Benjamin Delessert was appointed head of the Banque de France before he was 30 and held the post for 50 years. He was also a philanthropist who founded the Caisse d'Epargne, which today still enables people of limited means to accumulate some savings.

It was in the Hôtel Delessert that in 1852 preliminaries to making a match between Napoléon III and Eugénie de Montijo were conducted. A couple of years earlier the writer Prosper Mérimée had introduced Eugénie and her mother to his friend, Madame Gabriel Delessert, Benjamin's sister-in-law. By then Benjamin had been dead four years and buried in the old cemetery of Passy on rue Lekain (no longer in existence). His remains and those of the other members of his family were transferred to the new cemetery of Passy in 1961.

Continue to Place de Costa Rica and on to **RUE FRANKLIN** beyond it, if you wish to visit the **Musée Georges Clemenceau** at no. 8 (open from 2–5 pm except Mondays, Wednesdays and Fridays), home of the *Tigre*, as he was nicknamed, between 1896 and his death on 24 November 1929. This nostalgic place, where France's leaders met to prepare the peace talks after World War I, will give you an insight into the life of one of France's greatest statesmen, who had forged so much of the public life of the Third Republic. On display are his ink-well and quill pen, the uniform he wore when he visited the soldiers in the trenches, the pistols he used in no fewer than 22 duels (!), the pair of shears he used to prune his roses and his calendar, on which the entries stop on 24 November 1929.

Retrace your steps to Place de Costa Rica and walk into **RUE DE PASSY**, the village high street before its annexation to Paris, and one of its rare streets to be paved. Turn right into **RUE GAVARNI**, named after the 19th-century cartoonist, real name Sulpice Guillaume Chevalier. Transferred to south-west France in 1850 by his employers, he discovered the spectacular Cirque de Gavarni near Tarbes and was so dazzled by this rocky beauty spot that he adopted its name. Eventually he also bartered his trade for that of an artist and, like Daumier, contributed many of his works to the *Charivari*.

Turn left into **RUE CLAUDE CHAHU**, named after the Lord of Passy who turned Passy into a parish. At no. 9, on the corner of rue Eugène Manuel, stands a stunning Art Nouveau building dating from 1900, the work of architect Charles Klein and ceramist Emile Muller, who used fantastic thistle motifs to astounding effect.

Retrace your steps to rue Gavarni and turn left into **RUE DE LA TOUR**, where a long-lost medieval tower stood, which was later surmounted by a windmill. The crenellated tower that now stands

Rue Scheffer

on its site (at no. 86 further down), is a neo-medieval pastiche. An unassuming door at no. 28 to your right opens on to an astonishing haven nestling in the silent shade of ancient trees, one of the many secrets that Paris conceals from the casual eye. Another pretty alley is situated at no. 70, lined with elegant spacious houses, each standing in its own tiny garden.

Turn right into **RUE LOUIS DAVID**, named after the Republican painter who voted for the death of Louis XVI and who was exiled during the Restoration. On the right-hand corner of 13 **RUE SCHEFFER** stands another stunning Art Nouveau building, surmounted by spectacular parasol-shaped roofs.

Turn left into rue Scheffer and left into **Square Pétrarque,** built in 1927. Despite its profusion of eclectic 'neo' styles, an overall harmony prevails. Romantic lampposts complete the picture.

Retrace your steps along rue Scheffer. The famous poetess Anna de Noailles, née Princesse de Brancovan, lived at no. 40 from 1910 to 1933. A society lady, Anna was one of the backbones of Poiret's clientele, but also an active member of the Left Bank literati. Continue beyond rue Contambert into **Villa Scheffer,** at 51 rue

Villa Scheffer

Scheffer, a leafy alley yet again, enhanced by a picturesque little house and its adjoining turret, surmounted by a conical roof.

Retrace your steps, turn right into rue Cortambert and right again into rue de la Tour. An unattractive block now stands at no. 86, preposterously adjoining the reconstructed tower (now visible only from rue Desbordes-Valmore). The original medieval tower may have been used by Philippe le Bel when he came to Passy. A little further on on your left, the **Villa Guibert** displays eclectic architectural styles – from neo-medieval to Anglo-Norman, from Napoléon III to the 1920s – yet somehow it all fits together.

Turn right into **RUE EUGENE DELACROIX**. This was originally rue de la Croix, simply because it led to a cross on the corner of rue de la Tour. The cross was done away with during the Revolution. In a neighbourhood that celebrates so many painters, the shift to Eugène Delacroix in 1868 went unnoticed. The **Villa de la Tour**, on the right, was the home of the radical socialist leader Jean Jaurès in 1914, when he was assassinated by the extreme-right nationalist Raoul Villain at the Café du Croissant in the 2nd arrondissement on the eve of World War I. Next is the **Villa Souchier**, at no. 5 on your right, again a lovely, leafy nook.

Continue along rue Eugène Delacroix and rue Decamps, then turn left into **AVENUE GEORGES MANDEL**, a broad wealthy, residential avenue, of little interest to the pedestrian. Across the avenue is the **Lycée Janson de Sailly**, known for its academic excellence. Jules Ferry, the promoter of free education for all, picked out this site for a school that would pride itself on the teaching of the humanities, and Victor Hugo attended its inauguration ceremony.

Beyond rue de la Pompe the avenue is named **AVENUE HENRI MARTIN**, which originally was the name of the entire thoroughfare. Its eastern section was renamed in 1945 after the statesman Georges Mandel who was assassinated in 1944 by the militia in the forest of Fontainebleau. On the corner of rue de la Pompe on your left is the **Mairie**, erected by the Third Republic, undoubtedly the most lavish of Paris's 20 town halls, a match for the area it serves. Across the avenue, a little further on, lies **Square Lamartine**, which commemorates the poet and statesman who died on 28 February 1869 in a Swiss chalet situated on the site of 107/113 Avenue Henri Martin, conceded to him by the City of Paris. According to his niece, its well-kept garden was its only asset. The chalet was replaced by a beautiful *hôtel* at no. 107, which belonged to the famous art dealers Josse and Gaston Bernheim.

Square Lamartine contained an artesian well which supplied water to both the lakes and waterfall of the newly laid out Bois de Boulogne, and to the local population. Despite the enthusiasm of Saxon Kind, the initiator of the venture, it proved laborious – it took 11 years to drill the well (1855–66) and needed the injection of gas to get the water to spurt out. When it eventually did, it was to the detriment of the artesian well in Grenelle, the pressure of which diminished simultaneously for the obvious reason that Passy and Grenelle were part of the same geological stratum and shared the same water table. In the early 20th century locals could still be seen queueing up with bottles, flasks or pitchers to draw water, which had a constant temperature of 28°C, but an insipid taste.

Retrace your steps along Avenue Henri Martin and on to 43 Avenue Georges Mandel. This was still Avenue Henri Martin when the princely couple Edmond and Winnaretta Polignac were living in the opulent **Hôtel de Polignac**, on the corner of rue Pasteur-Marc-Boegue, the centre of musical creativity during the Golden Age of the early 20th century. Its famous rotunda-shaped music room, complete with mirrors in the fashion of Versailles, still overlooks rue Pasteur-Marc-Boegue. Here were performed the works of Gabriel Fauré, Ernest Chausson, Darius Milhaud, Igor Stravinsky and Maurice Ravel, by such artists as Wanda Landowska, to such guests as Marcel Proust. On one evening in 1927, the Princess played host to Henry James, Isadora Duncan, Cole Porter and Ezra Pound. Playing duets at the piano were two fellow-Russians who did not like each other – Stravinsky and Prokofiev. Winnaretta was concerned only with the music and ignored personal feuds.

Born to the American multimillionaire founder of the Singer sewing-machine factory, she was wealthy enough to be accepted by the blue-blooded aristocracy and accordingly married Louis de Montbéliard. However, when it became clear to her that she was lesbian, the two agreed to part ways and divorced. Divorce, however, was a drawback for a woman of society, an obstacle removed by Prince Edmond de Polignac, himself a notorious homosexual. At the time of their wedding Winnaretta was 28, the prince 59, and the marriage proved an ideal partnership, leaving the couple plenty of leeway to lead their own independent lives. Yet it was not devoid of deep, sincere, mutual affection and a shared love of the arts, which manifested itself in the quality of the paintings they collected and, above all, in the music and ballets performed in the wonderful music room on Avenue Henri Martin.

It was love of art that brought them together in the first place, during an auction where they fought tooth and nail over a Monet. Winnaretta had the upper hand and outbid the infuriated Prince, who originally cursed her to eternal damnation. Robert de Montesquiou, formerly her friend, took offence at not being invited to her intimate wedding, and called it a marriage between the dollar and the *sou*, between the lyre (the Prince was a fine musician) and the sewing machine! – a most unfair slander, Winnaretta being an accomplished musician. Cocteau himself entitled one of his poems *machines à coudre* ('sewing machines'), and it was set to music by Maxime Jacob. But Winnaretta knew how to rise above such taunts. When an embittered, impoverished noble acquaintance protested that his name was as good as Polignac, she retorted, 'Not at the bottom of a cheque!'.

On the whole she remained aloof to the personal enmities, mean sarcasm, gossip and slandering that unavoidably peppered the prodigious creativity of *salon* life, except in the case of the up-and-coming Chanel, who was denied access to her home, and the American composer Thomas Virgil, who was punished for being a most welcome guest of Gertrude Stein's. . .

In 1919 Winnaretta was widowed and free to enter the roaring, permissive, sophisticated Twenties as the independent and legitimate cornerstone of society, the champion of democratic modernity, even though her Victorian hairstyle might have suggested otherwise. Gone were the red velvet and the gold lamé of the old-guard *salons* frequented by the aristocracy. After she had promoted the music of Ernest Chausson and Gabriel Fauré, it was now the turn of Ravel, Stravinsky, Satie, the *Groupe des Six* and, of course, Diaghilev's *Ballets Russes*, whose productions demanded colossal funds. Her generosity knew no bounds, notably towards Satie. Following the premiere of *Parade* on 18 May 1917, when Jean Poueigh wrote that the ballet lacked everything – inventiveness, wit and professional skill – Satie sent him a postcard which read, '*Monsieur et cher ami – vous n'êtes qu'un cul, un cul sans musique*' ('Dear Sir and friend – you're nothing but an arse, an arse with no music'). Arguing that this constituted a public humiliation since the postcard came unsealed and could be read by all and sundry, including the concierge(!), Poueigh sued Satie and won the case. Satie had to pay 1,000 francs in damages and serve a week in prison, and it was Winnaretta who forked out the money. During his first appeal Cocteau raised his cane in a gesture against Poueigh's lawyer and was fined in his turn for 'making physical threats against a lawyer during the execution of his office'! Satie won the case eventually. In a letter written to Winnaretta from his home at Arceuil-Cachan, dated 10 October 1918, he confirmed his outstanding debt of 688 francs and 74 centimes (having paid out 311 francs and 26 centimes) and meekly asked his benefactress to allow him to keep the sum as an advance, owing to his poor finances in the wake of the war. Poor he was indeed, more than any of his friends ever realised, for he never allowed anyone into his flat. It was only after his death in the summer of 1925, when his flat was opened for an inventory, that his friends were staggered to discover the appalling destitution he had been living in – apart from his piano, a bed and a chair were his only possessions. Erik Satie had fallen fatally ill the previous January, after a life of heavy drinking of cheap wine, and it was Winnaretta who arranged for him to have a private room in the Hôpital Saint-Joseph in the 14th arrondissement.

Beyond her selfless generosity, Winnaretta's contribution to music and ballet in the first few decades of the 20th century cannot be overestimated. It was thanks to her that many famous pieces were written, for she encouraged her friends and major musicians of the time to compose music specifically to be performed in her *salon*. Ravel's *Pavane pour une Infante défunte*, for example, came into being in this way. There were also try-outs for Diaghilev's *Ballets Russes*, such as *Les Noces*. It must also be said to her credit that whenever she commissioned works, she merely provided the money and never interfered with the composers' ideas. The tragic events of World War II took Winnaretta to England, where she died in 1943. Today the **Polignac Foundation**, still based on these wonderful premises, carries on with her philanthropic work, providing funds to talented musicians at the outset of their careers.

Further along the avenue, on your right, runs the wall of the **Passy cemetery**, which can be entered through rue du Commandant-Schloesing to the right. Here lie, among others, the musicians Debussy, Fauré and Yves Nat, the painter Manet, the writers Tristan Bernard, Jean Giraudoux and Edmond Rostand, the actress Réjane, the *couturier* Poitou and the 'king' of perfume, Guerlain. Pioneers of the transport revolution are also buried here – Costes, who in 1930 undertook the first non-stop flight across the Atlantic from Paris to New York and Georges-Marie Haardt, who in 1924 headed Citroën's mission across Asia, the 'Yellow Cruise'. Two murdered statesmen also rest here – Sadi Carnot, assassinated

by an anarchist in Lyons in 1894, and Georges Mandel, mentioned above. The delightful Fernandel, real name Fernand Constantin, died in 1971, aged 68, and is buried here under a pink granite tombstone which cannot obliterate his unforgettable smile and the savours of his *Provençal* accent. On the cemetery wall, facing the Place du Trocadéro, is Landowski's impressive memorial to the victims of World War I. Opposite rises a statue of a dreamy Benjamin Franklin seated in an armchair. On the pedestal below can be read the superlative quote from the eulogy delivered by the orator Mirabeau on 11 June 1790: *Le génie qui franchit l'Amérique et versa sur l'Europe des torrents de lumière* ('The genius who set America free and showered on Europe torrents of light').

Continue to **PLACE DU TROCADERO**, once the site of the Couvent de la Visitation, founded by Henrietta Maria of France as mentioned above. Among other ladies of quality who stayed here was poor Louise de la Vallière, trying desperately to fight her love for the young Louis XIV and to escape the poisonous female tongues of the court. Her persistent royal suitor was hard to resist when he came to the convent in person and begged her to follow him back to the court. Twice she ran off, the second time taking shelter with the Carmelite Order on rue Saint-Jacques (in the 5th arr.), where she became Soeur Louise de la Miséricorde. By then the King had switched his amorous allegiance to Madame de Montespan and he made no effort to bring her back.

The Couvent de la Visitation was swept away during the Revolution. In 1813 Napoleon intended to replace it with an imperial monument, to match the Sun King's Palace of Versailles, above all, to outshine Russia's Kremlin – his *idée fixe* since the disastrous Russian expedition a year earlier. He instructed his architects Percier and Fontaine to create something 'a hundred times more beautiful than the Kremlin', an imperial city which was to include a palace for his two-year-old son, the King of Rome, two additional palaces for science and art, an imperial university and an archive. The gigantic project was to extend south to the Champ-de-Mars, across the Pont d'Iéna and as far as the Bois de Boulogne to the west. However, by 1815 the Bourbons were back on the throne of France and in 1823 they inaugurated here instead the Place du Trocadéro, which commemorated their victorious expedition in support of their cousin Ferdinand VII, whom they wished to see on the throne of Spain. In 1827 they put up on this site a cardboard model of the fort of Trocadero, next to Cadiz, which they had taken, and enacted that victory so as to efface Napoleon's project. Showing similar penchants to his uncle's, Napoléon III later considered erecting a bombastic statue – *La France Intelligente* – to watch over the six ministries that would be built around her, and also over the Ecole Polytechnique, which he intended to transfer here. He too, like his uncle, did not have time to carry out his project.

For the 1878 Universal Exposition, the Third Republic also mistook gigantism for grandeur and instructed its official architect Davioud to put up a 400-metre-long pastiche of a Hispano-Moorish palace, complete with two unsightly towers, which most Parisians found ghastly, including Proust, who referred to the 'ugly' monument in *La Recherche du temps perdu*. The monument was torn down in 1935 and replaced for the 1937 Fair by the present one, le Palais de Chaillot, the work of Carlu, Boileau and Azéma, an attractive example of the Modern Art style of the 1930s, and a successful companion to the Eiffel Tower. A spectacular show was staged here for the opening of the exhibition, with performers from all over the world, who danced against a background of exotic foreign palaces and the dancing waters of the floodlit fountains.

Today the western wing of the Palais de Chaillot is home to the Musée de l'Homme and the Musée de la Marine. The sleepy Musée de l'Homme was brought to the attention of the media in 1995, when the newly elected President Jacques Chirac proclaimed his intention to overhaul the museum and transfer here all the French collections of African, Oceanian and South American art. This is a pale contribution compared to the splurge of *Grands Travaux* during Mitterrand's reign, but France is suffering from a persistent recession and no ruler at present would dare to indulge in prodigal expenses, all the more so since Mitterrand's *Grands Travaux* have not always proved satisfactory.

Its eastern wing houses the Musée des Monuments Français, the Théâtre National de Chaillot and the Paris Cinémathèque and museum of the cinema. The theatre, which was designed by the illustrious Niermans brothers, was previously known as the Théâtre National de Paris (TNP) and gained worldwide fame between 1953 and 1961, at the time of Jean Vilar. The Cinémathèque was initiated by the enthusiastic film-lover Henri Langlois, after whom the museum of the cinema is named. Here are on display Niepce's first camera, Daguerre's glass photographic slides, Edison's kinetoscope, a reconstruction of Méliès's studio in the eastern suburb of Montreuil and legendary sets from such films as *Metropolis*. Before you call it a day, go to the centre of the esplanade between the two wings, an imposing site with its spurting fountain and graceful gilded statues. Rising across the river is the 'Iron lady' in full glory, particularly at night when set ablaze against the floodlit fountain. Between her feet, looming right in her axis, is the refined outline of the Ecole Militaire, marred, however, by today's unfortunate cluttered skyline.

The serene western section of the gardens rolling down to the Seine will sooth your tired feet and soul – nothing here intrudes on their sheer loveliness.

THE 17TH ARRONDISSEMENT

A VAST, elongated territory stretches across the north-western edge of Paris, ripped open by twelve railway lines creating an iron social divide that relegates the poor to the north and the better-off to the west. From the start, shabby grey tenement houses arose on the wrong side of the tracks, 'smelling of the shameful destitution of Parisian roomings', as Guy de Maupassant wrote in *Bel Ami*; his hero, Duranty, stood in the window of one of these houses and watched the tantalising new buildings of the recently opened rue de Rome, on the other side of that 'immense trench of the western railway', luminous at sunrise, as though 'painted with white light'. Despite the jarring discrepancy, the two sides of the tracks were united into one of the eight new arrondissements created and annexed to Paris by Haussmann on 1 January 1860.

Of all the 8 arrondissements, the 17th is Haussmann's creation *par excellence*; for, despite the 'deep chasm' that separated north from west, no arrondissement was as true to the new middle-class spirit of the Second Empire or promoted the values it stood for to the same degree. Understandably, it was not to the taste of someone like Paul Verlaine who, growing up in the 1850s and early 1860s at 2 rue Saint-Louis (now 10 rue Nollet) in Batignolles, described it as a neighbourhood of small, decent people where his father felt at home, 'pettily bourgeois, shabbily well-to-do, neat, niggardly, but as clean as can be'. The village, however, bore him no grudge and buried him in its cemetery, where his humble grave can still be seen.

Similarly, young Colette was put off by the whitewashed cleanliness of the middle-class area west of the tracks. Criss-crossed by broad, well-ventilated arteries, which had mushroomed overnight, it still bore the smell of fresh paint. At the turn of the century, her aunt was living on the new Avenue Wagram, 'in a magnificent, unattractive new block of flats' with a rapid lift. 'I rather disliked all those white walls,' remarked Colette. 'The drawing-room ... desperately carried on the whiteness of the staircase. White-painted woodwork, frail white furniture, white cushions with light-coloured flowers, white chimney piece. Good

'immense trench of the western railway'

heavens, there wasn't one single dark corner!' Needless to say, Aunt Wilhelmine Coeur greatly disapproved of Papa's living with 17-year-old Colette on the narrow, dark rue Jacob on the Left Bank. 'My dear,' she said to her brother, 'the new neighbourhoods are far healthier, far airier and far better built.' Of course propriety and respectability were the underlying virtues of these virginal *beaux quartiers* of western Paris, as against 'that dirty Left Bank where no nice people live'.

Carrying no tainted heritage or stigma from the past, the vast stretches of land, hitherto covered with cornfields, hunting grounds and meadows, became a land of opportunity for the emerging middle classes – four clear-cut strata which, within just a few decades, poured into the arrondissement, dividing themselves up neatly into four distinct neighbourhoods according to their wealth – west of the tracks the wealthy and the well-to-do, in Monceau and Ternes respectively; east of the tracks, in Batignolles, small employees, shopkeepers and pensioners, and further north in Epinettes, honest workmen. It was as neat a distribution as Haussmann's whitewashed avenues themselves.

Back in the early 19th century small Parisians had already been attracted to what was then the village of Batignolles-Monceau, situated beyond the toll walls, where they could enjoy better air combined with a lower cost of living. Thus, between 1810 and 1820 the number of its inhabitants increased from 498 to nearly 6,000.

The wealthy Plaine de Monceau, on the other hand, did not develop out of an independent nucleus but was the natural extension of the *beaux quartiers* that had erupted in the 8th arrondissement during Haussmann's feverish metamorphosis of the French capital, with Boulevard Malesherbes* as their backbone. And yet, there had been a *château* in Monceau, going back to the Middle Ages, around which a village should have logically developed. In 1429, Jeanne d'Arc, heading a numerous army, stopped there to rest, before resuming her advance on the gate of Saint-Honoré, by way of today's rue Lévis and rue du Rocher, through which she had hoped to take Paris, '*leur pucelle avec eulx et très grant foison char-iots, charettes et chevaulx*' ('their Maiden with them and chariots, carts and horses in great plenty'), according to the diary of an anonymous contemporary, *Le Journal d'un bourgeois de Paris*.

In 1753 the *château* was bought by the Farmer General Grimod de la Reynière as a country residence. Notoriously wealthy, La Reynière was already the owner of a magnificent *hôtel* on the corner of today's rue Boissy-d'Anglas and Avenue Gabriel in the 8th arrondissement, now occupied by the Embassy of the United States. He was equally well-known as a writer and gourmet, with a love for *haute cuisine*. Ironically, he died of indigestion after over-indulging in *foie gras*. The *château* gradually faded away through a process of sales and parcelling and disappeared altogether

* Boulevard Malesherbes had actually been conceived in 1800 by Napoleon.

unnoticed, in 1840. Its grounds extended roughly between what is now rue Lévis and Place Lévis and rue de la Terrasse and Boulevard Malesherbes.

Whether rich or humble, the new inhabitants of the area enjoyed the healthier quality of the air and the protection of the hill of Montmartre, which provided a natural barrier against the north wind. Sharing a taste for an orderly lifestyle, they went about their own affairs and, as much as possible, kept aloof from the turbulence that shook Paris in that century. When, during the 1871 civil war of the *Commune*, social unrest finally erupted into violence in the 17th arrondissement, it was to a large extent brought about by outsiders. Advancing towards the strategic target of Gare Saint-Lazare, which linked Paris and Versailles, the *Versaillais** pushed through the 17th arrondissement, where wine casks from nearby *brasseries* had been piled up into barricades, while the dead, after summary execution in Square des Batignolles, in Parc de Monceau and in front of the Mairie, were buried hastily in Parc de Monceau. The galvanising 'Red Priestess', Louise Michel, who headed a detachment of 25 women on Boulevard des Batignolles, later wrote in her *Souvenirs de la Commune*: '*Les Batignolles, Montmartre étaient pris, tout se changeait en abattoir. . .*' ('Les Batignolles, Montmartre were taken, everything turned into a slaughterhouse'). However, neither Louise Michel nor her disciple Hubertine Auclerc had a great following in the 17th arrondissement. When the latter, sporting the red revolutionary cap, came to deliver fiery speeches in the church of Sainte-Marie in Batignolles, now converted into a women's club and decked with red flags, few came to listen. La femme Lefèvre, the malevolent laundress from the wash-house of Sainte-Marie (an occupation notorious for bringing out the most violent instincts in the female populace of Paris) – a tall, lank, fanatical, trigger-happy *pétroleuse* (an incendiary woman during the *Commune*), sporting a pistol in her belt and vociferously inciting hate – became the terror of a predominantly law-abiding neighbourhood. Such were her murderous fury and thirst for blood, that news of her death on 22 May, while posted on the barricade of rue des Dames, was greeted with relief and even jubilation.

* The government forces, so called because the government's seat was in Versailles.

With the victory of the *Versaillais*, the Third Republic could stride out and proceed with the economic development of the 17th arrondissement, which, though boosted by Haussmann, was in fact the astonishing achievement of two brothers, Emile and Isaac Pereire, who can justly be claimed as its founding fathers. Of Jewish Portuguese extraction, they had come up to Paris from their native Bordeaux in the 1820s. Inspired by Saint Simon's concept of a harmonious industrial society based on social justice, and impressed by the development of the railway in Britain, they believed that in France too the railway would be the driving force of the new industrial society. They took over the 17th arrondissement and turned it into the cradle of France's railway and, as a result, the pacemaker of its economic and social revolution. Twin boulevards now honour the names of the two pioneering brothers equitably, a unique example in Paris's road network. These run on either side of the railway tracks that they built around Paris, known as la Petite Ceinture ('the little belt'). Also unique was the fact that this honour was bestowed during their lifetime.

The first railway tracks ran between Saint-Lazare and Saint-Germain-en-Laye. They were laid in 1835, after a relentless three-year struggle against doggedly unyielding financiers, politicians and bureaucrats. When Louis-Philippe finally promulgated a law allowing Emile to proceed with the venture, he stipulated that it should be 'at his own expense, risks and perils'. Opposition on the part of the scientific community also had to be overcome. When the optimistic Pereire chose to avoid the altitude problem of the hill of Monceau by means of two tunnels, the physicist Arago declared these would cause pneumonia and pleurisy! Others spoke of an inflammation of the retina. None of this happened, of course. Instead, a more spectacular and tragic accident took place on 6 October 1921, caused by the excessive traffic in the tunnels, ending with 102 casualties, 28 of whom died.

On 24 August 1837 Queen Marie-Amélie arrived for the inauguration of the railway at the Europe pier, north of Gare Saint-Lazare. Louis-Philippe did not accompany her on her journey to Saint-Germain, opponents of the project having used all their energy to persuade His Majesty that 'he could not expose his precious life to a journey fraught with dangers'. It was all right for his heroic queen and children (who would not let their mother travel

alone) to expose their own, however. Flowers and flags decked the
new train as it chugged along to the cheerful sounds of the brass
band of Batignolles. 'Nobody caught a cold in the tunnel, the
steam engine did not explode, the carriages were not derailed and
one could believe that a journey by rail was not necessarily fatal,'
commented Maxime du Camp. The next day the cabinet ministers, green with fear, put on a brave face and took a trip aboard the
train. Two days later the first fare-paying passengers crossed the
future arrondissement by train on their way to Saint-Germain. By
the following August this fashionable new mode of locomotion
was taking its first load of enthusiasts to Versailles and, in no time,
a merchandise station and workshops transformed the landscape
of the hitherto villagey Batignolles, singling out the 17th for a
destiny indissolubly linked to the railway and, later, to other
industries connected with transport, notably the automobile. By
1869, 13,254,000 passengers were taking the train at Saint-Lazare
yearly, 11 million of whom were travelling to the suburbs.

With his eyes riveted on England, the tireless Emile Pereire now
planned an underground railway for Paris, taking as a model the
Metropolitan underground line which had been opened in London in 1863. However, the minister Thiers was not endowed with
the same far-reaching imagination and vision as Pereire, and ac-
ceded to no more than an extension of existing lines, and on
strategic grounds only. He therefore gave Pereire permission to
build a railway line parallel to the 1840 fortification walls to speed
up the transfer of troops and ammunition – a mere 22-minute run
between the Cardinet bridge and Auteuil on the southern edge of
the 16th arrondissement. The fortifications, which had been
Thiers's initiative, proved ineffective against the Prussians, but the
Chemin de fer de Ceinture, or la Petite Ceinture, once completed
in 1864, played a significant economic role rather than military,
connecting the outlying neighbourhoods of the capital, just as its
visionary founder had conceived it.

Industries and workshops continued their expansion north of the
tracks, drawing a working-class population, who, however poor,
was bent on achieving a middle-class lifestyle. Simultaneously, west
of the tracks the *beaux quartiers* were expanding on the extensive
plain of Monceau, devouring its cornfields spangled with poppies

and cornflowers and furrowed by footpaths, where, according to Adrieu Marx, in fine weather, the Juliets of Batignolles would be seen arm in arm with the Romeos of Monceau. Once again the Pereire brothers were at the origin of this urban transformation, having by now branched off into finance and real estate. They had developed the railway network throughout France at a pace and to an extent that seriously frightened the French government, who were worried by their monopoly. Turning towards Britain once more, they had also come to control the seas, by means of the Compagnie Générale Transatlantique, the famous 'Transat'. There was no stopping the tireless brothers who by now had also set up a bank to finance new industrial projects, and later an insurance company. When the 1860 annexation triggered off the most spectacular real-estate activity ever undertaken in the city, they found themselves involved in the fever almost in spite of themselves: the Emperor had asked them to create the rue de Rivoli, the hotel and department store of the Louvre, the Rond-Point-des-Champs-Elysées, the Boulevard Voltaire in eastern Paris. . . to be followed by a lighting company for the streets of the capital. It was inevitable that the brothers should become the promoters of the 17th, their home territory, so much of which actually belonged to them. After ten years of preparation, work began around 1875 and soon the plain was covered with opulent freestone buildings, as shiny and new as the money of their occupiers. This was where the 'mushroom aristocracy', as Zola called them, lived, with plentiful servants and horses and carriages, which carried them daily to their places of entertainment, on the Grands Boulevards, on the Champs-Elysées and in the Bois.

Entertaining was also done at home: following the patterns of the waning old aristocracy, the mistress of the house liked to preside over weekly literary *salons* attended by the country's élite of literati, artists and musicians, many of whom had taken up residence here too. One such was the fashionable painter Ernest Meissonier, who had built himself a magnificent *hôtel* on the corner of rue Georges Berger (then Legendre) and Place Malesherbes (now Général-Catroux), soon to be followed by two of his disciples – Edouard Detaille, who settled in luxury next door, at 129 Boulevard Malesherbes, and Alphonse de Neuville at 14 rue Legendre around the corner. All specialised in military subjects, much in vogue in those bellicose times. Two years later the famous architect Jules Février built a magnificent mansion inspired by the Château de Blois for the wealthy banker of the Comte de Chambord, Emile Gaillard, also on Place Malesherbes. The composer Charles Gounod shared an *hôtel* on Place Malesherbes with his brother-in-law, the architect Pigny, while his colleague Gabriel Fauré, then director of the Conservatoire, lived at no. 154. Guy de Maupassant lived on Place Wagram and Claude Debussy at no. 10 of the neighbouring rue Gustave Doré. The composer Ernest Chausson was living at 22 Boulevard de Courcelles when he was killed in a bicycle accident in 1904, tragically cutting short a most promising career. Young Proust lived on rue de Courcelles. Other writers lived here too – Edmond Rostand, who wrote *Cyrano de Bergerac* at 2 rue de Fortuny; Alphonse Allais and Tristan Bernard at nos 7 and 9 rue Edouard Detaille respectively; not to mention Alexandre Dumas fils at 98 Avenue de Villiers. Actresses and singers followed suit, among them the legendary Sarah Bernhardt and the *café-concert* singer Yvette Guilbert, immortalised by Toulouse-Lautrec.

The sculptor Frédérique-Auguste Bartholdi lived here too, and it was in the 17th arrondissement, in the workshops and foundry of 25 rue de Chazelles, that he moulded the most important statue of modern times, *La Liberté éclairant le monde*, more commonly known as the Statue of Liberty. While travelling in Egypt in 1855, he had been impressed by the colossal dimensions of the monuments of Ancient Egypt. His friend Ferdinand de Lesseps was about to complete the Suez Canal and Bartholdi was commissioned to make a statue *Le Progrès apportant la lumière à l'Asie* (*Progress bringing light to Asia*), to stand at the entrance to the Canal. Bartholdi was disappointed when the project was abandoned due to a lack of funds, but he took the preliminary sculptures back to Paris in 1869 and used them for a new project, which would bring light not to Asia but to the wretched of Europe, who hoped for a better life in New York and beyond.

Bartholdi himself made the voyage to America in 1871, aboard the steamer *Le Pereire* (!), and chose the site of Bedloe's Island for the statue. Building on rue Chazelles began with the hand and torch, then came the head, which was exhibited on the Champ-de-Mars during the 1878 Universal Exposition. A huge crowd gathered along the streets during the transfer of the head to the Fair. *Le Petit Journal* reported on 30 June 1878: 'A colossal, fantastic head emerges in the opening of the Arc de Triomphe, while cries of 'Long live the Republic' resound in powerful volleys at the far end of the avenue.' Viollet-le-Duc, who was in charge of the metal structure of the statue, had died meanwhile and was replaced by Gustave Eiffel, who moved to the neighbouring rue de Prony, so as to be able to supervise the work from close quarters, anxious as he was about its colossal weight (200 tonnes) and fearing that the lady might not withstand the violent winds that occasionally sweep across the eastern coast of the United States.

On 24 October 1881 the yards at 25 rue de Chazelles were decked with American and French flags, ready for a ceremony presided over by the American Ambassador, who inserted the first rivet of the central pylon. For the next three years rue de Chazelles was the favourite outing for the inhabitants of the 8th and 17th arrondissements, who came to watch the progress the lady was making. At the beginning of 1884 she was all set, towering 46 metres above the plain of Monceau. On the 4th of July the brass band of Batignolles, which some 50 years earlier had celebrated the first train journey ever undertaken in France, came once more to the fore, when it struck up the American and French anthems on the occasion of the official presentation of the Statue – a somewhat belated gift from France to the young republic for its first centennial. The statue was then dismounted, dispatched to Le Havre, and, after floating for 25 days across the Atlantic, arrived safely in New York.

All the above artists, and many others, convened in the glittering *salons* of the Plaine Monceau. Leconte de Lisle and his *Parnassien* friends frequented the *salon* of the Marquise de Ricard at no. 10 Boulevard des Batignolles, while the members of the Academy were favoured by Madame Aubernon who invited them, in groups of twelve, to her weekly dinners on rue Montchanin (now rue Jacques Bingen). In order to express her respect for such honoured guests, her meals were accompanied by a dish of spinach, a far-fetched tribute to the green costume of the *Académicien*.

Not all the households of the Plaine Monceau could display such respectability, certainly not that of Emile Zola's Nana, the laundress's daughter from the gutter of La Goutte-d'Or, although she too was living in a magnificent home, on the corner of Avenue de Villiers and rue Cardinet. In a fluctuating society, where fortunes were made overnight, respectability and thinly disguised prostitution lived side by side, the latter 'advancing, gliding, dancing with the weight of its embroidered petticoats'. Brief notes jotted down by Zola in his notebook inform us of 'very well maintained *hôtels*' in the '*quartier Haussmann*', in particular on rue de Prony, with 'footman, powdered concierge, imposing staircase, huge landing, couch, armchairs, flowers. . .' Adrieu Marx acquiesces when he speaks of the '*belles petites*' who swoop down on the new quarters', adding that 'face powder has succeeded in replacing the dust of building plaster'. 'Semi-senile, debauched males were ready to abandon everything for an arse,' Zola jots down in his notebook. He also speaks of 'the pack behind the bitch who is not on heat', who spends as much as 200,000 francs a year, or, having recently bought a townhouse, now wants to sell it!

Around the year 1900 the 17-year-old Colette – Claudine in the novel – ran into her childhood friend Luce on Parc de Monceau. The poor country girl had been offered champagne, adorned in silk undies and stockings and set up by the sixtyish widowed husband of her aunt in a top-floor flat of a gleaming white building on rue de Courcelles. An enormous lift, lined with mirrors, carried Luce up to this flat, whose main items were a 1.5-metre-wide bed and a bathroom 'paved with tiles, walled with tiles . . . glittering, like Venice, with a thousand lights and more'. Not unlike Nana, Luce lapses occasionally into her native speech, which Colette finds 'priceless'. The seducer, like his forerunners, is depicted as 'hideous, fat and almost bald . . . he had a bestial look, with jowls like a Great Dane and big calf's eyes'.

Some cocottes, courtesans and demi-mondaines were the talk of the scandalised town, such as the fiery Andalusian Otero on rue Fortuny, for whom more than one suitor had given up the ghost and for whom William II of Prussia had written a play. Others, such as Louise Delabigne, now Comtesse Valtesse de la Bigne, knew how to worm their way into society. She too had ruined a wealthy suitor, but she had the talent and intelligence to know how to be accepted and became the friend of Manet, Courbet, Boudin, Alphonse de Neuville and Detaille, which earned her the nickname '*l'union des peintres*'. When she first came up to Paris from her native Normandy and went on the stage as Hebe in *Orpheus in Hell*, a critic said that she was as timid and as red-headed as a Titian virgin – but it did not take her long to lose both timidity and virginity nor, for that matter, to leave the stage and sell her favours elsewhere instead. From the arms of Prince Lubomirski, she flew to those of Baron Sagan, who financed the glorious mansion Jules Février built for her in 1876 on the corner of Boulevard Malesherbes and rue de la Terrasse and was subsequently ruined. It was her bedroom that served as a model for that of Zola's *Nana*. The highly acclaimed painter Henri Gervex used her as his model for the bride (!) in his painting *Le Mariage civil* (at least it was not a religious wedding), which now hangs in the Salle de Mariage (the wedding hall) of the Mairie of the 19th arrondissement. Thus Mademoiselle Valtesse has come down to posterity fortified by the Third Republic's attributes of chastity, matrimonial bliss and respectability. Middle-class morality, to which, after all, a quarter of France's households adhered, had the final word!

A decade earlier, far from the limelight of the Plaine Monceau, new ideas were fermenting in the humbler parts of Batignolles from which a new conception of painting emerged, which was going to have an unforeseeable influence on art and lead eventually to a revolution. A young generation of artists, with little money but plenty of creative enthusiasm, was eager to shrug off the shackles of academic tradition and its pompous, hollow search for ideals, and set out to capture the light in the present moment of daily life. Here, in the unpolluted neighbourhood of Batignolles, they found the exceptionally translucid quality of light necessary for their outdoor scenes, combined with a homely village atmosphere and cheap board and lodgings. They liked being close to the railway, the symbol of modernity, a subject for their paintings in its own right, and also a means of transport to the countryside, to Chatou, Asnières and Argenteuil, where they could experiment with outdoor paintings, producing the treasures that now brighten the walls of museums and galleries throughout the world. They also liked to gather at Café Guerbois (on the unlikely site of today's 9 Avenue de Clichy) under the inspiring guidance of their elder, Manet.

Manet had begun to frequent Café Guerbois on the then 'village' high street, La Grande-Rue, in 1863, on his way to Hennequin's, his paint and brush supplier, next door. On a Friday night, he would gather his artist friends – Fantin-Latour, Alfred Stevens, Astruc, the American Whistler – around two tables to the left of the entrance and engage in such stimulating discussions that Degas or Renoir would on no account miss them. The unkempt Cézanne, on the other hand, shied away from the band. Often when he turned up at the Guerbois he would sit at a separate table, feeling uncomfortable with the group 'who were dressed like notaries'. Monet regretted being away from Paris so often for, he said, 'one came out of these discussions with a more invigorated will and clearer thoughts'. What he could not yet have known or formulated was that these gatherings constituted, in fact, the laboratory of the Impressionist experience, where the notions of outdoor painting and of colour and light were discussed and confronted. As such the Café Guerbois could rightly claim the honour of being the birthplace of the Impressionist movement. At the time it was, for want of a better name, labelled *l'Ecole des Batignolles*, but soon the bourgeoisie, expressing their derision through the mouths of critics, gave the members of the movement the tag of 'Impressionists'.

Camille Pissarro was another member of the group, as was Frédéric Bazille, whose potential was snuffed out with his premature death, aged 29, on the battlefield of Beaune-la-Rolande in the Loiret in the 1870 war. A major painting of his, *Réunion de famille* (1867), brings out the spirit of comradeship within the Batignolles group. Bazille, a head above the rest of the group, is standing in the centre by his easel, showing his latest work to Astruc and Manet (it was actually Manet who painted Bazille's face). Alfred Sisley can be seen on the left, and Monet standing on the stairs, while their musician friend, Maître, is at the piano. A work by Fantin-Latour, *l'Atelier à Batignolles* (1870), now hanging in the Musée d'Orsay, also brings out that spirit. This was Manet's studio at 81 rue Guyot (now Médéric and Fortuny), in the Plaine Monceau rather than Batignolles, but that was before the speculation of the 1870s and Manet must have paid very little for this old house in the countryside. Besides, Manet was of bourgeois origin and socialised with both the Plaine Monceau crowd and his more modest fellow artists. It was on rue Guyot that Manet painted some of his most famous masterpieces – *Le Déjeuner sur l'herbe, Olympia, Le Fifre. . .* Some critics having detected a Spanish influence in these earlier works, referred to him sarcastically as 'Don Manet y Courbetos y Zurbanan de los Batignolles'. In Fantin-Latour's *Un Atelier* Manet is seen painting his friend Zacharie Astruc. A statue of the goddess Minerva symbolises the café – and neighbourhood – of La Nouvelle Athènes (see chapter on the 9th arrondissement), the international capital of art. The Oriental porcelain on the left is a reminder of the Impressionists' interest in Japanese art.

Zola and Nadar, staunch supporters of the movement, also attended the Friday night gatherings at Café Guerbois. Nadar had lent the group his studio on 35 Boulevard des Capucines for their first exhibition in 1874, while Zola, after Manet's exclusion from the Salon in 1866, had written on 7 May: 'Since nobody else is saying this, I am going to say it, I am going to shout it. I am so certain that Monsieur Manet will be one of tomorrow's masters that I believe I would have struck a good bargain had I the means today to buy up all his paintings. Manet's place is marked in the Louvre, like Courbet's, like the place of every artist with a strong, implacable temperament.' And when Manet was eventually exhibited at the Salon, Zola said: 'Do you know what effect Manet's paintings produce in the Salon? They simply burst the walls. All around them are displayed the sugary sweets of the artistic confectioners in vogue . . . gingerbread men and women made of vanilla cream.' In return for this support Manet invited Zola over to rue Guyot where he painted the writer. The portraits hung in his home in Médan until his death in 1905, when his wife gave them to the Louvre.

When, in 1874, Stéphane Mallarmé moved to no. 89 of the new rue de Rome, on the western and right side of the tracks, it was the proximity of the Lycée Condorcet, where he had been appointed as an English teacher, that had determined his choice rather than social considerations. By then his painter friends had migrated to the more central Nouvelle Athènes café at Place Pigalle, in the culturally ebullient 9th arrondissement. When the celebrated Tuesday gatherings began to be held in Mallarmé's home a few months later, *l'Ecole des Batignolles* had been officially renamed Impressionist, following their first exhibition, which happened to take place the same year. Fridays now replaced Tuesdays and were devoted mainly to poetry, predominantly symbolist. All these gatherings were part of the same phenomenon – the younger generation, be they writers, painters or musicians, were reaching out and groping for modernity and belonged to one and the same world: hence Mallarmé's portrait by Manet and Mallarmé's *Prélude pour un après-midi d'un faune* set to music by Debussy.

A century later the 17th arrondissement still bears the marks of its beginnings and the physical barrier of the railway tracks is even more visible now that the tunnels are gone (they were demolished after the 1921 catastrophe). While poor immigrants have naturally settled east of the tracks, in greater numbers in working-class Epinettes than in lower middle-class Batignolles, the western parts of the arrondissement, Monceau or Ternes, still appear to be largely inhabited by a family-orientated inward-looking bourgeoisie, behind the uninterrupted building façades that rise in regular alignments on either side of the main roads like some inconquerable fortresses. Few shops or cafés break the monotony, nor do pedestrians venture by to liven them up. In other parts of the arrondissement the pedestrian is rebuffed by the railway, which monopolises nearly 30 per cent of the area. Fortunately the tracks are gradually being roofed over, as has been the case on Boulevards Pereire, where a strip of recreational ground and some tennis courts have been laid out.

On the westernmost edge of the arrondissement, the impersonal Palais des Congrès, which opened at the Porte Maillot in 1974, adds no touch of intimacy or warmth to the area. Taking their usual pride in records and superlatives, its administrators trumpet its achievements in terms of figures: an area of 50,000 square metres, an auditorium of 3,650 seats, an exhibition area of 8,000 square metres, a yearly turnover of 1,500,000 francs . . . but little has been done here to create an inviting environment for locals, which takes more than opening yet another shopping centre. True, the Club Lionel Hampton on the top floor of Hôtel Méridien resounds nightly (except Fridays and Sundays) to good jazz, but it has that clinically comfortable atmosphere that is found anywhere and everywhere in the world. So where does Paris come into the picture? The answer is, in a few pockets that have happily preserved their villagey character; these we shall explore on our next walks.

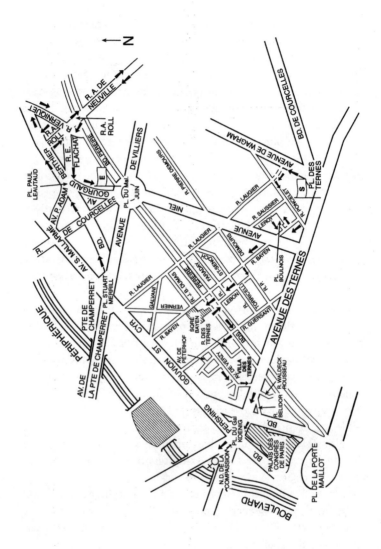

FROM PLACE DES TERNES TO BOULEVARD BERTHIER

A sunny Saturday morning is an exquisite time for a stroll in the area of Ternes. If you reach **PLACE DES TERNES** by Métro, you will be greeted as you come out of the station by Hector Guimard's vegetal, green archway, standing out against a blue sky, and by four green flower stalls disposed around the traffic island, bursting with dazzling colours.

Head north along **AVENUE DE WAGRAM**. As you cross Boulevard de Courcelles on your right, you will catch a glimpse of the Sacre-Coeur. A pleasant arcade at no. 67 bis, on the left-hand side of the avenue, leads to rue Poncelet (rue des Dames prior to the 1860 annexation, when the name could not be confused with rue des Dames in Batignolles, these being two separate suburbs). The arcade is no longer as countrified as it was when Dumas fils used it in his comedy *l'Ami des Femmes*, in which the heroine, the adulterous Madame Simerone, escapes the vigilant eyes of the detectives hired to unveil her goings-on, through 67bis Avenue Wagram, then emerges on rue des Dames (now Poncelet). Turn left into **RUE PONCELET** and continue beyond the street junction of rue Saussier and rue Leroy, where it becomes a picturesque pedestrian market, overflowing with an abundance of flowers and mouth-watering food – seafood, meat, fowl and game, cheeses and wines, vegetables and fruit – all of which mingle with the smell of freshly baked bread. Lined with old, rustic houses and serving predominantly old-timers, this spot has preserved the old Parisian touch that has all but faded away in the last two decades.

The pedestrian market spills into **RUE BAYEN**, to your right. Place Boulnois, to the right again, leads to a small sunny, sleepy square, shaded by a single tree in its centre. It is a scene out of provincial times – except for the many parked cars and an incongruous Japanese restaurant.

Retrace your steps and continue along rue Bayen. Ahead, rising above an arcade, is an elegant façade, dating from 1715, the only vestige of the former **Château des Ternes**, the grounds of which extended from today's rues Saint-Senoche, Faraday, Torricelli and Lebon, all the way to rue Jean-Baptiste Dumas (beyond Boulevards Pereire), at a time when this was a hunting territory.

The two brothers Habert arrived from Issoudun at the beginning of the 16th century. Being learned and intelligent, they were soon introduced into the highest circles and even into the court of Henri III. Pierre became secretary to the King and was ennobled, though not granted the right to be master of a fief, and when in 1548 he bought himself a large farm in Ternes, he was not allowed to add to it the insignia of the nobility. Confident of the King's favour, Pierre overlooked the law and converted the farm into a manor house with two turrets, a moat and a drawbridge. This aroused jealousy and scheming against him and his successors – all in vain, for in 1634, when Pierre's grandson Isaac was master of the place, Louis XIII promoted the domain into a fief, which granted him the privilege of levying taxes on the inhabitants of his estate, a privilege reconfirmed by Louis XIV in 1661. Habert, however, was then appointed Bishop of Rouergue (now Aveyron) in the south of France and, feeling a moral duty to reside among his congregation, sold up his estate. It is believed that Bossuet resided here soon after, when he prepared the *Oraisons funèbres* for both Henrietta Maria of France and her daughter Henrietta of England who died respectively in 1669 and 1670.

In the 18th century, when horse racing – the latest English fad – became the new favourite pastime of the high nobility, the racetracks were laid out on the nearby plain of Sablons, securing an aristocratic presence in Ternes. The great Duc de Montmorency built himself a magnificent stately home on the edge of the plain, and in 1776 a belvedere was built especially for the Queen, so that she could watch the races. The days of the countrified Renaissance farm turned manor of Ternes were gone.

The new landlord, Mirey de Pomponne, councillor and secretary to the King, replaced it with a splendid dwelling, as reported by his contemporary Germain Brice in his *Description de la ville de Paris*. Grégoire-Nicolas-René Masse, the next landlord, enlarged the building, adding a dining-room (an innovation in those days), a music-room and an orangery. It then passed on to Ange-Laurent de la Live de Jully, the brother-in-law of both the celebrated Madame d'Epinay, once the benefactress of J. J. Rousseau, and of

Madame d'Houdetot with whom Rousseau had been passionately enamoured. Madame d'Houdetot actually lived here from 1768 to 1771 and, in all likelihood the nature-loving Rousseau, whose writings refer to various outlying parts of Paris, frequented this place after his return from exile in 1767.

Madame d'Epinay was the companion of Baron Grimm, who had been Mozart's benefactor and left this unflattering account of de la Live de Jully: 'He was not possessed with much wit, or with much depth, but he was gentle and amiable in society, rich besides, an interesting figure, a bit pious, a bit of a musician, a bit of an engraver; one needs no more to be fashionable in the court and in Paris.' But de la Live de Jully was also a great art collector, and had works by Rembrandt, Van Dyck and major French artists in his collection.

In 1771 he sold the house to an American, Richard Codman, who sold it to yet another American, the Bostonian Robert Lyle. Owners kept changing during the unsettled times that followed, but the house and the extensive lavish grounds survived into the Second Empire, enhanced by a beautiful basin on whose waters floated genuine Venetian gondolas!

Today what is left of the grounds is a shrunken garden on rue Pierre Demours, studded with a few venerable trees, and another garden beyond the archway, now part of a home for the elderly. What is left of the Château is the only architectural vestige of the 18th century in this arrondissement. It now houses a crèche.

Turn left into rue Pierre Demours, which leads to **RUE LEBON** on your right, another picturesque street market, though quieter and less colourful than the one on rue Poncelet. The indoor market of Ternes, on the right-hand corner has been modernised and has somewhat lost its soul. Rue Lebon is also lined with solid neighbourhood restaurants, catering for a solid neighbourhood clientele.

Continue along rue Lebon to your right and across the twin **BOULEVARDS PEREIRE**, which commemorate the two pioneering brothers of the arrondissement, Emile and Isaac. With little respect for the past, the municipal authorities have of late renamed them Boulevards Periere nord and sud (and also added an unnecessary acute accent to the brothers' name). The boulevards run on either side of the railway tracks they had laid out around Paris, le Chemin de fer de la Petite Ceinture, now covered over with stretches of gardens and tennis courts. Continue into **Square Bayen**, surrounded by prosperous blocks of flats, some of which have direct access to the garden, offering the viewer a slice of life of middle-class Paris.

Retrace your steps and turn right into Boulevards Pereire and right again into rue Guersant, lined with bourgeois, homogeneous late 19th-century buildings. An iron gate at no. 39 on your left opens up into **la Villa des Ternes**, now home to a very select few, but once not beyond the means of the Montmartrois painter Steinlen. This is an opulent enclave, lined with substantial houses, varying from the homely rustic to the exquisitely pompous, underneath the shade of old trees. A profusion of rambling plants, flower-boxes and flower-beds complete the picture, while the noise of the outside world has been shut out. Only the occasional tinkle of a piano and the song of birds interrupt the blissful silence. However, if you come at the wrong time you may find the gate locked, in which case continue on and turn left into Boulevard Gouvyon Saint-Cyr and on to Boulevard Pershing. If you are fortunate to get in, you will leave by way of Avenue des Ternes.

Ahead is the **Palais des Congrès** dominated by the tall silhouette of the Concorde-Lafayette Hotel. As for the **BOULEVARD GOUVYON SAINT-CYR**, it was opened at the time of Louis XV and was then known as La Route de la Révolte. In 1750, when the King had long lost the favour of his people who had once nick-named him *le bien-aimé*, extravagant rumours had it that he had ordered the abduction and murder of children, so that he and his courtiers could bathe in bathtubs filled with their blood. A violent riot burst out on the road between Paris and Versailles, as a result of which this stretch of road was built as a diversion, connecting Versailles directly with Saint-Denis and Compiègne.

Cross over **PLACE DU GENERAL KOENING** and walk over to the little chapel **Notre-Dame de la Compassion**, standing incongruously on the edge of Paris, wedged between streets of zooming traffic, a surreal environment for a modest house of God. It did not always stand here, which at least would have justified this location historically. On the contrary, the chapel was transferred here in 1968 to make room for the Palais des Congrès, the site of the accidental death of Duc Ferdinand, Louis-Philippe's son and heir to the throne, which the chapel commemorates. On 13 July 1842, the Duke was riding his coach from the Etoile to visit his parents in Neuilly, when the horses bolted. The coachman was unable to keep them under control and the Duke jumped out of the dashing coach, slipped on the paving and broke his skull. He was rushed to Cordier's wineshop, the nearest house, but died there. Louis-Philippe ordered the blood-stained paving to be removed and the wineshop to be replaced by the commemorative chapel. Ingres was commissioned to design the stained-glass windows and the Baron de Triqueti to sculpture the Deposition. The recumbent statue is the exact size of the Duke and the tabernacle was laid on the altar on the exact place where his head lay when he expired. After the 1870 war and the *Commune*, the deserted chapel was occupied by squatters and ransacked by tramps, and would in all likelihood have disappeared if it had not been listed by the Caisse Nationale des Monuments et Sites historiques, at the request of the family. It was restored meticulously and transferred stone by stone to the present site. Few Parisians have heard of Duc Ferdinand and his fatal accident, nor have they noticed the tiny chapel when racing past it heading for the '*Periphérique*' (ring-road). Yet the chapel deserves attention – the primitive austerity of its stark stone walls, touched by the rays of sun that pierce through the stained-glass windows, make an appeasing setting for Ferdinand's tomb.

The PC (Petite Ceinture) bus runs to **PORTE CHAMPERRET** and will save your feet for the next section of the walk, an extensive stretch of often dull, deserted streets, to be undertaken by the tireless explorer only, who will be rewarded with exciting examples of turn-of-the-century architecture, then the homes of artists, singers, actors and the like.

BOULEVARD BERTHIER was their favourite, although it overlooked the fortification walls: they liked the fact that the air was clean and the street was attractive, combining a variety of houses of eclectic styles but of a uniform height which presented a pleasing harmony.

Notice, for example, no. 93, a brick-and-stone building with large windows and artists' studios, once inhabited by Enrico Caruso. While nos 89 and 85 were built of brick, no. 79 was of stone, and nos 77 and 75 are a characteristic blend of stone and brick, much in vogue at the time. A bright orange brick house at no. 67, across rue de Courcelles, is decorated with green enamelled ceramics, also typical of the time, while no. 65, with its pale blue bricks and blue ceramics, complements it nicely. More artists' studios follow at nos 63 and 61. No. 51, beyond Place Paul Leautaud, is an unusual house, all covered with bright green bricks, while no. 49 has an Alsatian-looking façade and is topped by a cheerful roof garden. Notice also the blue-and-white ceramic frieze at no. 45. **RUE ALFRED ROLL** to your right, displays several interesting Art Nouveau buildings: nos 14, 12 and 15 with its gorgeous Art Nouveau windows, and especially the humorous no. 6 with its two monkeys hoisted on top of its gables!

Retrace your steps to Boulevard Berthier. All the *hôtels* of the next block have survived, the first one, no. 33, having once been the home of Sacha Guitry. Yvette Guilbert's house once stood at no. 23bis, beyond rue Verniquet, an avant-garde building that many found shocking. It was demolished in the 1950s, a decade of architectural wreckage throughout the city. The red-headed landlady in her green dress and long black gloves, however, lives on thanks to Toulouse-Lautrec, as emblematic an item of touristy Paris as the Eiffel Tower.

Walk into **RUE VERNIQUET**. A pretty brick house has survived at no. 43, an Art Deco building from 1925 at no. 15 and an Art Nouveau building at no. 7. Turn left into rue Alfred Roll. The brick and stone corner house was the home of Madame J. Hatto, a famous opera singer.

Cross the Boulevards Pereire, where a row of *hôtels* has been preserved on the right-hand side. Between 1836 and 1885 Alphonse de Neuville had his studio at no. 89 Boulevard Pereire, on the corner of rue Alphonse de Neuville ahead. Alphonse de Neuville was one of the prominent painters of the Second Empire and the subsequent Third Republic. Specialising in military themes, he flattered the national ego of his contemporaries, especially after the catastrophic defeat of 1870, and was consequently catapulted to fame. The interior of his studio looked like a military museum and even contained a stuffed horse. His neighbour at no. 91 Boulevard Pereire, was Brisson, who had built Alfred Roll's *hôtel* on the corner of Boulevard Berthier and rue Edmond Flachat, to which we shall come later.

Continue into **RUE ALPHONSE DE NEUVILLE**. The entire block, from no. 15 to no. 3, has miraculously been preserved and displays a spectacular array of eclectic façades. Note in particular the beautiful Art Nouveau entrance at no. 15, and no. 3, product of a delirious imagination with its green dome, its two bombastic angels perched on the roof balustrade and its glittering gilding.

Retrace your steps and continue into **RUE EDMOND FLACHAT**, whose entire right-hand side has likewise been preserved. The young Edmond Rostand and his wife lived on the corner of rues Alfred Roll and Flachat before his plays *Cyrano de Bergerac* and *l'Aiglon* catapulted him to soaring success and into the Academie Française at the age of 33! Sarah Bernhardt had greatly contributed to the success of *L'Aiglon*, even though one critic spoke of 'some of the worst verses with which French poetry is afflicted'.

The Belgian painter Alfred Stevens lived at no. 20 rue Edmond Flachat. He was in great demand for portraits of society women, which secured him a substantial livelihood. Tristan Bernard lived at no. 22, a prolific writer, journalist and lawyer, whose humour and wit still live on. However, it is no. 32, at the other end of the street, that will capture your attention most, displaying one of the most fabulous façades in Paris of its kind: its enamelled brick, shining in different shades of green, is further embellished by magnificent ceramics. These are painted with ravishing motifs of lemon-tree branches laden with green foliage, yellow fruit and white blossoms, running gracefully along the façade against a deep blue background. Above, graceful irises decorate the pediment of the first floor window, while a frieze of delicate lilies runs under the roof. Even the three tiny windows of the attic are decorated with ceramics. On the second floor a lovely seated nude has been carved into the stone, between the two windows. The symmetry of the façade has deliberately been broken by the large window on the first floor, while two ancient-looking lions flank the entrance door to the house. How so many miscellaneous elements can fit into this small façade and still create such a harmonious whole is hard to comprehend, but it works.

No 34, the corner house opposite the Rostands', is a more modest neighbour and was once the home of the painter Alfred Roll. Although he did not live up to his ambition of becoming the Rubens of the 19th century, he was greatly honoured by the establishment and was commissioned to decorate the new Hôtel de Ville, which replaced Boccador's Renaissance building, burnt down by the *Commune*. The house bears a plaque by Chéret, engraved with a muse holding a palette and painting a picturesque little village huddling at the foot of a church.

Avenue Gourgaud, to the left, will take you to **PLACE DU MARECHAL JUIN** (previously Pereire), a picturesque roundabout where this walk will end.

LA PLAINE MONCEAU

In the latter part of the 19th century a colossal amount of the capital's wealth – usually freshly piled up – was concentrated in the area north of the Rotunda of Parc de Monceau, known as La Plaine Monceau, our next destination. Art and letters soon gravitated to and were nourished by it. Despite his immense popularity and wealth, the painter Meissonier was shrewd enough to sum up the artist's position in society: 'The artist must stay in his studio where he is King. What has he to do in a world where he is not cared for, and where his person is used as an ornament and is dished up to the guests?'

Ledoux's Rotunda, on the northern edge of **Parc de Monceau**, is our starting-point. This is one of the four monuments built for the toll gates of Paris to have survived (see 12th, 14th and 19th arrondissements). It also served as *pied-à-terre* to Philippe Duc d'Orléans, the future Philippe Egalité, landlord of the Parc de Monceau. The Duke occupied the first floor with its commanding view over the lovely countryside lying to the north, while the ground floor was allocated to the customs service. All the streets

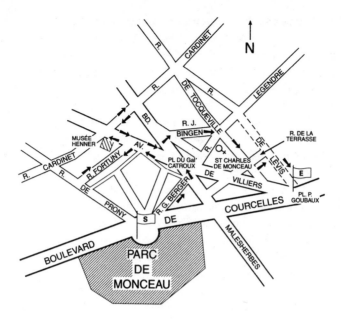

that radiate from the Rotunda were eventually lined with affluent homes. The broad **rue de Prony**, running to the north-west, became the stronghold of the *demi-monde*. Kept women were set up here by wealthy lovers belonging to the *monde*, who often maintained a comfortable respectability (*vivre bourgeoisement* as the expression went) within the family fold, just round the corner. However, the borderline between *monde* and *demi-monde* was not that clear-cut and depended largely on how high one had risen.

Walk into **RUE GEORGES-BERGER** which runs at a right angle from rue de Prony, heading north-east and leading to **BOULEVARD MALESHERBES** and **PLACE DU GENERAL-CATROUX** on its left. At nos 14 and 10 respectively lived the *Pompier* painters Alphonse de Neuville and Ernest Meissonier, then society's darlings, now forgotten by most. Both lived in sumptuous neo-Renaissance palaces, as ephemeral as their fame and as the 'mushroom aristocracy' depicted by Zola. Meissonier's dwelling was a colossal, red-brick Italianate palace, extending as far as the corner of 131 Boulevard Malesherbes and Place Malesherbes (now Général-Catroux). He wished it to be turned into a museum, but nobody wanted to preserve this white elephant and in 1894 it was levelled to the ground, outlasting the painter by three years only. At 129 Boulevard Malesherbes was the vast dwelling of their fellow painter, Edouard Detaille, who was popular for his military scenes. He occupied a colossal studio, with a ceiling high enough to hold a statue of a mounted cavalry horse.

Across the Boulevard, at no. 98, stood the sumptuous *hôtel* built by Jules Février (1876) for the Comtesse Valtesse de La Bigne (the red-headed Louise Delabigne, of unknown paternity, mentioned earlier), who, like many other *cocottes*, had used the stage as a jumping-off point for her social ascent, aged 15 and freshly arrived from Normandy. The site she picked out for her sanctuary was not just any site on the Plaine Monceau but the Place Malesherbes, its holiest of holies, where she mixed with leading bankers and Russian princes. Although her home was also the gathering place of artists, the Countess separated the sheep from the goats, admitting into her boudoir only those who could afford to keep her. When Dumas fils asked to see her celebrated bedroom, she replied, 'No, it is not within your means, *mon cher maître.*' And when she made an exception for Zola, it was merely on professional grounds, for he was then gathering material for his novel *Nana*, her fictitious *alter ego*. Zola was a reliable reporter, and provides us with a pretty accurate picture of that sacred place, notably of her celebrated bed, a gem created by the famous Cain and the focal point of her bedroom, which can now be seen on rue de Rivoli, at the Musée des Arts Décoratifs. The Countess may not have allowed her artist friends into her boudoir, but she willingly posed for them, and can be seen, for example, under an umbrella, next to Meissonier and Detaille, in the latter's painting *Le Régiment qui passe.*

Of all the former splendour of Place Malesherbes, no. 1 (no. 100 Boulevard Malesherbes) is the unique survivor, a solitary witness of a world that is no more. It was built, also by Jules Février, between 1878 and 1882 for the Baron Emile Gaillard, the banker of the Comte de Chambord and the Régent of the Banque de France. Emile Gaillard was also a great art collector, and it was largely in order to house his collection, which included paintings dating from the Renaissance, notably portraits of Henri II and Catherine de Medici and others from the early Flemish school, that he built himself this neo-Renaissance palace, inspired by the Château de Blois in the Loire Valley. It was furnished accordingly with genuine

16th-century furniture and served as a backdrop to a scintillating costume ball which Gaillard lavished on 2,000 guests on 11 April 1885. The next day the press reported: 'Two superb halberdiers, wearing the fleur-de-lys shield of France on their chests, struck the floor as the guests entered. The buffet was laid in the dining-room, a superb peacock as its central piece. Monsieur Gaillard was dressed as Henri II, in a purple satin costume.'

As in the case of Meissonier, no buyer was found for Gaillard's palace after his death on 4 May 1904. Neither the state nor the city of Paris was interested in acquiring the building and turning it into a museum and its Renaissance contents had to be auctioned off. It would probably have gone the way of its neighbours if the Banque de France had not bought it in 1923. Jules Février was duly grateful and paid the Bank a sincere tribute. Naturally, the glamour is gone, but at least the grand staircase stands, and its fireplace, a replica of the one in the Doge's Palace in Venice, has also been preserved. However, following a bomb attempt in 1985, the premises are no longer open to visitors.

On the corner of rue Jacques-Bingen stood an elegant mansion, decorated with Doric pillars, which was shared by Gounod and his brother-in-law, Pigny, from 1881 to 1893. Besides his collection of thousands of musical scores, Gounod set up a wonderful music room on the premises, 8 metres high, and complete with a genuine Cavaille-Coll organ!

Despite the wreckage wrought by insensitive developers and the passage of time, the Place du Général-Catroux (even the name Place Malesherbes has not been preserved), remains a haven of green lawns and shady, century-old chestnut trees, an oasis of tranquillity at weekends, when little traffic passes through. In spring bright tulips enliven it, later to be replaced by a blaze of rhododendron and azalea. The statues of Alexandre Dumas Père (on the western edge) and fils (on the eastern edge) grace the square at all seasons, as well as that of Sarah Bernhardt dressed as Phèdre, seated in front of the Banque de France. The actress is a later addition, a substitute for Grandpère Dumas, whom Poulbot had commemorated in his General's uniform, but who, being made of bronze, was melted down by the Germans during the last war. The statue of Dumas Père was made by Gustave Doré who, however, did not live to see its official inauguration on 4 November 1883, having died on 3 January

SARAH BERNARDT

Place Malesherbes (Général-Catroux)

of that year. Young Dumas did not forget him and went all the way to Père Lachaise cemetery, to meditate by his grave. Dumas Père, the greater of the two writers, has a mass of curly hair and seems to be in the act of writing; at his feet are three figures, absorbed in reading his adventure stories, while a splendid d'Artagnan is seated proudly at the back of the socle.

Sarah Bernhardt lived here too, just a block away to the west, on the corner (nos 35/37) of rue Fortuny and Avenue de Villiers, next door to Dumas's home at 98 Avenue de Villiers. Her home too was built by Jules Février, in 1876. Contemporaries declared it to have been a magnificent dwelling of exquisite taste, with harmonious brick and stonework on its façade, and a splendid interior staircase by Chéret. Here she assembled some magnificent *objets d'art* and also had an artist's studio (she was also a painter and sculptor). Nevertheless, within a few short years she was ruined and had to sell her house. The corner house at no. 37 was unforgivably demolished in 1960, but no. 35 is still standing. Sarah Bernhardt moved to 56 Boulevard Pereire – her home during her sensational success in *l'Aiglon*, but also during the declining years of her life – amid an incredible clutter, according to Maurice Rostand (son of Edmond). Among her medley of *bric-à-brac* and of genuine valuables were a monkey and a parrot, sharing an apparently peaceful existence in the same cage.

Head for **RUE FORTUNY**. Like rue de Prony, this was also a preserve of *cocottes*, among them two of the most notorious in the city – Geneviève Lantelme and Caroline Otero – who lived at nos 29 and 27 respectively. Both houses still stand. Whereas Caroline Otero caused some of her suitors to die of unrequited love, notably the explorer Payen, who offered her 10,000 francs for one night of her company, Geneviève Lantelme tragically drowned herself in the Rhine in 1918. The two neighbours hated each other thoroughly, yet they shared the same architect, Adolphe Vieil, who, innocently or maliciously, placed them behind almost twin façades. The street still has a spectacular array of *hôtel* façades, products of prolific and creative imaginations. All the building materials then in vogue – stone, brick, ceramic and wrought iron – participate in this excessive fantasy. Stylistic elements have been borrowed from the past, from Venice, Florence or Lombardy, from the Loire Valley, from Byzantium or elsewhere, to create an irreplaceable miscellany of an exquisitely decadent time. And yet, because the façades have been kept to the same dimensions and proportions, and because the use of polychrome ceramics has been repeated all along the street, a general harmony prevails and makes rue Fortuny an architectural period piece. Notice the blue and mauve ceramic frieze that runs along the brick façade of no. 13, once the home of writer Marcel Pagnol. Edmond Rostand also lived on rue Fortuny, at no. 2, to which he moved from the corner of rue Alfred Roll and Edmond Flachat (seen on the previous walk). It was on rue Fortuny that he completed *Cyrano de Bergerac*.

Retrace your steps and turn left on **AVENUE DE VILLIERS**. No. 43 now houses the **Musée Henner** in one of the area's few *hôtels* to have survived, providing a rare opportunity to see an example of their interiors, this one dating from the Second Empire. Despite the misleading name of the museum, the architect Félix Escalier did not build this mansion for the Alsatian painter Jean-Jacques Henner, but for the successful portrait painter of the Second Empire, Guillaume Dubufe, who had his studio here. Henner died in 1905 and in 1920 his descendants bought the mansion to turn it into a museum for his works, a happy initiative since Henner and the house were contemporaries and his works blend beautifully into it, conveying a feeling of historical authenticity even in the artificial environment of a museum.

Beyond the museum, on the corner of rue Cardinet, is the fictitious site of Nana's *hôtel*. Thanks to Zola's description, we can picture the real *hôtel* of Valtesse de la Bigne at 98 Boulevard Malesherbes: 'It was of Renaissance style, with the air of a palace, an imaginative layout inside, modern conveniences in a setting of deliberate originality.' **RUE CARDINET** is a typical, quiet, bourgeois street of the 17th arrondissement, the home of Debussy, at no. 58, where he worked on part of *Pélleas and Mélisande*. The opera was received by a tempest of disapproval when it opened at the Opéra Comique in 1902. Among other things, it was accused of being vapid and precious! Like the Impressionist painters, Debussy was misunderstood by the establishment, and as a student at the Conservatoire was reproached for 'loving music as much as the piano'! On one occasion his harmony teacher dropped the piano lid on his fingers, as punishment for having improvised on his favourite chords.

Retrace your steps on Avenue de Villiers and turn left, north of Place du Général-Catroux, into **RUE JACQUES-BINGEN**, once rue Montchanin and a stronghold of artists and literati. Among them was Guy de Maupassant, who lived at no. 10, which has since disappeared. At the street junction ahead, at no. 22 rue Legendre, the **church of Saint-Charles** stands on the probable site of the former entrance to the Château de Monceau, of which nothing has survived.

Continue right into **RUE DE TOCQUEVILLE**, running between proud, austere, fortress-like buildings, homes of the up-

and-coming bourgeoisie in the 19th century. The pleasant pedestrian section of rue de la Terrasse, to its left, leads to a different world in **RUE LEVIS** – a bustling market street, with colourful food displays and a sunny café terrace.

This is one of the most ancient routes of the arrondissement, believed to date back to Roman days, when it led in a straight line to Clichy. Abandoned after the departure of the Romans, it was not used again until medieval times, then a dirt road winding its way through the thick forest of Rouvray, which covered practically the entire arrondissement. This was the road taken by Jeanne d'Arc and her army of 12,000 men in 1429 when, following the coronation of Charles VII in Reims, she headed for the gate of Saint-Honoré, hoping to take Paris. In the latter part of the 19th century, when this was a working-class enclave in bourgeois territory, political meetings were held at no. 8, attended by such militant figures as Victor Hugo, Auguste Blanqui and Louise Michel, the 'Red Priestess' of the *Commune*; these were obviously quite different in atmosphere from the polished *salons* of the nearby Place Malesherbes. On one such meeting, held on 23 November 1884, Jules Ferry was called *'vermine'*, the National Assembly *'assemblée d'affameurs'* (assembly of exploiters) and Clemenceau *'moulin à paroles'* (chatterbox). There was also the customary battle cry, *'Mort aux bourgeois!'* followed by a street battle as those present spilled out into the open air.

FROM EPINETTES TO BATIGNOLLES

Lying east of the railway line – the wrong side – this area contains no trace of wealth, no evidence of past glory, no sign of social recognition, but you will be treading the soil where the first shoots of Impressionism appeared.

Start out from **PLACE DE CLICHY**, now the central roundabout of a busy commercial neighbourhood on the cheap side. In the early 20th century, Place de Clichy was a strategic junction between the Bois de Boulogne and Montmartre, society's two centres of gravity. *Brasseries* proliferated here consequently, a few of which are still holding their own around the Place, lit up by neon lights at night.

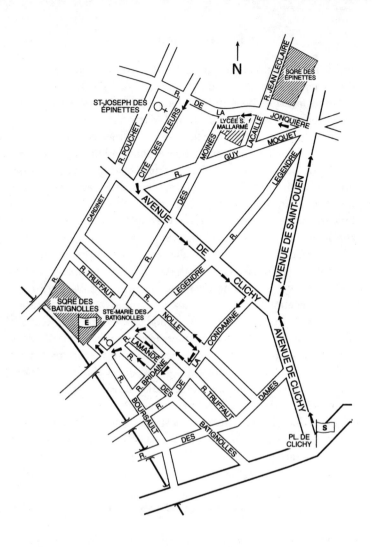

Walk into **AVENUE DE CLICHY**. The very plush La Taverne de Paris was located at no. 3, just off the Place; it was decorated by the most prestigious artists of Belle Epoque Paris – Steinlen, Willette and Chéret.

At no. 7 stood Le Père Lathuille – known worldwide thanks to Manet's painting – which went back to 1765. At the time it was one of the many *guinguettes* (open-air taverns) that sprang up beyond the toll barriers of Paris, where on Sundays and holidays lower-class Parisians gained a sense of freedom by way of cheap wine. By 1790, some substantial dishes were added to the menu – *lapin sauté* and *sole Moncey* – which could be eaten in merry company, under the branches of lilac trees, all the more exquisite in the month of May, when in bloom. Not surprisingly, it became a very popular establishment, often chosen for wedding banquets. On 30 March 1814, the place actually made the headlines and entered history books, when General Moncey, in charge of the defence of the Clichy barrier against the Allied forces, set up his command in this restaurant, a source of inspiration to Horace Vernet, who used it as backdrop for his painting *La Bataille de Clichy* (1820). The *patron* proved himself both patriotic and generous, feeding the troops abundantly and, above all, distributing to them his entire wine cellar – the ultimate act of heroism!

A less idyllic picture of the establishment is supplied by the caustic pen of a 19th-century writer who qualified its wine as suitable 'for washing the feet of horses'. The tables, he wrote, were wobbly and about to collapse and its countryside was reduced to 'one stump of Virginia Creeper, three nasturtiums and four Spanish beans'. He went on to describe its female clientele as Miss Lonelyhearts, 'misunderstood beauties' of 'missed opportunities' and 'lost futures', not unlike Manet's buttoned-up model, whom the lecherous suitor tries to loosen up. The latter was in fact the *patron*'s son, Louis Gauthier-Lathuille, from the Dragons regiment, who happened to be on leave in July 1879, when Manet stumbled on him in front of his house. Impressed by his dashing uniform, the painter wanted to fix it on canvas. By 1906 the establishment was converted into a *café-concert*, Le Kursaal, where such popular singers as Fréhel and Maurice Chevalier performed. The vogue of the *café-concert* was shortlived, overtaken by the cinema. In 1928, a first picture house was opened here, with the promising name of Eden, followed a few years later by another with a no less significant name, Les Mirages.

Manet's presence on Avenue de Clichy was no coincidence, for he had been frequenting the Café Guerbois at no. 9 (then no. 11, Grande-Rue des Batignolles) since 1863. Manet liked this typical suburban café, with its provincial decoration in Empire style, complete with five billiard tables, a garden and a bower, and got into the habit of stopping here every evening when he finished working in his studio. Here too the atmosphere was pastoral, so unlike that of the city centre, yet so close. Duranty, one of the eccentric characters who, along with the Impressionist clique, gravitated around the Guerbois, said, 'It's Dutch-looking, it's odd, it's quite a way from Paris.' The latter soon joined forces with Manet to make this their headquarters, a laboratory where new ideas fermented and would bring about a revolution in painting. The gatherings at Café Guerbois and the entrance of the Impressionists into public life both occurred in 1863, the year that thus marked the official beginning of their movement.

This was also the year of the first *Salon des Refusés*, initiated by Napoléon III after the panel of the official *Salon* had declined to exhibit thousands of paintings. The Emperor, who prided himself on his liberal and open-minded attitude, wished to give the reject-ed artists the same opportunity enjoyed by other artists, and de-creed that they be allowed to exhibit in the Palais de l'Industrie (see chapter on the 8th arr.), in galleries adjacent to those of the official *Salon*, and be allocated the same amount of space. The public should judge for themselves! This was of course to ignore the fact that the public – largely uncultivated *nouveaux riches* – had neither the finesse nor the experience to form their own judgements, and blindly followed the tyranny of officialdom. The Impressionists – Manet, Pissarro, Cézanne, and also their friends such as Whistler and Fantin-Latour – made the same mistake and naively jumped at the opportunity, only to become the laughing-stock of Paris. Manet provoked an outrage with his *Déjeuner sur l'herbe* and its scandalous nude – not an ethereal, mythical nude but a real flesh-and-blood nude, lying on the grass among the picnic things, surrounded by men in their town outfits. Worse was to come the following year with his *Olympia*, depicting an odalisque sprawling shamelessly on a bed, her clothing scattered around on the floor. But at least the *Salon des Refusés* gave valuable publicity to the clique from Batignolles and ensured that Manet's name would never be forgotten. This was exactly the tactic suggested by Zola, an energetic regular at Le Guerbois and a tireless spokesman for the *Ecole des Batignolles* – to shock the bourgeoisie. Manet, how-ever, never wished to shock the bourgeoisie and would have preferred its approval; if his art was revolutionary, it was not his intention to be that himself.

The Prussian War was to disperse the friends for a while. The generous Frédéric Bazille never came back. After the war, Le

Guerbois lost its appeal and was superseded by La Nouvelle Athènes, more centrally located, in the 9th arrondissement. A generation later the Brasserie Muller opened on the site, followed in recent times by a junk clothes shop, much the same as the many others that now line the Avenue de Clichy. You can catch bus no. 81 along the Avenue and get off at **GUY-MOQUET**.

Cross over into the perpendicular **RUE DE LA JONQUIERE**, a provincial street, winding through the humble village of Epinettes. The name Epinettes may have meant 'cheap wine', of which there was plenty in these parts. Rue des Moines on your left commemorates the monks of Saint-Denis, who used what was then a dirt road for their processions. The parallel rue des Dames was used by the nuns of the Abbey of Montmartre on the same occasions. As two parallels never meet, the idea was that female and male servants of the Lord would not meet either, so as to avoid undesirable consequences.

Continue along rue de La Jonquière and take the third turning to the left – a leafy place of enchantment, deservedly named **La Cité des Fleurs**. Unlike many other such nooks, which are jealously closed to outsiders, here everyone is welcome, as is shown by the presence of the parish **church of Saint-Joseph**, an early 20th-century domed edifice of reinforced concrete, sober, unassuming but luminous and in impeccably good taste.

In 1847 the owners of this strip of land imposed strict but beneficial regulations on each buyer, so as to ensure a pastoral environment. Every house had to have a front garden, with three flower-yielding trees. Houses, fences and gates had to conform to the same standard proportions, but otherwise each proprietor was free to choose for his house the architectural style he wished. Indeed, there is a proliferation of styles here, including combinations of all the 'neo' variants possible, with an evident predilection for the Italianate. Such a lovely street was bound to attract artists, among them Alfred Sisley, whose studio was at no. 27, the home of his mistress. During the last war some members of the Resistance also spied out this remote nook, believing the neo-Venetian façade of no. 25 would look innocent enough to provide cover for a printing house for forged papers. The vigilant Gestapo tracked them down nonetheless, rounded up all those who were present and shot them on the spot.

Turn left into Avenue de Clichy and right into **RUE DE LA CONDAMINE**, where the village of Batignolles begins, still sleepy on Saturday and Sunday afternoons. Unlike the streets of the Plaine Monceau and those around Boulevard Berthier, which glorify their *Pompier* painters, here it is the names of real-estate developers that tend to be commemorated, the artists of Batignolles having not yet gained public recognition. Thus Zola had a bungalow at no. 14 and Auguste Renoir shared a studio with his close friend Bazille at no. 9 (7 rue de la Paix at the time). Bazille was a very generous friend, always ready to support his needy companions with the substantial allowance he received from his well-to-do family, and often he put Sisley up in his studio. Renoir felt Bazille's death in the Prussian War very keenly for the rest of his life. The house still stands, though hermetically closed to outsiders.

You may wish to walk into **RUE NOLLET**, as drowsy today as it was between 1865 and 1870, when Verlaine lived at no. 10, feeling rather unhappy in this *petit bourgeois* atmosphere. The cartoonist Cham, born the Vicomte Amédée de La Noë, lived at no. 5. The son of a French Peer from rue du Bac, on the aristocratic Faubourg Saint-Germain, the Viscount refused to give up his artistic pursuits, to his father's horror, and joined the poor artists' stronghold at Batignolles, adopting the name of Noah's renegade son, Ham (Cham in French). He also abducted his family's cook, whom he was later to marry. The gatherings in his house included Emile Zola, obviously, but also the militant journalist Henri Rochefort, who, despite a working-class partisanship, was later to rally the right wing over the Dreyfus Case. Beyond rue Nollet, at no. 52 rue de la Condamine still stands a shabby-looking hotel, where Edvard Munch stayed at the beginning of the century.

Turn right into **RUE TRUFFAUT**, the heart of Batignolles, whose inhabitants were derided by many a Parisian as the occupants of small dwellings in keeping with their small horizons. A few buildings are worth noticing, notably the six-storey one at no. 33, enhanced by some blue touches on its brick façade, emulating the better-off *hôtels* in the western parts, or the charming no. 54 with its pleasant backyard, tended with the utmost care by generations of pensioners. Notice also the characteristic double flight of steps at nos 62/64 and the concierge's charming lodge, the size of a closet. Unfortunately, the little Mairie that was built here in 1830, when Monceau and Batignolles were briefly united into one suburb, has been demolished – more's the pity, since it was considered one of the loveliest suburban Mairies around Paris. A hideous building now houses the Mairie at 16–20 rue des Batignolles.

Turn left into rue Legendre, and left again into **RUE LAMANDE**, displaying a Louis-Philippe façade at no. 12. No. 11/13 still houses the Polish school, originally opened for émigrés during the troubled days of 1830. Turn right into rue Bridaine and right again into **RUE DES BATIGNOLLES**, the home of Edouard Manet throughout his career (like Renoir, he kept his home separated from his studios). Ahead is the white, provincial **church of Sainte-Marie** (so called because during its construction a 25-cm bronze statuette of the Virgin and Child was unearthed on the site). It was built in 1828 by Eugène Lequeux, when the church of Saint-Charles at 22 rue Legendre could no longer contain the growing number of parishioners of Batignolles. This was not an easy venture, for Batignolles was not a rich man's haven, and although Charles X and the Duchesse d'Angoulême helped raise the funds for the venture, for several years it had only a simple nave. Worse – it did not even have a bell tower, of which the locals were thoroughly ashamed: 'Is this a church that has no tower and consequently has no means of calling the faithful together for prayer?', protested a member of the committee in 1844. The bell itself proved altogether a humiliating issue. There were claims that it had been brought over from the little chapel of rue Legendre: 'Doesn't its only bell resemble those used in harbours to gather the workers?', it was asked. As a matter of fact, while the bell was being serviced in 1985 it emerged that it had a prestigious pedigree, having been cast in 1851 in the foundry of Hildebrand, purveyor to the Emperor. In 1888 the statuette of Mary was stolen and was never retrieved. Another Mary now rises above the altar, gloriously illuminated by the rays of the sun.

The little white church is set in exquisite provincial surroundings, taking you back several decades. In front of the church a picturesque crescent is lined with quaint houses; a pretty modern *salon de thé* and the old Café du Lion d'Or stand side by side, the latter's red awnings adding a cheerful touch to the drowsy street. Behind the church, **Square des Batignolles**, the gem of the neighbourhood, is one of the lovely gardens scattered about by Napoléon III's gardener Alphand. If you happen to come here at around 6 pm, you may wish to pop over to the railway bridge, west of the gardens, to watch the ceaseless coming-and-going of suburban trains and give a thought to Emile and Isaac Pereire, the pioneering brothers who brought the railway to France. Like all Alphand's gardens Square des Batignolles has lovely rolling lawns, shady trees, flower-beds, winding paths and a lake. A magnificent Belle-Epoque carousel has been set up here of late, complete with nostalgic music, providing pleasure to successive loads of the neighbourhood's children, seated astride its wooden horses, while the elderly residents rest on benches in the sun. Zola for his part did not care for the gardens and wrote in *Le Figaro* in 1867 that 'the gardens of the Temple (Square du Temple, in the 3rd arr.) and those behind the church of Batignolles have the picturesque aspect of gardens that retired grocers plant around their villas. . .'

Opposite the Square, south-west of the church, at no. 1 Place Charles Fillion, the restaurant Le Clos Sainte-Marie will prolong your journey into nostalgia on a warm summer evening, taking you out of Paris altogether.

Sainte-Marie-des-Batignolles

THE 18TH ARRONDISSEMENT

IN this age of assembly-line tourism, no package tour worthy of its name will bypass the 18th arrondissement, despite its inconvenient location on the northern edge of Paris. La Butte Montmartre, 129 metres above sea level and the highest summit in the Paris area, had offered the traveller a unique panorama of the city well before man-made monuments set out to compete. But when, at the turn of the century, it was further topped by a gigantic piece of neo-Byzantine architecture in the shape of a wedding cake, it became a tourist shrine. At its feet lies Pigalle, a rough designation for the boulevards that extend east and west of Place Pigalle, a nocturnal shrine of luring, flashing, neon lights, of sex and vice, an inevitable stopping-place on any 'Paris by night' tour, where coachloads of tourists are disgorged into the plush Moulin Rouge or, for those of scantier means, into some garish striptease joint.

The 18th arrondissement has been a place of pilgrimage since the dawn of time. Hill tops and summits had always aroused the imagination of people, who believed them to be the abode of divinities. The ancient Celts are believed to have attributed mystical powers to the hill of Montmartre and to have erected ritual megaliths on the sacred hill, under the guidance of the Druids. This was also a place of worship for the Romans who built here temples for the gods Mars, Mercury and perhaps Jupiter. But it was above all the martyrdom of a Christian, Saint Denis, that put Montmartre on the map as a sacred place of pilgrimage (*martyrium* was a cemetery for persecuted Christians, hence Montmartre and rue des Martyrs). The story of Saint Denis picking up his head after it had been cut off struck a chord wherever it circulated throughout medieval Europe, transmitted by troubadours and minstrels who sang in courts and castles. The story went that Saint Denis came to preach the gospel in Lutetia with his two companions Rustique and Eleuthère. The three men were arrested on the site of 25 rue Henri Barbusse, next to the Val-de-Grâce in the 5th arrondissement, the first of the seven stations of their martyrdom, during which they covered the area of the city from south to north. They were to have been put to death at the temple of Mercury at the top of Montmartre, but the soldiers, tired of climbing the steep slope, beheaded them halfway up the hill, on the site of the present 9 rue Yvonne-le-Tac. And there, lo and behold!, the holy man picked up his head, continued to ascend the hill till he came to a fountain on the site of what is now the Impasse Girardon, where he stopped to wash his blood-stained head, and then carried on north for another 'good league' (roughly 6.5 km or 4 miles). Only then did he collapse, expiring at the feet of the pious widow Catulla, who buried him on the site. No sooner was this done than corn grew on the grave, concealing it from those who would profane it, but not from Saint Geneviève, the patron of Paris, who had no difficulty in locating it two centuries later. Around AD 475 she set up an oratory on the grave, which became the nucleus of the famous Basilica of Saint-Denis. So much for historical accuracy!

According to other traditions, the bones of Saint Denis were found on the above-mentioned site of his execution. The remains of Christians were indeed concentrated in a quarry here, but whether Saint Denis was one of them cannot be verified. A chapel was erected over the quarry, probably around the 9th century, although the first mention of *sanctum martyrium* appeared only in 1096.

The identity of the Saint and the era when he lived (probably in the 3rd century) have given rise to similar confusion. In Hilduin's *Chronicles of Saint Denis* the name is spelt *Dionysii*, which suggests that the original Denis may have been no other than Dionysus, the god of wine, a plausible assumption in an area renowned for its wine. Could the names of the three evangelists, Denis, Rustique and Eleuthère, have been derived from a dedication on his temple – *Dionyso rustico eleuthero* ('Dionysus, rustic and free')? Or maybe Dionysus had simply lost his head from too much heavy drinking? In which case he would have plunged his head into the fountain to wash away his sin, or more prosaically, to recover from a hangover. The purifying quality of those waters was common belief at the time, as is attested by the saying: *Jeune fille qui a bu l'eau de Saint Denys, sera fidèle à son mari* ('A damsel who has drunk from the water of Saint Denys will be faithful to her husband'). Be that as it may, the chapel on rue Yvonne-le-Tac became a place of pilgrimages, the earliest of which dates from 1096. Among the innumerable pilgrims was Charles VI of France who came here twice, in 1391 and 1392, hoping to find a cure for his madness.

In 1133 an additional shrine was provided for pilgrims when the women's abbey was founded on top of the hill by Adelaide of Savoy, wife of Louis VI and sister of Pope Calixtus II. Pilgrims came to Montmartre not just from France but from all over Europe, among them Pope Alexander III, the Italian Saint Thomas Aquinas and Thomas à Beckett, the Archbishop of Canterbury. On 18 November 1169 Louis VII of France invited him and King Henry II of England to the Abbey of Montmartre in an unsuccessful effort to reconcile the two men. There were also magnificent processions between the Basilica of Saint-Denis and Montmartre every seven years, which were perpetuated from the time of Dagobert I, in the 7th century, until the Revolution. Most important of all, it was at the chapel on rue Yvonne-le-Tac that on 15 August 1534 the Jesuit Order was founded by the Spaniard Ignatius of Loyola and his companions.

In 1611, while repairs were being conducted after the destruction caused by the Wars of Religion, a flight of old steps leading to a vault was discovered. The words MAR CLEMIN DIO, engraved in the rock, gave rise to feverish excitement. Nobody questioned the authenticity of the inscription, which had to mean 'martyr, Clement (the Pope at the time of Saint Denis), and Denis'. This must surely be the place of martyrdom of Saint Denis. As many as 60,000 members of the court, led by Marie de Medici in person, came to pray at the holy shrine. A new abbey was built at the spot, which eventually took the place of the less accessible abbey on the top of the hill, founded back in the 12th century.

While the Butte Montmartre served the purpose of the religious authorities in times of peace, its strategic advantage could not be overlooked in times of strife. Thus, when Henri de Navarre set out to besiege Paris, he placed his battery on the top of the hill, which provided him with the opportunity to make the acquaintance of the Abbess of Montmartre, a 17-year-old brunette called Claude de Beauvilliers. A passionate liaison ensued, soon to be followed by many others, as the young nuns, inspired by the example set by their Mother Superior, surrendered their virtue to the valiant soldiers of the future Henri IV. These going-ons on the Butte shocked the righteous and the self-righteous down below, who referred to the abbey as '*le magasin des putains de l'armée*' ('the depot of the army's harlots'). It is reported that during mass at Lent the preacher castigated the young Vert Galant (Henri de Navarre) for having dallied with the Mother of the Church and cuckolded God! This affair soon came to an end, however, Claude de Beauvilliers having been foolish enough to introduce her phil-andering lover to her fair cousin, the blue-eyed blonde Gabrielle d'Estrées. . .

When Napoleon's allied foes defeated him and occupied Paris in 1814, they naturally took up position on the Butte Montmartre; 8,000 English troopers were stationed there as well as many Russian Cossacks. According to one story (challenged by some historians) their legendary penchant for alcohol led them to gather at La Mère Catherine's where they demanded a drink in Russian: 'bistro! bistro!' ('quick! quick!'), unwittingly introducing a new institution, which is still going strong to this day.

The topographical features of Montmartre and its remoteness from the centre of action had shielded it from most social explosions. But in 1871 a new page was turned in the history of the hill, hitherto reputed for its fresh air and rustic life. It was precisely its strategic position that now projected it into the limelight of French history and turned it into the tragic and bloody scene of the first act of the *Commune*.

In early March, infuriated by Thiers's humiliating capitulation to the Prussians, the people of Paris got hold of his troops' guns at Place Wagram and hauled them up the Butte Montmartre to safe haven. The Prussians did not stay in Paris, but the people of Mont-martre would not return the guns. This constituted an alarming threat to the authorities sitting in Versailles. On 18 March 1871, Thiers dispatched the 88th Brigade to Montmartre, but his soldiers defected to the rebels. Their General, Jules Lecomte, was arrested by the rebels and sentenced to death, after a show trial at the dance hall of Château-Rouge, (now 42/54 rue de Clignancourt), together with Général Clément Thomas. The latter was recognised by a child while strolling on Boulevard de Rochechouart in his morning coat and bowler hat, and was promptly assaulted and knocked out by an angry mob, unwilling to forgive his harsh conduct back in June

1848. Clemenceau, the Mayor of Montmartre at the time, could not contain the inflamed mob, who threatened him in his turn: 'Down with Clemenceau! Shoot him with the others. Go look for your whores, dirty bourgeois!' The dance halls of Montmartre – le Château-Rouge, l'Elysée-Montmartre, la Boule-Noire, le Moulin de la Galette – were converted into military headquarters and makeshift hospitals, while Montmartre itself became an entrenched camp. The skies of Paris were ablaze, for after the bombardment of the capital by the *Versaillais*, the *Communards* retaliated by setting fire to the Tuileries, to Thiers's mansion on Place Saint-Georges (in the 9th arr.), to the Hôtel de Ville, to the Cour des Comptes (replaced by the Gare, now Musée d'Orsay) and to other monuments. Reprisal was quick to follow – The Federal troops, led by Mac-Mahon, stormed Montmartre and turned it into a bloodbath. Louise Michel, the schoolteacher who had headed the *Communards* in this part of Paris (see also 17th arr.), and who had been seen on the last barricades at Place Blanche, wrote in her *Souvenirs de la Commune*: '. . . the Elysée-Montmartre was packed with dead bodies. . . And then, the Tuileries, the Conseil-d'Etat, the Légion d'Honneur, the Cour des Comptes, lit up like torches. . .'.

When in 1868 Jean-Baptiste Clément wrote the famous song *Le Temps des Cerises*, little did he imagine that three years later he would be elected Mayor of Montmartre and that his song would become the hymn of the *Commune*. In 1885 he dedicated his song 'to the valiant citizen Louise, the ambulancewoman of the rue Fontaine-au-Roi [in the 11th arr., one of the focal points of the *Commune*], Sunday, 28 May 1871.'

The enthusiastic support of the people of the 18th arrondissement for the *Commune* can be accounted for only by the social changes that had taken place there in the course of the 19th century, in particular during the Second Empire. As long as a scanty rural population lived here in harmony with the environment, however simply, there was no way it might have joined the political movements in the centre of the city. But when the Industrial Revolution was beginning to hit north-east Paris, the gateway to the big mining and industrial areas of the north and of the east, this section of Paris was doomed. Poor people thronged to these outlying *faubourgs* from the provinces, providing the necessary workforce for the new industries and hands and servants for the privileged bourgeoisie, comfortably accommodated within the city toll walls, the frustrating Mur de l'Octroi. To the east of the Butte Montmartre once lay the village of La Goutte d'Or, renowned for the quality of its wine, as its name indicates, and the village of La Chapelle, no less noteworthy for its beautiful roses. But now a Dickensian landscape had swallowed them up, shut off from Paris by the toll wall. It was a desolate wasteland covered with networks of railway-tracks, ominous chimney stacks belching their black smoke into a leaden sky, decrepit hovels in which the dregs of society huddled at night to escape the cold and criminal hands; a nerve-racking environment, punctuated by the chugging of trains to and from Gare du Nord, soon to be joined by the rattling of the elevated Métro. This lumpen proletariat often existed on an empty stomach, inhaling the poisonous air, polluted by factories and steam-engines and reeking with the putrid smell emanating from industrial, chemical waste and the slaughterhouse of La Villette. What else could they do but fuel their bodies and drown their souls in absinthe, the plague of 19th-century working-class Paris.

In *L'Assommoir* Emile Zola describes with photographic precision the life and environment of the 18th arrondissement. It was his intention, he said, 'to paint the fatal degeneration of a working-class family in the foul environments of our *faubourgs*'. The life of the heroine Gervaise rotates around the red-brick wash-house of La Goutte d'Or, the centre of working-class life, where among laughter and giggles, gossip, bickering and even vicious wrestling, cocky, sharp-tongued, sturdy laundresses tried to preserve moral integrity, a hopeless attempt in a depraved world on the verge of decay and disintegration. Seeing the glittering wealth displayed shamelessly on the Grands Boulevards beyond the wall, only a few blocks away and yet so far beyond their reach, the poor girls of the *faubourgs* inevitably ended up on the streets. There they became ready prey for brutal, callous pimps, while their male companions got sucked into a life of crime, protected by the dark recesses of the wall and by the veil of the pitch-black night. Gervaise could hear the piercing screams of victims being murdered behind the wall, and when her man, Lantier, failed to return one night she dreaded finding him stabbed to death in one of its damp, dark recesses.

In 1860 the walls were pulled down, the outer *faubourgs* were incorporated into Paris; La Goutte d'Or, La Chapelle and the Butte Montmartre, became its 18th arrondissement. Like the Grands Boulevards, which had replaced the city walls at the time of Louis XIV, the Boulevards Extérieurs became a new pleasure-ground, catering overall, though not entirely, for the masses. Some adventurous bourgeois liked to come here at night, to rub shoulders with the riff-raff and experience new emotions. Hence the Boulevards that girdle the 18th to the south became the thrilling meeting place of the rabble and the middle classes. Here, for the moment, they could secretly transcend all social taboos and pair off with the forbidden mate – the bourgeois husband with the enticing demimondaine, the bourgeois wife with the virile hunk. In Manet's painting *Le Père Lathuille*, the stuck-up, primly dressed young woman in the café (mentioned in the 17th arrondissement, but situated practically on the edge of the 18th) is wooed by an impassioned young man wearing a moustache – a symbol of virility at the time, to the extent that Maupassant devoted an entire short story to this facial decoration. Maupassant likewise tells us in *Bel-Ami* of Madame de Marelles's irresistible attraction to this neighbourhood and its places of pleasure, such as the shady Reine Blanche, where she finds thrills mingled with terror, an escape from the posh, uneventful Café Anglais on the Grands Boulevards.

Paris society had always thrived on new thrills and Tout-Paris thronged to the opening of the new cabaret, Le Chat Noir, in 1880. Its founder, the bohemian Rodolphe Salis, collaborated with Emile Godeau, who brought with him from the Latin Quarter its literary spirit and humour, adapting it to the new environment. The Montmartre genre, with its crude, cocky wit was born: 'God created the world, Napoleon the *Légion d'Honneur*, but I made Montmartre!' Salis rightly claimed. Debussy, Steinlen and Willette, who had painted the famous poster for the cabaret, could be seen here, as well as the future Edward VII, who seems to have frequented every establishment of Belle-Epoque Paris. However, Le Chat Noir was located next to the Elysée-Montmartre and the Boule-Noire on the Boulevard de Rochechouart, and this was lower-class territory. If a bourgeois wished to come here, he had better keep a low profile. Pestered by undesirable visitors, Salis eventually moved his cabaret a few blocks south, to the safer environment of rue Victor-Massé in the 9th arrondissement. Aristide Bruant, who was one of the performers at Le Chat Noir and was immortalised by Toulouse-Lautrec in his black, wide-brimmed felt hat and red-neck scarf, took over the old premises on Boulevard de Rochechouart where he opened his own cabaret, Le Mirliton. This time there was going to be no social segregation and the bourgeois rushed in, delighted to be the butt of Bruant's jokes. Night after night, top-hatted, monocled men had their airs and graces dragged in the mud in his verses, while their bejewelled companions were urged to dump their strait-laced gentlemen and instead go after one of the he-men that were prowling around. When one such woman, with her husband's encouragement, did just that, it ended in a bloodbath: disgusted both by her husband, who was hoping vicariously to regain his failing virility, and by the common brute, she ended by murdering them both in the beautiful setting of her *hôtel particulier*.

Le Chat Noir made a splash but it was the opening of the Moulin Rouge, on 5 October 1889, that was to mark Montmartre as the Mecca of pleasure and entertainment, literally the world over.

The Moulin Rouge was a sensation from the very start, and its opening was no less a historic event than the completion and inauguration of the Eiffel Tower. Both were timed to coincide with the 1889 World Fair, a key date since it also commemorated the first centenary of the French Revolution. The nightclub's founder, Charles Zidler, was a brilliant entrepreneur who had started out as a butcher on the oozing banks of the Bièvre, in the 13th arrondissement. By choosing the year 1889, Zidler and his partner Joseph Oller (who a few years later opened the prestigious Olympia in the 9th arrondissement) turned the opening of the Moulin Rouge into a national event! The same nationalistic fervour that surrounded the technological excellence of the Eiffel Tower surrounded the glamour of the female bodies at the Moulin Rouge, as they paraded to the sound of the *Marseillaise*, all decked in tricolours for the occasion. Outside, on the Boulevard, the bright red mill with its rotating sails was an irresistible invitation. the Montmartre writer Mac Orlan described 'the vermilion mill with its slow turning, blood-coloured sails. . . One felt snapped up by the inexorable jaws of the night.' The Moulin Rouge offered 'Gay Paris' what it really wanted – not social protest but glitter and flash and, above all, a display of female flesh – the exotic flesh of belly dancers within a huge model elephant (there was an elephant fad in 19th-century Paris), and frilly thighs furiously beating out a provocative French cancan known as *chahut*. The Boulevards outside the Moulin Rouge, with their treacherous, flashy electric lights, where scandalous luxury mingled with utmost misery, were bound to deprave and corrupt. Sex and crime could provide easy money and abolish social barriers. Many a wealthy, foolish gentleman, washed by champagne and wheedled by a coquette, found his *hôtel* broken into within the next few days. Many a bejewelled lady, drawn irresistibly into the arms of an unknown seducer, found herself stripped of her valuables by the break of dawn. It was Edith Piaf's job in her earlier days to spy out the land, spot out a likely prey and inform her man of the victim's whereabouts; after the initial seduction, she would be stripped of her booty, not without first putting up a useless struggle. This was the price paid for poaching in underworld territory.

For underworld territory it was and still is. With a fluctuating population, constantly replenished by fresh arrivals from the provinces and foreign countries, and having for address but some dubious hotel, the 18th arrondissement inevitably prospered on crime. There was the notorious *bande à Bonnot*, who organised the first bank robbery on rue Ordener, on 21 December 1911, and the no less notorious *apaches*, who terrorised the eastern half of Paris, using knives rather than revolvers, which they spurned, because they liked their victims to bleed properly ('*il fallait que ça saigne*'). There were sleek, black-haired, black-suited Argentines who tangoed the first part of the night away before carrying out their evil designs. During the Great War and soon after American soldiers became engaged in racist brawls with Senegalese and other Blacks. There were gigolos and there was an international white slave trade, whose victims were carried off to the heart of Asia and to the pavements of Cape Town, often with the help of ageing ex-prostitutes. But all this was child's play, according to Jack Diamond and other Chicago gangsters who toured Europe in 1929 in order to extend their network and find new outlets. On visiting the 18th arrondissement, they commented on the phoney band from

Pigalle trying to emulate Al Capone but never even matching Borsalino. When absinthe and ether gave way to cocaine, and when the Corsicans entered the scene after World War II, then you were talking big crime and big money, crime on a professional scale that could at last rival Chicago.

An international community of anarchists moved about in this underworld, feeling at one with the population that had ignited the *Commune*. Indignant at the shrieking social injustice that stared them in the face, they were determined to bring about the fall of the corrupt society that permitted it by blowing up as many of its members and institutions as possible. Although their initial motivation was noble, it was not always easy to distinguish between them and common criminals, nor between them and the poverty-stricken artist community of Montmartre. Thus Picasso's 'band' was put on the file by the police, while the Cubist painter Juan Gris was arrested when he was mistaken for one of the daring bank robbers on rue Ordener.

The environment of the 18th arrondissement favoured crime and dirty dealings: warehouses stood empty beside railway tracks, stretches of wasteland covered the east of the arrondissement, and in the west there was the steep maze of narrow streets of the Butte Montmartre. The Butte also provided ample hiding space in its quarries and caves, which had been the den of bandits and runaways throughout history. Political opponents also sought refuge here, among them Marat, when for a while the tide of the French Revolution turned against him. As a result Montmartre was even renamed Mont Marat for a time. During the June 1848 insurrection, the dictatorial Cavaignac sent his troops to the quarries of Montmartre to quash the last pockets of resistance still holding out.

Although thugs and ruffians scoured the hill, making use of its nooks and recesses and causing disturbances at the Moulin de la Galette (especially at weekends), and despite occasional stabbings or fatal shootings, the Butte Montmartre preserved the countrified, homely simplicity that had already appealed to Jean-Jacques Rousseau in the 18th century. When in the first half of the 19th century the brilliant society of finance and the arts settled in and around the newly opened quarter of La Nouvelle Athènes at the southern foot of the hill (see the chapter on the 9th arr.), the Butte

La Butte Montmartre

Montmartre exerted an appeal on those in search of a secluded getaway. While the poet Nerval stayed on the Butte for a year only, Berlioz made it his permanent home. Later Degas liked to walk up the hill and observe the laundresses, who loathed the man and called him 'a dirty old *voyeur*'. Van Gogh lived on rue Lepic for a while, but it was Renoir, more than any of his contemporaries, who found on the Butte his ideal of a harmonious village life, unspoilt as yet by the encroaching progress of the city. Here he found vigorous, rosy-cheeked people soaking up the fresh air, as opposed to their depraved, sallow-faced, sickly counterparts drowning in absinthe down below. It was these idealised people, with their velvety complexions and best Sunday clothes, that he painted in his *Bal du Moulin de La Galette*.

When, at the turn of the century, a wave of artists flooded the hill, it was as much the availability of cheap housing that determined their choice as the pleasant environment or the genial, classless population. For they were a bunch of bohemians living from hand to mouth, who had to make do with seedy, musty hotel rooms infested with fleas, hardly better than what they would have found at La Goutte d'Or or La Chapelle: colourless, peeling walls, faded bed sheets, or no sheets at all, foul and fetid mattresses, not to mention the latrines... The artists' headquarters, Le Bateau-Lavoir, where Picasso and others were living, were hardly more inviting – no wonder Picasso left them and moved to a spacious flat on Boulevard de Clichy as soon as he could afford to do so.

Unlike Mac Orlan, Poulbot and Maurice Utrillo, who remained in Montmartre all their lives, capturing its atmosphere in their works, Picasso, Matisse, Modigliani, Braque, Apollinaire and Max Jacob had much more universal preoccupations and were never part of the village. Montmartre offered them cheap food and board, as well as models among the congenial local people – or on the models' market of Place Pigalle when they could afford it – but it was totally alien to the revolutionary fermentation that was taking place at the Bateau-Lavoir, which led to the birth of *Fauvisme*, *Cubisme* and abstract art, and culminated in 1907 in Picasso's outrageous *Desmoiselles d'Avignon* (painted in his studio at the Bateau-Lavoir). Besides, except for Max Jacob, they remained here altogether for less than a decade and by 1910–11 had migrated to Montparnasse.

In 1920 a bunch of genial, free-spirited, somewhat eccentric villagers of Montmartre followed the desire of Rodolphe Salis and declared the hill a free commune, to be headed by a democratically elected Mayor. The old friends, by now residing in Montparnasse, were called upon to participate in the elections. Several electoral lists were made up, among them the Cubist list with Picasso, Max Jacob and Archipenko. A monkey by the name of Existence was also on that list... The Dadaist list was led by Francis Picabia,

André Breton and Tristan Tzara. On their programme were the following steps to be taken: 'to remove, to wipe out, to destroy, to wreck, to eliminate.' The Cubists wanted skyscrapers but the traditional locals – Suzanne Valadon, Poulbot – opposed them and suggested instead cancelling the months of December, January and February, installing an escalator uphill, a chute downhill and a conveyor from one bistrot to another! Their party obtained 57,835 votes! They also wanted to put an end to the tourist invasion by restricting the number of visitors allowed into Place du Tertre to 100,000 at any one time!

The tourist invasion had in fact taken on alarming proportions. The trouble began in 1919, with the completion of the gigantic, meringue-like Sacre-Coeur. This national shrine was conceived by the Church to expiate the crimes of the *Commune*; the locals retaliated by simply ignoring it and continuing to worship in their old parish church of Saint-Pierre de Montmartre, one of the three oldest churches of Paris (1134) and the only vestige of the first abbey. But the nation supported the project, funded through national subscription. Since the 'conservationists', led by Clemenceau, failed to defeat the bill in the National Assembly, and the lovely hill of Montmartre was clearly doomed to eternal punishment and disfigurement, the 'Savagists', one of the electoral lists of the Commune of Montmartre, now suggested transforming it into a swimming pool!

Visitors seem to like the shrine: postcards bearing its picture top the sales list among Paris monuments. They also do not seem to mind being penned into kitschy Place du Tertre, perhaps because they are unaware that just around the corner lies a heavenly village of pastoral charm, inhabited by genial locals or discerning outsiders, often from the world of the arts. Olivier Messiaen and Arthur Rubinstein were once among them. It is also one of the rare spots in Paris relatively safe from the covetous designs of building companies – the danger of landslides as a result of the unrestrained exploitation of its quarries in the past preserves it from excessive constructions.

Down the hill, traditions have also been maintained. The bright red sails of the Moulin Rouge still rotate slowly every night, even though today they lure busloads of grey-suited Japanese rather than Anglo-Saxons or Russian dukes. The sex industry flourishes conspicuously along the Boulevards, while the central island is periodically occupied by fairground stalls, a hangover from the early years of the century when Picasso used to come down the hill to the celebrated Medrano Circus, next to which lion tamers, boxers and wrestlers displayed their muscular bodies. The cabaret Les Deux-Anes maintains the old *chansonnier* witty tradition of Montmartre, whereas the Elysée-Montmartre and La Cigale, further east, offer pop concerts. The music shops of Pigalle sell electric guitars and drumkits to suit modern tastes. A century ago a 'musicians' market' was held here, where conductors would recruit players for their orchestras.

Petty and serious crime still abound here too – from pickpocketing and the sale of stolen goods on the 'thieves' market' of La Goutte-d'Or (including stereo systems and video machines) to the more sophisticated forging of identity papers, carried out at the back of some café, not to mention drug dealing.

Above all, this has remained a neighbourhood of a floating, migrant population, as can be deduced from the incredible array of cheap luggage on sale along the Boulevards. No fewer than 30 nationalities are living at La Goutte-d'Or, at present predominantly from Black Africa. With their colourful costumes, and the multitudes of traditional fabrics piled up in their shops or dangling from street stalls, they have added a new touch to the overwhelmingly rich palette of Paris. However, like the rest of Paris, which is in the process of gentrification, La Goutte-d'Or is intended for demolition. Another 'village' is to be wiped off the map of Paris in the name of safety, hygiene and social fumigation.

WHERE TO WALK

MONTMARTRE

If you can spare time for just one walk in countrified, away-from-it-all Paris, Montmartre should be your choice, provided you are fit – the climb up its maze of sloping alleys and steep flights of steps can prove quite demanding! Here a picturesque view unfolds at

every corner and a new surprise awaits you at the top of every flight
of steps. Here also, above the thick veil of pollution that shrouds
the rest of Paris, the air has remained almost as fresh and the light
almost as limpid as when Renoir painted the healthy, native girls of
the village with their velvety skins. And except for the immediate
environs of the Sacre-Coeur and Place du Tertre, which are packed
with tourists and cluttered with the usual paraphernalia of the
tourist trade, Montmartre is surprisingly uncrowded. However do
not come on a dull day – Montmartre craves for a ray of sun, and if
you can make it in the earlier part of the morning, all the better –
you will capture that unique atmosphere when Parisian life stirs

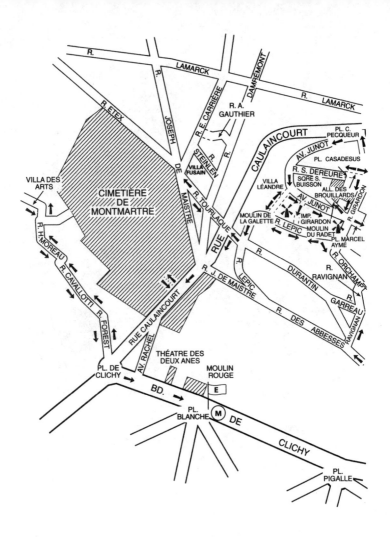

into its daily motion. But then a splendid sunset over the roofs of Paris can also be an unforgettable sight. . .

Although the hill of Montmartre covers a very small area indeed, it cannot be explored in a single itinerary. Use your sense of adventure to stroll beyond the suggested walk. And do not feel bad about leaving out some spots – there will always be 'a road not taken' in Montmartre.

Anvers Métro Station is our starting point. It is situated on the **BOULEVARD DE ROCHECHOUART**. At no. 84 is the **Elysée-Montmartre**, where La Goulue, once the star of le Moulin Rouge,

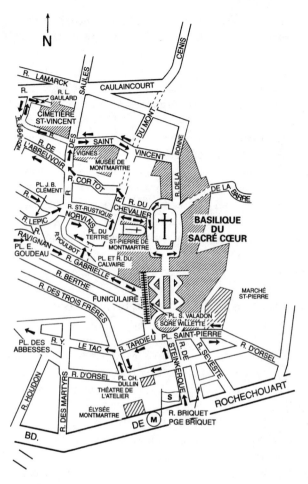

started her career. Today its stage is used by international pop
stars, reflecting the cultural changes that have occurred in the city.
Walk into **RUE STEINKERQUE**, due north, in whose cheap
brothels Picasso and his friends experienced a certain aspect of
Paris in their younger, bohemian days. Towering pompously
ahead is the Basilica of Sacre-Coeur with the pleasant gardens of
Square Willette rolling downhill at its foot. You will come to
PLACE SAINT-PIERRE, a neighbourhood garden, enhanced by
an antiquated carousel complete with prancing horses, which is
said to be two centuries old. A nostalgic street organ churns out old
melodies as it goes round. Place Saint-Pierre played a more

strategic role during the 1870 siege of Paris, when Nadar, the famous photographer and Jack-of-all-trades, used it as a base to launch a good number of balloons to enable the city authorities to communicate with the provinces. It was in one of them that Gambetta took off in order to reorganise the army of the Loire, while Clemenceau, then Mayor of Montmartre, and Victor Hugo waved farewell to him from below. To your right is the celebrated **Marché Saint-Pierre** − a bedlam on a Saturday afternoon − offering the largest and cheapest choice of fabrics in the capital. Black Africans and white French housewives rub shoulders with dressmakers and film or theatre dressers, while Arab men buy glittering fabrics for their women sequestered back home. Pablo Picasso did the same in 1904, when he came here to glean cheap cloth for his attire.

Square Willette is named after the Montmartre painter who helped to promote the romantic image of Montmartre, with its village shepherdesses, Pierrots and Harlequins, cheap copies of which have been circulating throughout the world since the turn of the century. It is a piece of historical irony that his name should have been given to the gardens of the Sacre-Coeur, in view of his fierce objection to this house of God: 'It is not possible that God, if he exists, should agree to live in there. This stupendous jumble has been built by the Devil, and for the Devil.' He entered the basilica one day, followed by some tipsy fellow-artists, and went round it chanting: 'Long live the Devil!'.

PLACE SUZANNE-VALADON, the strip of garden adjacent to Square Willette to the west, also commemorates a major member of Montmartre's artist community, a painter in her own right, but also the model and fickle mistress to several of her fellow-artists, from Edgar Degas, Puvis de Chavanne, Toulouse-Lautrec and Renoir to Erik Satie, whose heart she broke beyond repair. She dealt even more roughly with her own son, Maurice Utrillo, the Montmartre painter *par excellence*. Who his father was no-one ever knew for sure. He became hopelessly alcoholic by virtue of his grandmother's habit of putting him to sleep during his infancy with the help of a little alcohol. Suzanne Valadon had no qualms about locking him up in his room, at no. 12 rue Cortot, while she shared the fat profits from the sale of his highly appreciated paintings with her lover Utter, her son's contemporary. The *ménage à trois* with their screams and shouting matches and fits of violence, were notorious on the hill. The art dealer Bernheim took pity on Utrillo and bought a townhouse in his name on Avenue Junot. The *ménage* moved to this new address, where Utrillo was sequestered once more, but at least in greater comfort and with a more entertaining view from his barred window.

It is on Place Suzanne-Valadon that the Montmartre funicular railway starts its ascent. First built in 1903, it ran on coal and had a slim chimney that puffed out smoke as it laboured to the top of the hill. The new funicular, inaugurated in 1991, is not even remotely romantic, but it has greater speed and greater capacity, and it spares the feet of those who do not wish to or cannot climb the 225 steps up rue Foyatier, running parallel to the railway. We, for our part, suggest the long way round.

Retrace your steps on Place Saint-Pierre, continue along rue Tardieu and turn left into rue des Trois-Frères. It will lead you to the picturesque **PLACE CHARLES-DULLIN**, a typical Montmartre square, shaded by trees and home to a pretty theatre, **le Théâtre de l'Atelier**, once the famous Théâtre de Montmartre. Like all the suburban theatres around Paris, it was founded by Seveste, who had been given exclusive rights over them by Louis XVIII in gratitude for having found the remains of his brother Louis XVI. The actor Charles Dullin started out a pauper, reciting poems by Baudelaire and Verlaine in the neighbourhood's cabarets, to make ends meet. Scorned because of his deformed back and his nasal voice, he received an unhoped for stroke of luck when the director of the Théâtre des Arts in nearby Batignolles happened to hear him at the Lapin Agile one night. He hired him on the spot to play in *The Brothers Karamasov*, a role that marked the beginning of a brilliant career. For 30 years his name was associated with the Théâtre de l'Atelier, where he excelled in the roles of Molière's *The Miser*, *Volpone* and *Richard III*. Above all, it was Jean Cocteau's *Antigone*, with costumes by Chanel and sets by Picasso, that made history on this stage and the entire Tout-Paris was present on the night of the première. Later, it was Charles Dullin in his turn who introduced an unknown actor by the name of Jean-Louis Barrault, then as wretchedly poor as Dullin had been and living in the neighbouring Bateau-Lavoir.

Retrace your steps on rue des Trois-Frères and turn left into **RUE YVONNE-LE-TAC** (previously rue Antoinette). The convent at no. 9 is located on the supposed site of the decapitation of Saint Denis, after which he is said to have picked up his blood-stained head and proceeded up the hill, a miracle commemorated by a chapel which was probably built in the 9th century. When the new abbey of Montmartre was built here in the 17th century, after the rediscovery of the holy shrine (it had fallen into oblivion during the War of Religions), the chapel became part of the abbey.

On 15 August 1534 Ignatius of Loyola and his six companions (from France, Navarre, Spain and Portugal) took a vow of poverty and chastity in the chapel crypt, with the determination to devote their lives to the salvation of heathens and Christians alike, making it the cradle of the Jesuit Order, or the Society of Jesus as they came to be known in 1537. In 1541 they elected Ignatius their father superior. A 19th-century plaque commemorates the event inside the chapel (the original 17th-century plaque disappeared during the Revolution): 'This was the cradle of a great religious order which acknowledged Saint Ignatius of Loyola as its father, and whose mother was Paris and the year of salvation was 1534, 15 August.'

Continue along rue Yvonne-le-Tac. The entrance to the abbey was located at no. 23. Its grounds extended as far as rue des Abbesses, rue des Trois-Frères and rue Ravignan up until the Revolution, when the abbey was looted and desecrated, and its grounds divided into small plots and sold off. Gone were the magnificent entrance door and cloister, while the chapel and the *sanctum martyrium* were turned into a gypsum quarry, fetching substantial profits for its new owner. The Jesuits' efforts to find the legendary crypt were fruitless. They came back here several times in the 19th century but were always unsuccessful. Eventually they bought the sacred site where they put up a wooden chapel. They later conceded it to the Auxiliary Ladies of Purgatory who replaced it with the present one.

Ahead is **PLACE DES ABBESSES**, named after the 43 abbesses of Montmartre, the last of whom, Louise de Montmorency-Laval, was guillotined on 2 July 1794 – a 71-year-old lady, decrepit, deaf and blind, she was accused of having 'plotted deafly and blindly against the Republic'. This is yet another picturesque corner of Montmartre, shaded by trees and decked with characteristic items of

Place des Abbesses

Belle-Epoque paraphernalia – a pillar-shaped billboard, known after its inventor as Colonne Morris, a graceful Fontaine Wallace and, above all, Hector Guimard's spectacular Métro station.

Place des Abbesses was still on the edge of civilisation at the time. Beyond it lay the wilderness of Montmartre. At this point all passengers would alight from their coaches and continue the journey on foot, a slippery hazard in winter. The town hall of Montmartre stood on the corner of Place des Abbesses and 14 rue des Abbesses. During the troublesome year of 1870–1 Georges Clemenceau was its Mayor. The poet Verlaine married here on 11 August 1870, aged 26, although he would never become a family man.

Walk into rue des Abbesses and turn right into **RUE RAVIG-NAN**, which climbs up into the even more countrified **PLACE EMILE-GOUDEAU**, named after Rodolphe Salis's partner at the famous Chat Noir. An Edenic garden planted with exquisite fruit trees lay here in the 19th century, a remnant of the grounds of the abbey. Among them was a pear tree of such gigantic dimensions that a famous *guinguette* (open-air café) was opened under its branches, named Le Poirier Sans Pareil (The Peerless Pear Tree). It was closed down because of a landslide, but a hotel on the corner of the newly opened rue Berthe perpetuated its name for some time.

At no. 13 rue Ravignan, just off Place Emile Goudeau, stood **Le Bateau-Lavoir** (so called because it resembled a wash-house), the birthplace of Modern Art. Here in 1907, from the clutter of slummy studios and from among an extraordinary jumble of junk, emerged a scandalous masterpiece, a milestone in the history of art – *Les Demoiselles d'Avignon*. Picasso had already painted at Le Bateau-Lavoir the last of his Blue Period paintings and all those of his Pink Period. But now, under the influence of Cézanne, the *Fauves*, and above all Braque, whose works were deridingly referred to by one critic as 'cubist', a revolution was fermenting which was to change the very concept of art and have repercussions worldwide. And it was taking place here, precisely in Picasso's junk-filled studio, 'the central laboratory of modern art', as Max Jacob described it.

Unlike Renoir and other 19th-century predecessors, it was not the pure air and pastoral charm of Montmartre that had attracted Picasso and his friends to the hill but down-to-earth practicality: Montmartre was cheap! Here they could find a roof for a song and a meal for a trifle. Naturally, they were not averse to the genuine simplicity and lack of conformity of the people, but this alone would not have kept them here. The fact is that they left Montmartre as soon as budding success enabled them to do so, and although they superficially befriended the locals, they never became integrated into Montmartre and almost never integrated Montmartre into their art. It was not the brothels of rue Steinkerque that Picasso had in mind when he painted *Les Demoiselles d'Avignon* (nor that charming town of Provence, for that matter) but a bordello he knew in Barcelona; and although the circus scenes on the Boulevard at the foot of the hill – both inside

Le Cirque Medrano and in the open air – did inspire his work, the village on the hill hardly ever did.

It was when Picasso was living here that he painted the portrait of Gertrude Stein. Every day the very overweight American writer would cross the whole of Paris and climb up the exhausting steps of Montmartre to sit for Picasso in his studio. The ruthless artist had no qualms about making his admirer repeat this ordeal 80 times in a row. On the other hand, he showed great generosity towards le Douanier (real name Henri) Rousseau because here was someone he respected. The celebrated banquet that was lavished upon Rousseau at Le Bateau-Lavoir in December 1908 was instigated by Picasso and was organised in his studio by his warm-hearted companion, Fernande Olivier. Apollinaire meant the banquet as a hoax, for he regarded Rousseau as a second-rate painter and a simple soul (after all, he had been formerly employed as custom-house officer at the toll gate of Brancion, hence his nickname Le Douanier), but Picasso meant it in earnest, as a consecration of his career. Apollinaire was dispatched to Rousseau's house in the 14th arrondissement, at the other end of Paris, from where he escorted the elderly painter by coach all the way to Le Bateau-Lavoir. The entire artistic community of Paris was invited to the banquet, including its international celebrities, Alice B. Toklas and the Steins. The village scroungers gatecrashed the banquet and made the most of the occasion, stuffing both mouths and pockets. Meanwhile, the enchanted Douanier sat enthroned at the table under the chandelier. As he dozed off in contentment, the wax began to drip from the chandelier and piled up on his bald head, much to the delight of the assembled guests. The banquet turned out to be the major social event of the Paris art world in the first decade of the 20th century and remained imprinted in the participants' memory for many years to come.

André Malraux, de Gaulle's enterprising Minister of Culture, to whom we owe much of the restoration of the historic Marais, was aware that Le Bateau-Lavoir was a historic landmark and intended to have it listed. Unfortunately, he did not have time to do so, for on 12 May 1970 the building was devastated by a fire. It took only a couple of minutes for this wooden structure, the temporary home of Gauguin, Van Dongen, Aristide Bruant and many others, to burn to ashes. Among the artists who were living there at the time were the sculptor Laurent Guyot and the painter Daniel Milhaud, son of the composer Darius. A new building now stands on the site, doing its best to rekindle the flame of the one-time Bateau-Lavoir.

Continue on rue Ravignan. Ahead to your left is the pretty **PLACE JEAN-BAPTISTE CLEMENT**, named after the Mayor of Montmartre during the *Commune* and the author of *Le Temps des Cerises*. A cherry tree was once planted here in his honour.

Turn right into **RUE GABRIELLE**, a countrified street ending in a flight of steps among shady trees, from where you can enjoy the gliding passage of the funicular plying up and down the railway track. Picasso's first studio was located at no. 49 and the Jewish poet Max Jacob's monastic room at no. 9. When the artistic community left Montmartre for Montparnasse, around 1910, he alone clung to Montmartre and wrote on the walls of his room, '*ne pas partir à Montparnasse.*' It was also in this room that he had an illuminating revelation after which he converted to Roman Catholicism. This did not help him much during World War II – on 7 March 1944 he was deported to Drancy, the antechamber of the death camps, never to return. He was 68.

Retrace your steps and notice on your right bits of the Sacre-Coeur rising above the steep slope. Turn right on **RUE DU CALVAIRE** – a long flight of steps which will take you further up the hill. It is named after a cross that stood here when this was the path that led from the lower to the upper abbey. A breathtaking view of Paris rewards you at the top, where you will also discover the tiniest square in Paris, the **PLACE DU CALVAIRE**, exquisitely atmospheric in the morning, before the daily invasion of tourists. No. 3 on your left is a fine example of Art Deco architecture. This was the home of painter Maurice Neumont, one of whose works can be seen in the museum of old Montmartre at 12 rue Cortot. La Terrasse Patachou on your right is a delightful place to rest one's tired feet in fine weather, steeped in flowers and affording a spectacular view of the city.

Turn left into **RUE POULBOT** where at no. 11 you can visit the **Espace Dali**, an art gallery devoted to Salvador Dali. The street leads to **RUE NORVINS**, once the village high street, supposedly some 900 years old and the oldest street in the village. If you turn left on rue Norvins, you will come to the junction of rues des Saules and Saint-Rustique, the most famous of Montmartre's landscapes, next to the Sacre-Coeur, thanks to Utrillo's recurrent paintings of this picturesque spot. **La Bonne Franquette** on the corner of the narrow rue Saint-Rustique was frequented by Sisley, Cézanne, Zola and later Picasso. It was immortalised by Van Gogh in a painting entitled *La Guinguette*, which now hangs in the Musée d'Orsay.

At no. 22 rue Norvins stands a beautiful 18th-century mansion, **La Folie Sandrin.** In the early 19th century it was turned into a mental home, run by Dr Blanche, among whose celebrated patients was the poet Gérard de Nerval, who later hanged himself from a lamppost in one of the narrow alleys east of Place du Châtelet (since cleared by Haussmann), precisely on the site of the present Théâtre de la Ville. It was during his stay here that he wrote his masterpiece *Aurélia*. When the Russian battalion occupied Montmartre in 1814, its chief had the idea of establishing his headquarters in the beautiful surroundings of this clinic, but the highly-strung inmates, upset by the din of the battle, raged and fretted and greeted his men with such hysterical agitation that he gave it second thoughts, packed up and set up his headquarters elsewhere.

Retrace your steps and continue along rue Norvins. At no. 6, La Mère Catherine, founded by Catherine Lamotte in 1792, is traditionally believed to be the place where the word 'bistro' was coined, as reported earlier. At no. 2 the hotel-restaurant Le Bouscarat was also frequented by the artists of the hill.

You will now have reached **PLACE DU TERTRE**, where Montmartre's tourist industry congregates. Multitudes of T-shirts, Toulouse-Lautrec reproductions and portrait painters mingle in a sea of red-chequered tablecloths under garlands of electric bulbs, like some vast backdrop of a French operetta, punctuated by an old French song and the drifting sound of a piano or an accordion wafting through open restaurant windows. In days of yore Place du Tertre was the village square, where many of its social functions were filled. This was the site of the village gallows before the building of the new abbey in the 17th century, where justice was dispensed by the Abbess of Montmartre. Likewise, when Montmartre was endowed with its first municipality during the French Revolution, the town hall was established at no. 3. When, in 1920, following the initiative of Rodolphe Salis, the eccentric community of Montmartre declared its independence as the *Commune Libre*, they too made Place du Tertre their seat, at no. 19. You may remember from previous pages that the 'traditionalist' electoral list wanted to limit the number of people allowed into Place du Tertre at any one time to 100,000 – undoubtedly the most clear-sighted item on their agenda! Essentially, the main activity of the *Commune Libre* was the organising of village fêtes such as the yearly wedding of Poulbot and his companion, a ceremony that was perpetuated even after the couple had been formally wed. But the *Commune Libre* was also a democracy led by a Mayor. All the people of the hill were encouraged to take part in the elections, as well as old friends who were living in Montparnasse by then. On 24 December 1898, well before the rise of the *Commune Libre*, Louis Renault climbed up the Butte Montmartre in his newly invented car, finally pulling up in front of no. 21.

Turn left into **RUE DU MONT-CENIS**. It is believed that back in 1436 the village shop was located on the corner of rues Norvins, Saint-Rustique and Mont-Cenis and was owned by a certain Jehan Doulcet. For over a thousand years, from the time of King Dagobert in the 7th century up to the French Revolution, this was the road that led to the Basilica of Saint-Denis. Every seven years, at the beginning of May, a procession of monks from Saint-Denis would climb up the steep path to the Abbey of Montmartre. Four monks dressed in red would lead the procession carrying the head of the saint, which the abbey's nuns would come to kiss. The last procession took place in 1784.

Before 1686, the entrance to the abbey was on the site of no. 2. At present the **church of Saint-Pierre de Montmartre** is its only vestige, one of the three oldest churches in Paris, along with Saint-Julien-le-Pauvre in the 5th arrondissement and Saint-Germain-des-Prés in the 6th. It holds the tombs of Queen Adelaide of Savoy, the wife of Louis VI who had founded the abbey in 1135, and of Marie-Louise de Montmorency-Laval, the last Abbess, who was guillotined in 1794. There are even four marble pillars from the

Roman temple of Mercury that had once occupied the site. While work on the Sacre-Coeur was in progress, disfiguring the once-pastoral hill, someone came up with the extravagant project of demolishing the old church, so that the newly opened Avenue Junot could be extended to the Sacre-Coeur. Though unable to prevent the construction of the Sacre-Coeur, Willette and his friends at least saved the ancient church of Saint-Pierre.

In 1794 Claude Chappe's first telegraphic semaphore was fixed to the church because of its elevated position. It relayed signals between Paris and Lille. A second semaphore, installed later, transmitted signals between Paris and Strasbourg in the record time of 6 minutes. When Napoleon came to visit the semaphore in 1804, he had to leave his horse lower down the hill on what is now Place Emile-Goudeau, where he tied it up to one of the trees, and make the rest of the steep climb on foot. Some prominent local figures are buried in the churchyard, among them the sculptor Pigalle, the navigator and explorer Louis-Antoine de Bougainville, the first Mayor of Montmartre, Félix Desportes, and some of the Debrays, the dynasty of millers who had owned the famous mills of the hill. The churchyard however can be visited only on 1 November, the Day of the Dead in the Catholic calendar.

Turn right into **RUE DU CHEVALIER DE LA BARRE**, on the northern side of the **Basilica of Sacre-Coeur**, named after the 19-year-old knight who in 1766, at the hands of the Church, was tortured on the wheel and beheaded for having omitted to uncover his head before a holy procession. By naming the street after the young knight, who had been the victim of religious intolerance, Clemenceau and the Montmartre community could at least symbolically express their fierce opposition to the moral order of Catholicism and to the Sacre-Coeur that embodied it. Built by the architect Abadie, in a national bid to expiate the sins of the people – that is, the *Commune* – the National Assembly passed the bill to permit the building of the Sacre-Coeur in 1873, which proves that beyond religious fervour lay political interests. The cornerstone was laid in 1875, but because of the enormous budget entailed in such a gigantic enterprise, a national subscription had to be launched and the building was completed only in 1919. The official inauguration had taken place in 1890, attended by three million of the faithful.

Five years later, on 16 October 1895, the church bell – aptly the largest in the world, weighing 17,535 kg – was installed; 28 horses and a huge crowd of people joined forces to haul it up the hill, accompanied by a procession carrying torches. The local people were unimpressed and deprecatingly called the campanile 'the minaret'.

During the *Commune* rue du Chevalier de la Barre was still known as rue des Rosiers due to its abundance of rosebushes. A cottage stood at no. 36, in the backyard of which the first bloody incident of the *Commune* took place, the execution by the *Communards* of the Général Lecomte and of Clément Thomas on 19 March 1871. After his victory Thiers deliberately set up a court-martial in this very house, where the bookbinder Louis-Eugène Varlin, one of the founders of the First International, was condemned to death. He was shot a couple of metres away, probably on the corner of rue de la Bonne. His last words were, '*Vive la République! Vive la Commune!*'

Retrace your steps and turn left into rue du Cardinal Guibert towards the entrance to the Basilica of the Sacre-Coeur, which affords one of the most spectacular views of Paris.

Having taken the measure of the colossal monument, retrace your steps and turn right into rue du Mont-Cenis, then left into **RUE CORTOT**. Erik Satie, the musician and desperate suitor of Suzanne Valadon, lived in a tiny room at no. 6* from 1890 to 1898, only a few houses away from his heart's desire, who lived at no. 12. Today no. 12 houses the **Museum of old Montmartre**, well worth a visit. The lovely old house belonged in the 19th century to Claude de Rosimond, an actor who, like Molière, wrote many of the comedies he acted in. On 31 October 1860 he collapsed and died on the stage while playing the lead in Molière's *Le Malade Imaginaire* – just as Molière had departed two centuries earlier! The list of artists who at some point lived or had their studios here is quite impressive – Renoir, who painted *Le Moulin de la Galette* and *La Balançoire* here, followed by Gauguin's disciple Emile Bernard, and later still by Van Gogh. Othon Friesz lived here at the same time as the turbulent trio of Suzanne Valadon, her lover Utter and her son Maurice Utrillo, and would undoubtedly have had some juicy stories to tell. Another neighbour, the painter Galanis, recorded an incident that was

* Can be visited by appointment. Tel. 01 42 78 15 18.

typical of the notorious *ménage*: 'One day I narrowly escaped being killed by an iron flung at full swing through the courtyard by Utrillo. The iron went smashing through the glass roof of my studio and landed on my drawing table.' Raoul Dufy, André Salmon and Francisque Poulbot also lived here. Today the museum houses nostalgic memorabilia and organises temporary exhibitions in the cosy setting of a private home. You can see a reconstruction of Gustave Charpentier's music room, in which he had composed his operetta *Louise*, depicting the life of Montmartre. Charpentier never lived here but he used to come up to visit his friend Renoir. You can also see the original sign from the cabaret Le Lapin Agile, which was painted by the cartoonist André Gill (the one at the entrance to the cabaret is a copy). There are also some original posters by Toulouse-Lautrec of La Goulue and le Moulin Rouge, as well as furnishings from famous Montmartre cabarets. There is the extra pleasure of a delightful view overlooking rue Saint-Vincent and its vineyard, and of the museum's exquisite garden where you can rest.

Continue along rue Cortot, which becomes RUE DE L'ABREUVOIR beyond its intersection with rue des Saules. On the right-hand corner is a bright pink cottage with bright green shutters, red geraniums and coloured electric bulbs, like something out of an operetta once more. This is La Maison Rose, where Picasso stayed when he first arrived in Montmartre in 1902; obviously the premises have been spruced up since. Rue de l'Abreuvoir has retained the rustic aspect and quiet atmosphere of the days when horses were brought to drink in its trough(*abreuvoir*) at the bottom of the street. When you reach it, turn round for a lovely view of the street, climbing up the slope. At the intersection of rue Girardon, rue de l'Abreuvoir narrows down into a mere alley, L'Allée des Brouillards, leading to the '*château*' by the same name – a bourgeois, sleepy, provincial dwelling steeped in greenery and much appreciated by Gérard de Nerval, who wrote, 'What seduced me in this stretch of land sheltered by large trees was, first of all, the remnant of a vineyard, which brought to mind Saint Denis.' Later, the Casadesus family of musicians came to live here; they are remembered in the tiny Place Casadesus on your right. Left of the alley is the Square Suzanne-Buisson. Its fountain, supposedly the one where Saint Denis cleansed his blood-stained head, has recently received a statue of Saint Denis carrying his head to remind us of the miracle. It seems, however, that the fountain was actually situated north of the garden, in what is now the Impasse Girardon. If you step back left of the statue, you will notice the tip of the sails of **le Moulin de la Galette** above the tree branches.

Cross the garden and turn left into **AVENUE JUNOT**, along the afore-mentioned **Impasse Girardon**. On your left is **PLACE MARCEL-AYMEE**, home of the author of *Le Passe-Muraille*, hence the sculpture built into a wall, a tribute by his friend Jean Marais. Both Marcel Aymée and the musician Inghelbrecht, the founder of the National Radio Orchestra, the ORTF, lived in the corner house at no. 2.

Continue along rue Norvins and turn left into **RUE DES SAULES**, named after the willow trees that once grew on this watery spot. On your right is Montmartre's vineyard, a neat, bright-green patch cheerfully tilted downhill towards rue Saint-Vincent, but against all logic, exposed to the north! This is because it was planted in 1934 by Montmartre's merry yet incompetent intelligentsia to revive old traditions. Their knowledge of wine growing was limited indeed, and unaware that grapes need four years before they can be pressed for wine, they went on to organise the first grape-picking ceremony the following year. The ceremony was held all the same and was honoured by the presence of both the President of the Republic, Albert Lebrun, and the Minister of Agriculture, Henri Quenille, who were offered the first two bunches of grapes. The grape-picking ceremony has been repeated every October since, except during World War II. The wine is pressed in the cellar of the Mairie and sold at auction in April. The labels of the bottles are painted by local artists and the money raised is used for charity, a tradition initiated by the artist Poulbot for the children of the hill, whom he had loved and fostered, and immortalised in his paintings.

Opposite the vineyard across rue Saint-Vincent, at no. 4, stands the most famous of Montmartre's cabarets, the legendary **Lapin Agile**, once the hub of bohemian nightlife. Outsiders also came here at times to bawl out bawdy songs, even students from the distant Latin Quarter; but the man who stole the show was *le patron* himself, Frédéric Gérard, better known as le Père Frédé, who leased it from Aristide Bruant, its owner since 1903.

When it opened in 1860 it was called Au Rendez-Vous des Voleurs, and later Le Cabaret des Assassins. However, when the painter André Gill painted the famous sign of the funny-looking rabbit jumping out of the saucepan with a bottle of wine in its hand, the place was renamed Le Lapin A. (=André) Gill, eventually corrupted to Le Lapin Agile. André Gill was also a poet who composed and sang protest songs bashing the bourgeois, the police and the establishment at large, in good old Montmartre tradition. Frédé also used to sing, scraping an accompaniment on an untuned guitar. Originally a fishmonger, he would go down to les Halles every dawn, dressed as a Breton fisherman and accompanied by Lolo, his donkey, which would help him carry his fish up the hill. When Frédé turned innkeeper, Lolo was made redundant and became the mascot of the cabaret. Frédé grew a fantastic beard and wore a red scarf around his head in summer and a Trappist fur hat in winter. His Burgundian wife Berthe was a wonderful cook and prepared a two-franc menu, which, though cheap, was well beyond the means of most local clients. The warm-hearted couple never turned away hungry mouths. Frédé was very friendly and said *tu* to everyone, but kept an eye on both drunkards and thugs – he did not want to get into trouble with the police, who had already closed down his previous Montmartre cabaret, Le Zut, and he had no hesitation in throwing Modigliani and Utrillo out when he deemed it necessary. Even he could not altogether eradicate brawls and fights, often ignited by alcohol. Frédé's own son-in-law, Victor, was shot dead one fateful night, '. . . shot down at the counter by a bullet right in the head; they [the cops] turned a deaf ear', according to writer Dorgelès. Victor apparently had encroached upon the pimps' territory.

A warm, cosy atmosphere permeated the cabaret on cold winter nights, with the fire glowing in the hearth and the snowflakes falling outside. Pictures lined the walls, masterpieces such as Picasso's *Harlequin* side by side with unspeakable rubbish – Frédé was not exactly a discerning connoisseur. When he was a little short of money a few years later, he simply sold the *Harlequin* for the ridiculous sum of 5,000 francs. The fortunate buyer was Rolf de Marée, the founder of the *Ballets Suédois*.

The chapter cannot be closed without mentioning the greatest of all hoaxes perpetrated in the history of modern art, and the hero of the hoax was no other than Lolo! The writer Dorgelès did not think much of the Cubists and the *Fauves* and believed that any ass could produce the same results. In order to prove his point, he tied paint-brushes to Lolo's tail and stuck a canvas underneath. Lolo obliged by swishing his tail energetically, probably just to get rid of the un-comfortable burden, but as a result created an impressive abstract work of art, although some unkind witnesses claimed that the art critic André Warnod, who was present, contributed by guiding the donkey's tail. Be that as it may, the painting was certified by a bailiff and dispatched to the 1910 Salon des Indépendants, under the title *Sunset over the Adriatic* and signed by a fictitious Italian painter named Boronali. It seems that one dictionary of painting, published in 1939, mentions him as a 19th-century painter of the Italian school, born in Genoa, but with no date of birth. . . Lolo's work attracted press reviews that referred to '*Un tempérament encore confus de coloriste*' and '*un excès de personnalité*' ('His palette betrays a temperament that is still confused' and 'an exaggerated personality'). Today the painting belongs to a private collector, whose name has not been disclosed. It was exhibited at the Grand Palais in 1955, during an international exhibition entitled *Le faux dans l'Art et dans l'Histoire.*

Turn right on **RUE SAINT-VINCENT** and walk along the vine-yard to **RUE DU MONT-CENIS**. The drab corner block of flats at no. 24 is a shameful replacement for the one-time lovely house and garden of Hector Berlioz. His Romantic friends – Chopin, George Sand, Liszt and Delacroix – used to come up from the 9th arrondissement to visit him here, and it was also here that he composed *Harold in Italy* and conceived the idea of the opera *Benvenuto Cellini.*

Retrace your steps and continue down rue Saint-Vincent beyond rue des Saules. On your right is the old **cemetery of Saint Vincent**, which in 1831 replaced the churchyard of Saint-Pierre de Mont-martre. The entrance is on rue Lucien-Gaulard down the road. Many of Montmartre's artists rest here – the writers Marcel Aymée and Dorgelès, the musicians Inghelbrecht and Honegger, the painters Boudin, Steinlen, Utrillo, Emile Goudeau from Le Chat Noir, to mention some.

As you leave the cemetery, cross Place Constantin Pecqueur

ahead and walk into **AVENUE JUNOT**, the most elegant street on the hill and a delight for lovers of Art Deco. Turn right into **Villa Léandre** at no. 25, once the home of Max Ernst. This is a gorgeous little alley, lined with impeccably kept gardens and houses, miraculously kept open to the visitor. Its dark, shady, unkempt neighbour at no. 23 is just as delightful and leads directly to rue Lépic (the gate down the steps is always kept open). However, you should first have a look at no. 15, the best example of Art Deco in the avenue. It was built by the Viennese Adolf Loos in 1926 for the Dadaist Tristan Tzara. No. 13 was the home of Francisque Poulbot, a kindly man who set up a playground for the children of Montmartre in the garden. **Le Hameau des Artistes** at no. 11, another lovely alley, is hermetically sealed to outsiders; so is the adjoining luxury residence, which has incorporated the historic windmill, **le Moulin de la Galette**, once a place of pleasure for the youths of the hill and a source of inspiration to artists such as Renoir and Toulouse-Lautrec. Today, the property (and the windmill) are surrounded by a high-tension electric fence and guarded by a radar. At least it was saved from demolition in 1979 by a group of determined local residents.

The first written mention of a windmill in Montmartre dates from 1344. By the 17th century there were about 30 windmills on the hill. It was at that time that some miller had the idea of serving home-made pancakes (*galettes*) to the clients, while they were waiting for their flour to be milled (see also chapter on the 14th arr.). The idea caught on and wine was soon added to the menu, so that the windmills attracted revelling youths, for the wine 'set their hearts, heads and legs astir'. Le Moulin de la Galette, known at the time as Blute-Fin (for the fine sifting of its flour) was notorious for its goings-on: '*Il se fripe plus de jupons qu'il ne se blute de farine*' ('More skirts are crumpled than flour is sifted'), as one contemporary observed.

Retrace your steps to no. 23, walk down the steps to **RUE LEPIC** and turn left. At no. 83 stands the only other surviving windmill of Montmartre, **Le Moulin du Radet**, now a restaurant, La Cuisine de Jeanne, a charming place where in good weather one can eat in the little garden. This is a good place to stop before you make your way towards the extensive and less appealing foot of the hill. La Divette du Moulin across the street, at no. 98, is a more modest restaurant but pleasantly unpretentious and caters to genuine locals.

As you retrace your steps and make your way down the steep rue Lepic, try to picture the car race held here during those eccentric days – the winner was the one who arrived last! No. 64, on the corner of rue Tourlaque, displays an early 19th-century white façade with graceful niches, quite unusual in these parts. If you want to spare a thought for Vincent Van Gogh, you may push on as far as no. 54, where he lived with his brother Theo, before you turn into **RUE TOURLAQUE**. At no. 22, **la Villa Fusain** is yet another famous artists' quarters, its shady garden dotted with sculptures. Many of its picturesque studios were recovered from the 1889 World Fair. Renoir had a studio here at one time, Steinlen, Derain, Bonnard lived here, while other artists, Picasso and Vlaminck among them, visited the place regularly. Hopefully you will find the entrance door to this exquisite nook unlocked.

From here on, proceed only if you are interested in exploring the historical and cultural merit of the area.

Retrace your steps to **RUE CAULAINCOURT** and turn right. Continue downhill to the junction of **rue Joseph Maître** which runs along the cemetery of Montmartre on your right. In his younger days Fritz Lang lived in a wretched room at no. 14, drawing and selling postcards in order to make ends meet. Continue along the steel bridge that hangs over the **cemetery of Montmartre**, built on the outskirts of Paris in the early 19th century, when the cemeteries of the capital were closed down. Situated north of the city, it was then called le Cimetière du Nord. A flight of steps leads to the entrance at **no. 10 Avenue Rachel**, named after the great actress who is buried here, alongside many of France's artistic and literary set, from painters such as Degas and Fragonard to theatre men such as Lucien and Sacha Guitry, Louis Jouvet, Frédérique Lemaître – the idol of the Boulevard du Temple – and the two masters of vaudeville, Feydeau and Labiche. Among the musicians is Berlioz, laid next to both his wife and mistress Harriet Smithson, the librettists Henri Meilhac and Ludovic Halévy who collaborated on such favourite *opéra bouffes* as *La Belle Hélène* and *La Vie parisienne*, as well as Jacques Offenbach, who composed the music.

As you leave the cemetery, turn right into Boulevard de Clichy, diagonally right into rue Forest, and on to rues Cavallotti and

Hégésippe-Moreau, where the famous **Villa des Arts** is located. The painters Corot and Théodore Rousseau lived here in the 19th century, followed later by Cézanne and Signac. Cézanne's well-known dealer, Ambroise Vollard, endured here an ordeal similar to Gertrude Stein's at Le Bateau-Lavoir, being required to sit for Cézanne in his studio 114 times. At least he did not have to climb so many steps.

Retrace your steps and turn right into Boulevard de Clichy and on to **PLACE DE CLICHY**. At no. 14, the historical **Brasserie Wepler** was very popular with Picasso and his friends who preferred it to le Lapin Agile with its second-rate artists. The establishment has kept its typically gigantic Belle-Epoque dimensions and décor.

Retrace your steps. On the corner of rue Caulaincourt and **BOULEVARD DE CLICHY** stood the famous Hippodrome until 1931 – a gigantic establishment that could seat up to 5,000. Like today's Palais Omnisport at Bercy, its range of shows was extremely varied – from animal taming and ju-jitsu, to Erik Satie's *Parade*: the first Cubist ballet, with choreography by Massine and sets by Picasso. But already in 1910 huge crowds came here to be thrilled by the early motion pictures. The Gaumont cinema replaced the Hippodrome. In 1945 it put on a ballet called *Les Forains*, a tribute to Picasso in his Blue Period, which had been inspired by this neighbourhood. At no. 62 was the cabaret Les Quatre Gats, where many a *chansonnier* began his career. This place too was frequented by Picasso and his friends, and in 1907 Alfred Jarry's *Ubu Roi* was premièred here. At no. 100 Boulevard de Clichy a well-known *chansonnier* cabaret, Le Théâtre des Deux Anes, still stands, one of the last heroic survivors of a glorious past, where social protest and satire blend with exuberant joie de vivre.

As you reach **PLACE BLANCHE** at the end of the next block, you will notice on your right the bright red sails of **le Moulin Rouge**, rotating as if in slow motion to beckon the passer-by. The presence of this shrine of sex in the heart of the red belt contrasts sharply with the lofty Sacre-Coeur at the top of the hill.

Of all the figures associated with Le Moulin Rouge, La Goulue was unquestionably the most famous. Having run away from home and dried glasses in the taverns of the '*fortifs**', she fetched up one day at the Grand Véfour at the Palais-Royal, where a crowd

---

* The fortification walls built around Paris in 1841 by Adolphe Thiers.

of admirers offered her champagne and poured gold coins on her hair. From there they took her to the Elysée-Montmartre on Boulevard de Rochechouart, where she became a dancer until in 1889 Zidler swept her off and catapulted her to stardom at Le Moulin Rouge. By that time l'Elysée-Montmartre was no longer the fashionable dance hall it had been before the *Communards* turned it into a revolutionary club.

With La Goulue as the star of the opening show at le Moulin Rouge, l'Elysée-Montmartre was definitively dethroned. All the upper crust of Paris, financiers and artists, were invited to the opening, and everybody turned up. With its lavish setting, its exquisite garden and exotic dancers moving about inside a huge model elephant, Le Moulin Rouge was to put Montmartre on the map like never before. Everything about it seemed to hit the right note: its sails were a reminder of the pastoral past, while their bright red colour signalled the promise of fun and entertainment; this was just what Belle-Epoque Paris was seeking, and La Goulue was going to give it to them. Dancing a wild and uninhibited *chahut*, a provocative form of French can-can, she was an electrifying presence and brought down the house when, with a stretched leg raised, she knocked off one of the men's hats. She is said to have even favoured the Prince of Wales with this treatment. For several years she reigned over Le Moulin Rouge, outshining the other dancers – Grille-Egout, Nini Patte-en-l'Air, Cri-Cri, Môme Fromage – and forming a stunning partnership with the extraordinarily unprepossessing, yet splendidly tall and supple Valentin le Désossé ('boneless'). The name and image of the plump, fair-haired Alsatian girl, who had started life as the daughter of a laundress at La Goutte-d'Or, crossed the Channel and the Ocean: from Whitechapel in London, to the Bowery in New York, all the girls emulated her hairdo, which was made known to the world by her admirer, Toulouse-Lautrec.

But La Goulue was soon deposed by Jane Avril, who in turn ceded stardom to Yvette Guilbert. Alcohol was to a large extent responsible for her undoing, and before long the rosy, bubbly face of the energetic Alsatian became swollen and red, her body limp and overweight. When, during a performance in 1892, she stumbled and collapsed on the floor, she was fired! From there she descended into limbo, going from one menial job to another and finally to some brothel where she worked as a servant and then to the slum belt of the 18th where she tried to survive selling rags. She died a total wreck in 1929 at the hospital of the wretched, Lariboisière.

LA GOUTTE-D'OR

A tiny patch of Africa transplanted to Paris – La Goutte-d'Or – will enchant the adventurous traveller in search of something exotic. The neighbourhood is also one of the last remnants of genuine working-class village life. Despite desperate struggles on the part of local associations to rescue it from the hands of technocrats determined to 'clean up' the area, demolition has already begun and the usual characterless buildings of our times are cropping up, notably the new police station, easily distinguishable by its tricoloured flag.

Saturday morning is the best time to come here, when the local population is disproportionately inflated by streams of North Africans surging into the neighbourhood from the entire Paris area. The fun begins virtually inside the **Métro station of Barbès-Rochechouart,** or even before you get there, during the train ride itself! When the train pulls in at the station, you will be disgorged onto the platform and swept along with the human tide through the station's long corridors, among a jumble of stalls, vendors and goods; eventually you will be spilled out into the open air, where the ever-growing throng continues its inexorable advance, flooding both causeways and pavements. A closer look will bring to your attention huge carrier-bags carried by this multitudinous crowd, each bearing the name TATI. Indeed, TATI is where most of them are heading, on this their weekly shopping expedition, for TATI is the main attraction of the intersection of Boulevards Barbès, de Rochechouart and La Chapelle, loosely referred to as Barbès. This is the empire of junk clothing, and it has turned Barbès, both above and below ground, into the most gigantic bazaar in France, where total chaos prevails. Although this territory has in effect been entirely taken over by the hordes of pedestrians, motorists have not renounced their right to use the road and make brave attempts to pass through, only to end up in endless queues of cars and buses. It is nothing short of amazing that the Paris Transport Authority, the

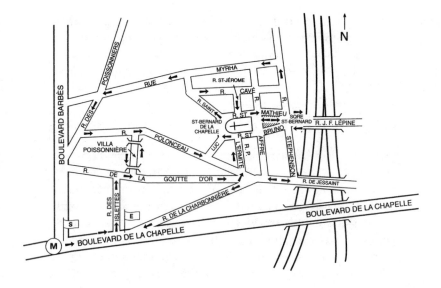

RATP, has not provided an alternative route for buses, at least on Saturdays.

TATI is not only the main clothes supplier for the poorer sections of Paris, it is also the main tourist destination for relatives from North Africa, who spend the better part of their visit to Paris burrowing among cheap goods piled up on innumerable counters. Middle-class French locals also shop at TATI's occasionally, but not at Barbès (there are a couple of other shops in the city), and often for the fun of it – it is always exciting to find a bargain for the price of a cup of espresso, which will look nice as long as it is new.

If you want a real taste of the atmosphere, join the crowds and arrive by Métro, but keep an eagle eye on your belongings. Once on the street, walk east into **BOULEVARD DE LA CHAPELLE**, where a colourful food market is held under the elevated railway tracks – a pretty sight, though the air is filled with the incessant clattering of passing trains.

Turn left into **RUE DES ISLETTES**, where the famous wash-house of La Goutte-d'Or stood, a red-brick building, reeking with steam. It is around this working-class hub that the life of Zola's Gervaise rotated and from where his Nana set out on her journey up the echelons of society. La Goulue, a creature of real flesh and blood, was also the daughter of a laundress from La Goutte d'Or – Zola's characters are all true to life.

Turn right into **RUE DE LA GOUTTE-D'OR**, at present predominantly North African. The first North Africans came here in the early years of the 20th century, but the big wave of immigrants arrived in the 1950s, often to work in the automobile industry. By the end of the decade the Goutte-d'Or was so heavily populated with Algerians that it became the headquarters of the FLN during the Algerian war. Today the street is lined with food stores and cafés, but you will rarely see a woman among the customers, even though some of the goods on display in the shops are clearly there for them, notably the candy-coloured, heavily machine-embroidered fabrics suitable for bridal wear.

In the middle of this North African enclave, behind an iron gate at no. 42, is **la Villa Poissonnière**, an incongruous countrified alleyway sloping gently down towards you, decked with the same romantic street lamps as those that decorate la Butte Montmartre: it seems to have been placed here by mistake. On either side stand charming old houses, some attractively embellished by ceramics, each with its exquisite, pocket-size garden filled with the twittering of birds. The site is believed to have been the property of a winegrower when this was open countryside, ideally situated on its sunny slope rolling gently to the south. Indeed, in the Middle Ages the wine of La Goutte d'Or had attained such renown that during a European contest at the time of Saint Louis it shared third prize with the wines of Alicante and Laconia. The first prize went to Cyprus, the 'Pope' of wines, and the second prize went to Malaga, the 'Cardinal' of wines. The wine of La Goutte d'Or was crowned the 'King' of wines, which also tells us something about the position of the royal authorities in the hierarchy of medieval Europe and their struggle to gain independence from Rome. It was customary at the time for the City of Paris to present the King with wine from La Goutte d'Or on his birthday.

The hubbub of present-day reality will hit you as soon as you step back into rue de la Goutte-d'Or. Ahead, at the intersection of rues de la Goutte-d'Or and Polonceau, is a pleasantly tree-shaded triangle where the local men meet socially on a sunny day, re-creating the atmosphere of their North African homeland.

Turn left into **RUE PIERRE-L'ERMITE**. The church of **Saint-Bernard de La Chapelle** at the end of the street is a 19th-century copy of a 15th-century style. Most Parisians had never heard of this remote church until the summer of 1996, when it made the headlines as a stronghold of resistance to the energetic measures of expulsion taken by the government against African workers devoid of work permits, known as *sans papiers*. Having occupied the church, they engaged in a long-haul hunger strike, supported by the media and by a substantial portion of the public and humanitarian organisations, members of which joined them in the church. Early in the morning of 23 August, they were taken by surprise, when the police stormed the church and dislodged the strikers with their customary brutality, heedless of public opinion.

The sculptured bourgeois façade at no. 3 is evidence that well-to-do people – successful shopkeepers and suppliers of other services to the poor – lived so close to the slums. In the courtyard of no. 4 a climbing vine is a reminder of the time when La Goutte-d'Or was a hamlet of vine growers.

Turn right into **RUE SAINT-LUC**. A pleasant compound built around a pretty courtyard is to be seen at no. 11.

RUE CAVE, on your right, honours Monsieur Cavé, an important figure in the industrial development of 19th-century France, and bread-provider to nearly 1,000 inhabitants of La Goutte-d'Or, who worked in the workshops he set up on the wasteland of La Chapelle. The son of a poor farmer from Picardy, he had come to Paris on foot, without a penny to his name. He built a marine steam engine that increased the speed from Calais to Dover to 13 knots, an exceptional achievement for those days. Other pioneering industries were set up here, notably François Calla's foundry, where a good number of Paris's street-lamps and monuments were melted down, such as the pillars of Sainte-Geneviève's university library in the Latin Quarter, some of the fountains of the Champs-Elysées and Visconti's lovely fountain at Place Louvois (in the 2nd arr.). There was also the plant founded by Antoine Pauwel, elected Mayor of La Chapelle in 1845. In 1856 a young unknown engineer was picked out by the firm to build the railway bridge of Bordeaux. His name was Gustave Eiffel.

A sign reading *hôtel familial* at no. 32 underlines the fact that this is a territory of uprooted migrants and has been so since the reign of Louis-Philippe, when the neighbourhood's population shot up from 2,000 to 11,000! The few cottages, notably the one concealed behind a huge tree and overflowing with rambling ivy at no. 26, are further reminders of a pastoral past.

Turn right into rue Saint-Jérome and left into rue Saint-Mathieu, running north of the church. The pleasant **Square Saint-Bernard** in front of the church enhances the small-town drowsy atmosphere. Beyond is the railway bridge, a gruesome landscape of steel and iron. Somehow, even in this unlikely Dickensian landscape a bright green vine has found itself a place in the sun.

Retrace your steps and walk north along rue Stephenson. From the corner of rue Cavé you will get an excellent view of the Sacre-Coeur and the eastern slope of Montmartre.

Turn left into **RUE MYRRAH**, the gateway to Black Africa. This is no Place du Tertre but a genuine neighbourhood catering for genuine locals, who have their traditional African costumes made to measure, for example at no. 25. Here slender African women walk down the street in their traditional headdresses and robes, often with a baby tied to their backs. West Indians have also moved in here and have opened a fast-food restaurant, Mac Doudou, at no. 42, which serves their own ethnic food. There is also a Bulgarian restaurant at no. 57, as well as a kosher butcher's.

Turn left into **RUE DES POISSONNIERS**, where the **Marché Dejean** is held, a dazzling feast for the eye. Black Africa, the West Indies and Haiti all converge here, offering a riot of choice sea produce and exciting fruit, such as cannot be found anywhere else in Paris. (Some of the stores, however, are owned by Asians, and African fabrics are usually made in Holland!) There is also a travel agent at no. 14 rue des Poissonniers, advertising package pilgrimages to Mecca: the neighbourhood is predominantly Muslim. Espace Kata on your right is an extraordinary old-time plush cinema turned into a penny shoe bazaar, where the entire African population of the Paris area seems to be supplied with footwear for as little as 15 francs a pair.

Turn left into **RUE POLONCEAU**, the borderline between Black and North Africa and the social hub of La Goutte-d'Or. Here stand its Mosque and Koranic school, at no. 53, and also a youth club. A

Buddhist temple occupies a rustic old house at no. 38. Rue Polonceau runs into rue Jessaint, a wholesale centre for North African food, which supplies restaurants and embassies with meat, spices, chick peas and semolina, with which they concoct delicious couscous and tajines.

Retrace your steps and continue downhill along **RUE DE LA CHARBONNIERE** diagonally to the right. It will lead you back to Boulevard de la Chapelle where this walk will end. The street has been dubbed the 'thieves' market', as stolen goods are rumoured to be disposed of here, but only those with inside knowledge or flair are aware of the fact.

Rue Myrrah

THE 19TH ARRONDISSEMENT

BEFORE 1986, when the site of the main slaughterhouse and the premises of the livestock market of Paris were metamorphosed into, respectively, a science museum and a multipurpose entertainment hall, as part of the new 35-hectare Parc de la Villette, the only reason for a bourgeois from western Paris to come all the way to these remote infamous parts of north-eastern Paris was the prospect of a gastronomic meal at Le Cochon d'Or, Au Boeuf Couronné or Dagorno on Avenue Jean Jaurès. Such establishments took pride in the quality of their meat, freshly supplied from the slaughterhouse of La Villette, on the other side of the canal, which they served in copious chunks. It was the 'in' thing to savour Gargantuan portions, especially during the Third Republic, when the consumption of food was a respectable occupation, a daily ritual celebrated around the dining table, described by Emile Zola as the altar of a family townhouse in the *beaux quartiers* of western Paris. Zola's memory, incidentally, was honoured here in 1930, on the occasion of the 50th anniversary of the gatherings that used to take place in his home in Médan, *les rencontres de Médan*, as they came to be known. Léon Hennique was the only survivor of those gatherings to have attended the anniversary celebration. Excursions to La Villette were not a family affair but an all-male experience – this was no neighbourhood for honest middle-class wives or daughters. On the other hand, potbellied lawyers, doctors, politicians and entrepreneurs of all sorts, as well as artists, writers and actors, thoroughly enjoyed themselves here over a meal that could consist of ten courses and took several good hours to absorb. How many people today could face a meal consisting of five different meat specialities, such as *ris de veau normand, queue de boeuf limousin* or *veine de boeuf charolais* preceded by a consommé and followed by the inevitable *salade de saison* and *plateau de fromages*, and still be able to tackle a *tarte aux fruits*? The writer Francis Carco and the gastronome Escoffier seemed to cope all right when they gathered here in 1935 with other members of the Académie du Goût, for a feast presided over by Curnonsky, *le prince des gastronomes*. Needless to say, those feasts were always accompanied by an assortment of

wines of the best vintage, as well as by vintage Calvados, which is known to help the digestion.

The guests hardly noticed, let alone cared about the surrounding poverty, the shrieking hunger, the mass carnage of cattle, sheep and especially pigs (the pork section was dubbed *l'Enfer*. . .). Chewing away in a Belle-Epoque setting, which exuded self-confidence and prosperity, they ignored the fact that the 19th arrondissement was the headquarters of the feeding and evacuation industries of the capital and resembled a gigantic sewer, although the municipal dump had by then been transferred to the forest of Bondy, east of Paris. Even the headquarters of the *Pompes Funèbres* were set up in the 19th arrondissement, at 104 rue d'Aubervilliers, on the site of the early municipal slaughterhouse as it happened. The rag warehouses too were set up here, debouching the clothing waste of the capital to the ragpickers who operated in the '*zone*'' – the slum belt of Paris, now the stretch between the Boulevards des Maréchaux (Extér- ieurs) and the Boulevard Périphérique. Also near by, but beyond the diners' attention, were sugar refineries and gasworks which belched their noisome fumes into a steel-tainted sky hanging heavy above. And while they were titillating their palates with a full- bodied scarlet Bourgueil or Chinon, a few blocks away, at 'le Bistro des Miracles', nicknamed after Victor Hugo's notorious Cour des Miracles, less distinguished customers were gobbling down a trans- lucid, vinegary wine known as *rouquet*.

These customers were known in their own jargon as *pilons* ('wooden legs' and, by extension, 'beggars') or *pièges à poux* ('flea traps'), wretched tramps who did not take off morning coats or top hats as they came in, but shed a stick or a pair of crutches, working tools with which they hoped to arouse pity among charitable passers-by, as they hung around the elevated Métro stations of northern Paris.

It was the geography of the 19th arrondissement that predisposed it to host the infrastructure of a fast industrialising Paris. Situated on the north-eastern edge of the city and having two canals and a basin, it was doomed to become the gateway to the heavily industrialised regions of northern and north-eastern France. It was also conveniently remote from the city centre and thus a suitable place to dump waste, along with the dregs of society.

When Napoleon created the Bassin de la Villette, his main object was to divert the waters of the river Ourcq in order to feed the fountains of Paris, which he hoped would outdo those of glamorous Rome. A thrilled crowd attended its inauguration ceremony on 2 December 1808, cheering, '*Vive l'Empéreur!*' At a time when recreational grounds were scarce, Parisians were enchanted by the lake, the refreshing trees planted along its banks against a backdrop of pastoral meadows to the north, and also by the majestic vista to the south, up to the Rotunda designed by Nicolas Ledoux. Compared by some to the water pools of Versailles, the Bassin de la Villette was appreciated even by the privileged of western Paris. In spring and summer lovers and families relaxed on its green banks, on cold winter days adults and children went skating on its immaculate ice that glittered in the crisp air under a canopy of blue sky.

Three centuries earlier, Henri IV had also been driven by aesthetic considerations when he wished to bring an air of Venetian grace to his intended Place de France (see chapter on the 3rd arr.) by means of an elegant canal between the river Ourcq and the Seine, a project which was nipped in the bud by his assassination. Louis XIV also showed interest in the idea of a canal but both his ministers Colbert and Riquet (the latter had built the Canal du Midi) died before they had time to carry out the plan. Louis XVI was caught unawares by history, and Jean-Pierre Brullée, who was entrusted with the project in 1790, at his own expense, was ruined in the process. So it was Napoleon who finally took charge of a venture originally conceived in 1520, at the time of François I.

Napoleon's waterways, however, soon found a more profitable use than providing pleasure to idle Parisians, having come in good time for the great industrial revolution of the 19th century. By 1830 the Canal de l'Ourcq, of Saint-Denis and the Bassin de la Villette proved a tremendous asset as a means of transport in addition to rue de Flandre and la Route d'Allemagne (now Avenue Jean-Jaurès), which had led respectively to the north and to the east since Roman times. Rue de Flandre was, in fact, an extension of the Roman road that became rue Saint Martin and rue du Faubourg Saint-Martin in medieval times, itself built on the axis of the Roman city's *cardo* on the Left Bank (rue Saint-Jacques). During works on the Canal de l' Ourcq in the early 19th century, a vase was found containing 2,500 Roman coins from the early 4th century and believed to have been hidden here by a native during the Germanic invasions. The new waterways were built between those two arteries, benefiting from the topography afforded by the vast plain of La Villette that lay between the hill of Montmartre to the north-west and that of Belleville to the south-east. Flowing across the suburb of La Villette, the two canals met at right angles and headed for what is now Place de Stalingrad, then the north-eastern edge of the city, where the two roads also converged. The canals became the life-blood of the arrondissement, carrying on their waters all the wares from the north and east of France (notably coal for domestic fires) to be stored or processed along the Bassin de la Villette – 'the general warehouse of the capital'. Here also began the Canal Saint-Martin, which headed south through eastern Paris to meet the Seine.

It took but one generation to transform rural La Villette into a sordid area, and it was largely the cross-shaped waterway that was responsible for its martyrdom. When Napoleon came over for the inauguration in 1807, two thirds of its land were still covered with corn, barley and oats. Orchards, vineyards and vegetable gardens completed the scene, alongside meadows where grazing cows provided milk for the 2,000 villagers of La Villette. By 1830 the pleasure-seekers of the Bassin de la Villette had been replaced by sweating stevedores and dockers, and dreary sheds, warehouses and barns lined its once green banks. Among other things stored here was the cereal of La Villette, its major crop since the Middle Ages, which thrived on the vast plain.

Like many medieval villages on the outskirts of Paris, La Villette grew as a ribbon development along the two ancient roads, mainly along rue de Flandre, where it was known as La Grande Villette, and to a lesser degree along the Route d'Allemagne, which was known as La Petite Villette and was more of a hamlet. First mentioned in 1198 as part of the domains of the community of Saint-Lazare – *villa nova sancti Lazari Parisiensis* – it appeared again two centuries later in a deed of Charles V, dated 1374, as *La Villette sainct Ladre* (Lazare) *lès* (near) *Paris*. In 1407 it was referred to as *Longueville* in keeping with its strung-out development along the main road. Largely exposed to the outside world, La Villette was attacked and besieged by the troops of Henri IV in 1590. Three years later, while stopping over in the house of Emeri de Thon at La Villette, Henri IV declared his intention to convert to Catholicism. Following this, a truce was signed between him and the Catholic League on 31 July and made public the next day '*à son de trompes et cri public*' ('to the sound of horns and public cry'), thus putting an end to the civil war. Louis XV also passed through this north-eastern gateway of Paris after his victory over the Dutch and the English at Fontenoy (Belgium) in 1745, but, unlike his ancestor, failed to stop at the house that had been prepared for him and merely rode past it. It was also through La Villette that Louis XVI was brought back to Paris from Varennes, where he was recognised, disguised as a valet, during his attempt to escape abroad with his family on the night of 21 June 1791.

In 1814 La Villette made news once more when it became the sad scene of France's capitulation to the Allied armies, signed on 1 March next to the Rotunda at the present Place de Stalingrad. The following day the Allies entered Paris through the barrier gate of La Villette, with the Tzar of Russia and the King of Prussia at their head. Twelve days later the Comte d'Artois and future Charles X followed suit as Lieutenant General of the kingdom of Meaux. When he next entered the capital, on 6 June 1825, it was with great-er ceremony, however: seated with his family in the royal carriage, he was coming from Reims after his coronation, the last monarch of France to have celebrated this 1000-year-old ritual. A triumphal arch had been erected at the barrier of La Villette, where the King was met by the Prefect of the Seine and presented with the keys to Paris before the colourful ranks of the National Guard.

Charles X was inflexible and unimaginative and did not last long. Under his successors, the bourgeois Louis-Philippe, and later

Napoléon III, the wheels of the industrial revolution turned ever faster. By 1860, the year of its annexation to Paris, La Villette numbered 65,000 inhabitants struggling to survive in Dickensian conditions. 150 firms had been established here and 15,000 vessels used the port, transporting 40,000 tons of merchandise per year. A final blow was dealt to the neighbourhood on 1 January 1867, when the new Paris slaughterhouse opened, followed on 22 October by the livestock market. And yet, by some ironical coincidence, on 1 April of the same year, les Buttes-Chaumont, among the most enchanting gardens in Paris, were also inaugurated in the arron-dissement – a juxtaposition of events that exemplified Napoléon III's contradictions. In his *Guide du Promeneur*, Delaforgue wrote that, 'At the top of the list of wonders of the new Paris, one must, without any doubt, rank the park of Buttes-Chaumont.' He went on to praise this 'graceful paradise' with its magnificent, sweeping views and its countless beauty spots that even 'the least impres-sionable tourist does not tire of admiring'. This was not, of course, Parc de Monceau and no nanny would be seen here pushing a stately pram, but the Emperor was full of good intentions, if unable to resolve his contradictions. For while he made these recreational grounds available to the people of eastern Paris, he had also aggravated their poverty by annexing the area to the capital and subjecting them to taxes, from which the suburbs had hitherto been exempted.

Furthermore, when Haussmann gutted the centre of Paris, the middle classes, whom the naïve east had hoped to lure, turned their backs on this fast-deteriorating area and migrated to the west. After all, the neighbourhood could no longer boast the rivulets and springs which had at one time watered the slopes of Belleville. One by one the windmills disappeared and in no time the hill was covered with hovels. Dismayed, the locals watched the real-estate market plummet and were plunged into a state of despair and anger, ready to explode: the only people who had moved to their area from central Paris were the poor! A decade of turbulence followed, during which time the area's inhabitants gained the rep-utation among the self-righteous bourgeoisie of western Paris of being 'the scum of the earth'.

On 8 May 1870, the 19th arrondissement voted *en masse* against the Emperor's plebiscite and after Napoléon III's defeat by the

Prussians joined forces with the *Commune*. Working-class aware-
ness had already been rife at La Villette during the 1848 revolution,
but, with little experience and no organised leadership, their
insurrection had swiftly been quelled and many of the rebels found
themselves deported to Algeria. By 1870, however, three sections of
the First International had been established in Belleville (by some
strange fluke also in 1867), two in the 19th, one in the 20th.

Social discontent had already been bubbling in Belleville since
the Restoration. The Napoleonic wars had impoverished its inhabitants, and in the open-air *guinguettes* the Bellevillois, stimulated
by ample quantities of cheap wine, gave vent to their anti-royalist
feelings in the form of subversive refrains, notably those of the
poet Béranger. By the late 1840s the poverty was such that the
municipality had to make special provision for the allocation and
distribution of bread, while three newly-founded revolutionary
clubs signalled the ever-growing social unrest among the Bellevillois. During the 1848 Revolution, hundreds of them had rushed
down the slope to join their fellow Parisians in the centre of action
and put an end to the French monarchy. There were many more of
them by 1870, and they were better organised. With such charismatic and persuasive leaders as Gambetta and Henri Rochefort,
successively their deputies to the National Assembly, the militant
journalist Jules Vallès and the hot-headed Flourens, who led the
suicidal riots, they could stand up for their rights and hope to be
victorious, especially after Napoléon III's capitulation to the
Prussians at Sedan on 4 September. And when the riots culminated
into the *semaine sanglante* ('bloody week') of 21–28 May 1871, the
Communards set fire to all the installations in the Bassin de la
Villette – the docks, warehouses, factories and lofts, all collapsed
under a glowing sky. Sugar, cotton, oil, wood, cashmere and
alcohol went up in flames – even the deep dark waters were ablaze.

Seven years later the 1878 Universal Exposition brandished in
the face of the world the definitive victory of the bourgeois Third
Republic. When the festivities were over, the pavilions proved
handy replacements for the time-worn installations of the port of
La Villette. The children of the defeated *Commune*, prostrate and
weakened by their diet of absinth, which had long since replaced
the fresh milk of cows, roamed this dismal, ominous wasteland.
Crime was their only prospect. Their victims were often the

neighbourhood's young females whom they would round up and offer as game to their fellow men. The brutality and callousness of these pimps was notorious and once caught in their noose, the girls had little hope of escape: those who put up a resistance could be stabbed, and other working women were also vulnerable when loaded with their scanty weekly wage. Violence thrived among the butchers too, notoriously hot-tempered, and fights between trigger-happy pimps and butchers, knife at the ready, were not uncommon. Who knows how many victims ended up in the oozing waters of La Villette? Seven criminals from La Villette were sentenced to death between 1872 and 1900.

> *La dernière fois que j'l'ai vu*
> *Il avait l'torse à moitié nu*
> *Et le cou pris dans la lunette*
> *A la Roquette*

> The last time I saw him
> He was stripped to the waist
> And had his neck trapped in the guillotine
> At the prison of La Roquette,

wrote Montmartre's celebrated *chansonnier*, Aristide Bruant.

The upright citizens of Paris, the target of Bruant's derision, shuddered with terror at the mere mention of La Villette and Belleville, but the immigrants who came here in search of livelihood or refuge could not afford to be so fussy. As always in Paris, the newcomers had to make do with the outlying arrondissement before being allowed the privilege of venturing further in, a pattern that still persists. Sixty-seven ethnic communities – the widest spectrum in the French capital – have taken up residence in the 19th arrondissement since the latter part of the 19th century: Poles, Russians and Yugoslavs; Armenians, Turks and Greeks who had fled from one another back home and were reunited in this small area, where the former distinguished themselves once more in making excellent shoes; Jews fleeing persecution in eastern Europe and later in Germany, who brought to Belleville their clothing trade; Black Africans and North Africans, who fill the air with the smell of exotic spices; Far East Asians who have turned the northern half of Belleville into the second largest Chinatown in Paris, with lush food stores and restaurants catering to local compatriots, which is a guarantee to the visitor of value for money and genuine atmosphere. Even the street names have followed the trend – Morocco, Algeria, Indochina and many other foreign countries, towns and regions are remembered here. Scattered through the arrondissement, too, are many mosques, churches of various denominations and synagogues. At the state primary school on rue Tanger nearly half of the pupils are of North African extraction. The school even offers bilingual instruction in Arabic and French to both its Arab and French pupils.

The 19th arrondissement is also the stronghold of the more traditional segment of the Parisian Jewish community, notably its residential parts around the Buttes-Chaumont and Avenue Secrétan. Fellow Jews have long been present here and the oldest and most established school in the community, Ecole Lucien de Hirsch at 70 Avenue Secrétan, goes back to 1901. However, lately they have moved here in great numbers, attracted by the area's greenery, altitude and healthier environment.

In 1993 the then Mayor of Paris, Jacques Chirac, was invited over to the inauguration of the arrondissement's 20th synagogue. In 1691, when Jews, Protestants, suicides and actors were denied burial, the inn-keeper Camot allocated a portion of his backyard to the Jews at a special price. In 1773 the property belonged to Matard, a skinner by trade, who, despite Jewish protestations, also buried carcasses of animals on the site. In March 1780, Jacob Rodrigues Pereire, one of Louis XVI's interpreters, succeeded in buying the site on behalf of the Jewish Portuguese community, obtaining from the King, for the first time since the expulsion of the Jews from Paris in 1394, a pledge that it would be officially recognised as a Jewish cemetery, provided the deceased were buried by night and discreetly. Pereire himself became one of the first to be laid there the following September. However, the cemetery fell into disuse after 1810, when Napoleon abolished the restrictions that had hitherto weighed on the Jews; from then on, they were buried, like the rest of the population, in the new cemeteries on the edge of the capital. The tiny old cemetery is still in existence, hidden behind no. 44 rue de Flandre, some thirty silent tombstones, on an area 35 metres by 10, behind a locked gate. It is the property of the Jewish Consistory, which does allow visits.

The Jews are not the only ones who have discovered the virtues of the 19th arrondissement. By the late 1970s, when the shortage of space in the affluent west had become alarming, it dawned on the public authorities that a real-estate reservoir was still available in the east. It also dawned on them that once cleared of the stigma of the last century, the area could display to advantage its obvious assets, namely, its gardens and waterways, its sunshine and lesser pollution. As part of this thorough clean-up, it was decided in 1979 to do away with the slaughterhouse, and the following year the idea of opening a science and technology museum in their place was put forward. By the same token, the harbour of La Villette, which in the early 20th century had employed as many as 2,000 stevedores, was to cease trading and to be restored to its original recreational function. Its vacated warehouses were to be given over to aspiring artists who would add a cultural dimension to the area. The only flaw was that, as usual, the plan was rash and not thoroughly thought out. Admittedly the science and technology museum, La Cité de la Science et de l'Industrie, enjoys 35 hectares of surrounding open-air space and sits cleverly moored in the water like some gigantic vessel. Admittedly, too, this showcase of French technology is the largest museum of its kind in the world, thus greatly flattering to the French national ego. Likewise, it boasts an overwhelming number of visitors – over 4 million a year – and has become one of the unmissable sites on the Paris sightseeing tours. Coaches and buses bring over their daily load of foreign tourists, most of whom are unaware that but a few decades ago, animals were dragged here to be butchered. Altogether 18% of international visitors to Paris get to La Villette, an impressive figure considering the remoteness of the site.

However, its success is only partial, or, as some critics put it, the vessel is pitching in an all too customary financial chasm. Indeed, most visitors treat the museum as part of a day's outing to the Parc de la Villette and wander exclusively through the sections that are free of charge. Only 5,000 of the 15,000 daily visitors buy an entrance ticket; many only use the *médiathèque*, which is free of charge, or give the children a one-off treat at the Planetarium or the Inventarium, a cheaper alternative to Disneyland. Others just use the car park! Indeed, overwhelmed by the gigantic size of the place, the visitor feels disoriented and ends up by riding the reassuring escalator that takes him to Explora, the real heart of the futuristic museum. Concepts of space and light, the universe and the weather forecast, techniques that defy nature by growing plants without soil are among the thrilling experiences that await visitors inside. School parties run around pressing on any button they can lay their fingers on: whether they will have come out wiser we do not know, but at least they will have let off steam. The unemployed of the northern and eastern suburbs, in search of new outlets, also have a go at the museum's numerous gadgets. All this is a far cry from the initial ambition, expressed in 1985, 'to create an establishment whose cultural mission is to make accessible to all members of the public the development of science, technology and industrial know-how.'

Opposite the science museum, the 36-metre-diameter sphere of the Géode mirrors the surroundings of sky and land, turning blue or silver-grey according to the weather. Inaugurated in 1986, it boasted the largest circular screen in the world, 1,000 square metres. One million spectators a year climb aboard for a three-dimensional sensory voyage, into the bowels of the earth, into the outer reaches of space or around a car racetrack. Another attraction is the Cinaxe, a heart-stopping, high-tech experience where, for 20 minutes, visitors are moved about in rhythm to projected visual clips. A ride on the *Argonaute* submarine, though less novel a concept, provides an equally potent thrill for some.

One vestige has also been salvaged from the past – La Grande Halle, south of the Canal de l'Ourcq, the work of Victor Baltard's student Jules de Mérindol – a remarkable structure that used to shelter the livestock market. It has been beautifully converted into a multipurpose hall for exhibitions and various performances. Its renovation is one of the architectural success stories in the French capital, thanks to the talents of Philippe Robert and Bernard Reichen, who have made the conversion of old industrial constructions their speciality.

Also on the southern side of the Canal de l'Ourcq is the Zénith, Paris's most popular temple to rock and pop. It is a makeshift structure which was put up in 1984, temporarily it was then thought, at the trivial cost of 40,000 francs and within the record time of 12 months. Many *Grands Projets* of the last decade or so, which have so shamelessly exhausted public funds, could learn from the success of the Zénith, which responds to the cultural aspirations of today's youths and where Eric Clapton, Ray Charles and Miles Davis, among others, were given an ecstatic reception by their 9,000-strong audiences of fans.

In autumn 1990, the Paris Conservatory (Conservatoire National Supérieur de la Musique et de la Dance) moved to the Parc de la Villette, the first element of La Cité de la Musique, which was completed in January 1997 with the opening of the museum of music. Thus the Parc de la Villette was also to become the centre of musical research and education for the future, although again the overambitious project was carried out in a chaotic way and without sufficient funds. Architecturally speaking this has unquestionably been a successful venture, owing to the immense talent of Christian Portzamparc. Young musicians like the vast premises, all shining and new and an improvement on the cramped former Jesuit school on rue de Madrid, north of Gare Saint-Lazare, their previous home.

For the non-specialist the main attraction of La Villette, however, remains its infinite and varied activities and festivities which embrace, literally, everything. All kinds of aquatic activities are on offer, from crash courses in motor-boating or intensive canoeing to an idle cruise. Those who prefer to stay on dry land can take a 109-km bicycle ride along the Canal de l'Ourcq, as far as La Ferté Milon. This is also the mecca of world culture, as light-weight and transient as much of this age. On special occasions spectacular water festivals are staged on the Bassin de La Villette. Laser and synthesisers reign supreme in these high-tech-oriented parts, which have long discarded their innocent lanterns and pompoms. The new generation hardly resembles the blood-stained butchers and sweaty, ruddy dancers in the *guinguettes*, and are more likely to be thrilled by pyrotechnics than by the traditional *Fête du Boeuf Gras*, which celebrated the fattest and most select ox of La Villette in the days of the livestock market. This was the highlight of the year, when decorated carts, disguised merrymakers and a boisterous band followed the imposing animal down the streets, watched by the entire arrondissement in a trance.

In 1987, in keeping with contemporary trends, Bernard Tschumi set out to design a park that would have a certain cerebral interest. Admittedly it has some attractive spots, such as the bamboo garden, but most of the extensive stretches are impersonal and arid, with 'designer' benches that are hardly suitable for the weary bodies of the elderly. Nor are the red geometric, paltry metal structures intended as sculptural decorations and much vaunted as one of the park's highlights, worth writing home about. Supposedly reflecting the spirit of pop art, they only serve to reinforce the emotional vacuum created by today's urban environment. Dubbed preposterously *folies*, they are no match for the neo-classical Second Empire *folie* of les Buttes-Chaumont, the Sibylline temple that crowns its dramatic cliff. Unlike les Buttes-Chaumont neighbourhood, La Villette has not yet become a hospitable environment, which perhaps explains why the vicinity of the Rotunda has become the city's hottest night-time centre for drug traffic, in particular crack. But the Rotunda is also the pride of La Villette, one of the four surviving monuments Nicolas Ledoux built for the city's toll gates and the only monument in the arrondissement bequeathed by the *Ancien Régime*. It should be seen after dark, preferably from the footbridge of the Bassin de la Villette, when it gleams magically across the water, standing out splendidly against a black sky.

WHERE TO WALK

FROM BELLEVILLE TO PRE-SAINT-GERVAIS

Because Belleville had been a nest of social unrest, the unsympathetic authorities seized the opportunity during the 1860 annexation to run a dividing line through rue de Belleville, its high street, relegating the northern part to the 19th arrondissement, the southern part to the 20th. The following walk, from the northern part of Belleville to the suburb of Le Pré-Saint-Gervais, is a strenuous one, to be undertaken only by the enterprising visitor. If you have come a long way, you may decide to combine it with the second walk, which explores the neighbourhood of les Buttes-Chaumont. If you must opt for one or other of these walks, we suggest you leave out the first one.

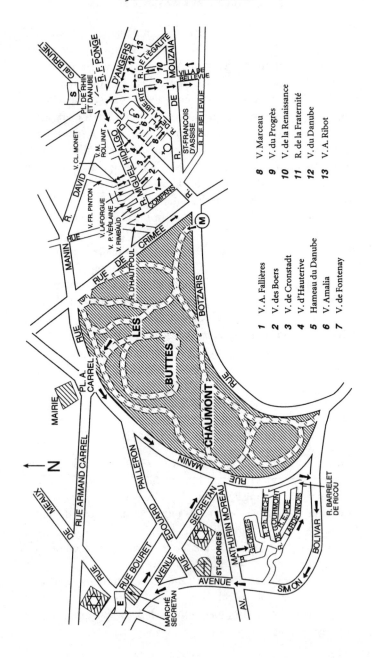

1 V. A. Fallières
2 V. des Boers
3 V. de Cronstadt
4 V. d'Hauterive
5 Hameau du Danube
6 V. Amalia
7 V. de Fontenay

8 V. Marceau
9 V. du Progrès
10 V. de la Renaissance
11 R. de la Fraternité
12 V. du Danube
13 V. A. Ribot

Head for **PLACE DES FETES**, best reached by Métro when coming from the centre of the city. As its straightforward name indicates, this was the centre of festivities of Belleville. As the cinema became the favourite form of entertainment among working-class Parisians, it was in Place des Fêtes that, in 1907, the first picture-house opened, in a makeshift conversion of a café, large enough to seat 200 spectators. Since electricity had not yet reached Belleville, a gas engine and a dynamo answered the need for energy. Sadly, the house was torn down the following year to allow for the extension of the Métro. The 19th arrondissement was in fact the birthplace of the film industry, for it was in his home at no. 55 rue de la Villette that Léon Gaumont installed his first studio in 1896, shortly after the first astonishing, public showing of *La sortie de l'usine Lumière* in the Salon Indien of the Grand Café (see chapter on 9th arr.). Belleville was soon to number a dozen picture-houses, bearing such names as l'Epatant, le Féerique, le Paradis and also Cocorico (after the French mascot). Place des Fêtes was still a picturesque spot 30 years ago, when it was surrounded by humble, even derelict houses, but which kept a low profile and blended in with the unpretentious gardens and the picturesque kiosk in the centre. Today, unsightly high-rises – a rash solution for an acute housing problem – thrust their necks impudently upwards. Only on market days – Sunday, Tuesday, Friday mornings – is the illusion of a village fête perpetuated, when the food stalls, extending full circle round the gardens, make splashes of bright colours.

One nook, however, has been salvaged due south of the Place des Fêtes. It is tucked away behind nos 11 and 15 **RUE DES FETES** and can be reached through a narrow passage between the two buildings. Before walking in, notice the incongruous 17th-century *hôtel* at no. 11, proudly displaying its characteristic wrought-iron balcony and slate roof, a reminder that in pre-industrial days this was a desirable area where the city dweller could enjoy commanding views and a healthier air than in central Paris. A number of privileged Parisians built themselves houses on the heights of Belleville. In the 18th century, the famous Favart of the Opéra-Comique is known to have owned at least five different houses here. Even at the time of Louis-Philippe no one could have predicted the economic and social upheaval that would cause Belleville's decline.

A cobbled passageway at no. 13 leads to an enclave of some 20 bungalows, on either side of a central alley, each with its own pocket-size garden. This *cité-jardin* had the merit of providing a pleasant environment for people of modest means, quite unlike the concrete jungles of today. With its picturesque octagonal kiosk and Art Nouveau glass canopy, venerable shady trees and jumble of bushes, creepers and flowers, this is now a sought-after oasis of tranquillity, way beyond the reach of lower-class Parisians.

Retrace your steps. Turn right into **RUE AUGUSTIN-THIERRY** where a small garden, **le Jardin du Regard de la Lanterne**, is named after the round stone structure on your right, which shelters the first of several, successive inspection- or peepholes (*regards*) built above the medieval aqueduct of Belleville, running here 2.5 metres below ground level. These were built in order to check the level of the water and they were always kept locked to prevent the water from being harnessed or stolen. The opening in its lantern-shaped roof allowed for the circulation of fresh air, which ensured a better quality of water. The iron rings that until quite recently were fixed to the wall served to tie the aldermen's horses when they came on their annual inspection round.

The aqueduct of Belleville was built under Philippe Auguste for the use of the religious communities of Saint-Martin-des-Champs and the Temple. However, the King demanded that some of its water be diverted to the three public fountains of the city, which were located in the area of Les Halles. Together with the aqueduct of Pré-Saint-Gervais, which was built at the same time by the Order of Saint-Lazare, they constituted the bulk of the water supply of the Right Bank until the early 19th century, which explains why the inhabitants of Paris disposed of only one litre of water per day each, and accounts for the filth and stench of the capital's streets. The aqueducts were overshadowed by the newly opened Canal Saint-Martin and fell into disuse altogether in 1865, when Belgrand endowed Paris with a modern network that piped water into private homes – more than three centuries after London had been supplied with the same service!

Turn left into rue Compans and right into **RUE DU PRE-SAINT-GERVAIS**, which leads to the former village by the same name, today a suburb of Paris. You will soon reach the summit of

Belleville, 128.5 metres, less than one metre short of the summit of Montmartre and of Paris, although the Bellevillois swear to the contrary. Two streets fork out at the junction ahead, rue des Lilas on your left, rue des Bois on your right. In pre-industrial days, the area was indeed covered with meadows (*prés*), woods and lilacs. In 1901 a lovely house of elegant proportions, surrounded by an exquisite garden, could still be seen on the site of the drab block of flats at no. 32. This was the country house of François Soufflot '*le Romain*', nephew of the famous architect of the Panthéon. Other artists, now less widely known, came to live here too. Among them were two friends of the writer Eugène Dabie, the author of *Hôtel du Nord*, who would have probably also been forgotten had it not been for the movie made out of his novel by Marcel Carné. Eugène Dabie used to come over from the Hôtel du Nord by the Canal Saint-Martin, which was run by his parents. Today all that is left is a pocketkerchief patch of garden with three ugly concrete benches.

Continue down rue des Bois and turn right into **rues Emile Desvaux and Paul de Kock** – an unexpected delight: from an Anglo-Norman chalet to a copy of Bauhaus, or a fairy-tale crooked cottage with pink shutters and bright blue frames – every resident has given vent to his creative individualism and his gardening talents. Not surprisingly this was a stronghold of painters, who came to be known as the *Ecole du Pré-Saint-Gervais*, of whom, admittedly, few outsiders have ever heard. If you happen to walk by during the day, you may chance upon Orthodox Jewish schoolboys coming out of their school in these unlikely surroundings, tangible evidence that the southern part of the arrondissement has in recent years become a stronghold of Jewish Orthodoxy. You may have also noticed at the entrance to this enclave the names of three residents who were shot by the Germans in 1942, 1943 and 1944, respectively, as members of the Resistance – a large number for such a small enclave, but then this was a patriotic, working-class area, with strong anti-German feelings going back to the 1870 war. When you leave rue Emile Desvaux you will see on your left their names indicated once more, not just as victims of the Nazis – the usual formula in Paris – but of the *Bosches!* This working-class life is portrayed in the novels of Paul de Kock, who died in 1871 and after whom one of the streets is named. The self-righteous bourgeoisie of western Paris was shocked by his crude, licentious literature, which today would make an altar-boy smile. Admittedly, he did not write great literature, but he was very prolific and produced some 250 works.

Turn left into rue de Romainville and right into **Passage Montenegro**, a modest alley with crooked paving, a window bursting with red geraniums at no. 8 and a bright vine climbing at no. 11.

Turn left into **RUE HAXO**, running downhill due north. From here you will enjoy a sweeping view of the northern suburbs and the countryside and understand why the village was once called Bellevue. Cross over Boulevard de Sérurier and **BOULEVARD D'ALGERIE**. The latter traces the *zone non aedificandi*, the unbuilt strip of land, 200 metres wide, that surrounded Thiers's fortification walls (the '*fortifs*') and was known as *la zone*. Its denizens, the *zonards*, ragpickers and other destitute people, vanished only 30 odd years ago when the Boulevard Périphérique was built.

The fortification walls, built in 1841, ran parallel to the inner toll walls until the 1860 annexation, when the latter were torn down. The fortification walls were torn down in their turn in 1919, until when they also served as substitutes for the toll walls (Boulevard Sérurier now runs on their site while Boulevard de la Villette, the south-western border of the 19th arrondissement, has replaced a section of the old toll walls). In 1914, when the tax collectors posted at the gates stopped travellers into Paris with the standard question, 'Anything to declare?', the poor women would reply, 'A husband at war and three children to feed', enough in those days of penury to make the functionary melt. Initially the *zone non aedificandi* was meant to be replaced by gardens, but the housing problems in Paris were too acute and low-rental red-brick blocks of flats were built around the city in their stead. Here, however, an attractive garden did spring up – Square de la Butte du Chapeau Rouge, to be visited later.

Continue along **AVENUE DE LA PORTE DU PRE-SAINT-GERVAIS**. The white building sprawling on your right is **l'Hôpital Robert Debré**, a children's hospital named after the renowned surgeon, son of a rabbi and father of Michel, one of General de Gaulle's most loyal companions. On the eve of World War I, Jean Jaurès held desperate peace rallies in this stronghold of radical socialism, to no avail. As the war dragged on, the area was divided up into allotments by hungry Parisians who raised meagre crops to feed their families.

Take the subway crossing under the Boulevard Périphérique and walk across rue Alexander-Fleming, the border of the city of Paris. On your right, adjoining the ring road, stands an 18th-century *regard*, which served the aqueduct of Pré-Saint-Gervais. The romantic poet Charles Nodier, a one-time curator of the Arsenal Library (in the 4th arr.), used to come all the way from the centre of Paris to rest by its side.

Walk into rue André Joineau for a brief detour beyond the city boundaries to the suburb of **Pré-Saint-Gervais**, where you will be able to recapture much of the atmosphere of the outlying arrondissements as they were a mere 30 years ago. On your left stands the festive, somewhat provincial **Mairie**, displaying a profusion of red geraniums, while neat lawns and patterns of flowers roll like carpets at its feet. The site is worthy of any town-hall square in any small town of sleepy France; the star-studded blue flag of the European Community, hoisted next to the tricolour, is a reminder, however, that this is the end of the 20th century and that France is determined to make European unity work. The modern-style telephone booth and the police uniforms designed by no less than the House of Balmain are further indication that France is also determined to shed her laid-back image of pre-technocratic days.

When, on the eve of World War I, the indefatigable Jean Jaurès set out on his peace mission, he came here too to exhort the citizens to renounce the folly of war. He was, of course, preaching to the converted: the Pré-Saint-Gervais was then and still is a socialist stronghold, holding its own within what was until recently overwhelmingly communist territory, known as '*la banlieue rouge*'.

Opposite the Mairie can be seen another *regard*, built by the Order of Saint-Lazare over the aqueduct of Pré-Saint-Gervais. The aqueduct supplied water to the fountains of rue Saint-Denis, the main axis of the city up to the 1820s, but lost its *raison d'être* with the opening of the Canal of Ourcq. Thiers's fortifications ran right through it, dealing it a final blow.

The doorway at no. 63 will lead you into a charming enclave, in itself a good enough reason to have come all this way! Another doorway at no. 73 opens into an enchanting network of leafy alleys bearing the names of chestnut trees, acacias and sycamores, with exquisite gardens and houses of eclectic styles on either side. Time seems to have stood still here since 1816, when a contemporary writer spoke of this haven of greenery 'away from the whirlpools of the capital'. In 1800 another writer recommended going to Pré-Saint-Gervais to dine on a fresh lawn.

Exit by way of Avenue des Marronniers, then left on Avenue du Belvédère. If you take the tiny cul-de-sac **la Sente des Marchais** you will reach a car park with a flight of steps, which leads to Avenue Jean Jaurès. Cross into Avenue Edouard Vaillant. On your right is another *regard* and, beyond it, a steep alley lined with rustic houses, **la Sente des Cornettes**. Rose bushes and geraniums will reward you for your climb. At no. 17 stands a cottage built more than 40 years ago entirely out of broken roof tiles.

If, before retracing your steps, you turn right into Avenue Faideherbe, you will come to the drab suburb of the Lilas, a flat area like the rest of the extensive plain lying north-east of Paris, where large-scale industrialisation replaced the cornfields of earlier times, bringing, inevitably, a dismal air to the landscape. The Pré-Saint-Gervais, being hilly, escaped a similar fate to a certain extent.

Retrace your steps to the junction of Boulevards Sérurier and d'Algérie, either of which leads to the entrance of the gardens of **Square de La Butte du Chapeau-Rouge**, on RUE ALPHONSE AULAND. This was still part of the *zone* on 25 May 1913, when Jean Jaurès came here too on a peace rally. 'We have a formidable problem to resolve,' he said to 10,000 people, 'formidable because we have to fight against war without jeopardising the independence of the nation.' Jean Jaurès was assassinated for his convictions on 31 July 1914.

The gardens were laid out in 1939, the only patch of the 33-km-long belt around Paris to have escaped being built on. Those who live in the vicinity have the hilly terrain and the memory of Jean Jaurès to thank for this pleasing setting for their recreation.

LES BUTTES CHAUMONT AND THEREABOUTS

PLACE DE RHIN ET DANUBE, the starting point of our next itinerary, is close to Métro Danube. (If you come from La Butte du Chapeau Rouge, where the previous walk ended, take the Boulevard Sérurier, west of the gardens, then rue David d'Angers.)

This is a lethargic spot, with shady old plane trees, a provincial little hotel and two equally provincial cafés, survivors of a more leisurely past. The centrepiece of the roundabout has been planted with corn, a reminder of the area's agricultural past. Who else but the French would have thought of erecting in the middle a statue of a beautifully shaped peasant woman reaping the corn? Next to this 'village green' are the traditional baker's and butcher's, but also a video club lit by neon lights, the only noticeable sign of contemporary life.

West of Place de Rhin et Danube, on the site bounded by rues du Général Brunet, David d'Angers and Compans, there used to be a horse market which was done away with in 1878. In 1889 it was decided to build here a network of countrified alleys and bungalows, one of the very rare examples of a successful housing estate in a working-class neighbourhood, quite unlike the vandalism perpetrated around Place des Fêtes. The enclave extends south beyond **RUE DE MOUZAIA,** which is loosely considered as its backbone and its point of reference. The other major streets are named Egalité, Liberté and Fraternité, substitutes for unkept promises down the years.

Make your way into **RUE MIGUEL HIDALGO** and the countrified havens on either side, notably **Villa d'Hautrive,** on your left, with its examples of Art Deco, followed by **Villa de Cronstadt** and its romantic street-lamps. It continues into **Villa Marceau,** with a bourgeois corner house which was obviously built for a prosperous resident. If you have come here in early spring, you will be greeted on by silvery-mauve clusters of wistaria; if somewhat later, by bright roses. There is a charming miniature garden at no. 6, and a profusion of creepers at no. 7 and another picturesque pocket-handkerchief garden at no. 9.

Turn left into **RUE DE LA LIBERTE** and left once more into **Villa de Fontenay.** Neither Monet nor Renoir would have sniffed

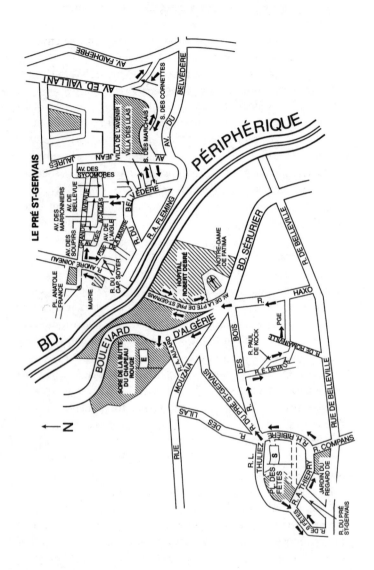

at the pale yellow house at no. 10, steeped in luxuriant vegetation and drowsing behind its closed green shutters in the heat of a still summer day. The roof over the garage of no. 8 seems about to collapse under the weight of rambling creepers. An attractive iron gate and a bower lead to the tiny garden at no. 6.

The celebration of nature continues on the parallel **Villa Amalia** (right on rue du Général Brunet and right once again). Some wanton clematis peep into the street through the latticed wall at no. 7. If you are intrigued by the sound of trickling water behind the wall, and in turn peep through, you will delight in a miniature Japanese garden, complete with rockery and pond, waterlilies and goldfish.

Retrace your steps and turn right into rue du Général Brunet. **The Hameau (hamlet) du Danube,** on your right, is barred to outsiders, but its neat red roofs and red geraniums can be enjoyed from behind the gate.

Continue to Place de Rhin et Danube and turn right into **RUE DE LA FRATERNITE.** An attractive Art Nouveau piece of green ceramic at no. 5 reads '*l'oeuvre de la bouchée du pain* ('the morsel of bread charity'), harking back to the days when this neighbourhood shrieked with hunger.

Turn left into **RUE DE L'EGALITE.** The corner house at no. 2 is an attractive example of 1920s architecture. **Villa du Progrès,** to your right, is also shedding its working-class heritage: the overhanging wistaria is a sign of gentrification. No. 10 has been taken over by Pop Art and resolutely painted orange, bright blue and apple green. An old-timer was standing idly across the street on our last visit and we wondered whether he appreciated this artistic revolution.

Beyond rue de Mouzaïa, the alley becomes **Villa de Bellevue** and climbs up the steep slope lined with arching roses, cascading honeysuckle and some exquisitely decorated bungalows.

If you are not satiated with lovely sights, you could meander back through **Villa de la Renaissance, Villa du Danube** (or **Villa Alexandre Ribot**), before turning left into rue David d'Angers, past Place de Rhin et Danube and along rue Miguel Hidalgo. At the end of the street a last cluster of alleys commemorates Monet, Verlaine and Rimbaud. Walk into **Villa Claude Monet** which boasts an 'Anglo-Norman' chalet with a substantial terrace overlooking a steep flight of steps. **Villa des Boers,** across the street, allows no cars. Its elegant street-lamps and the church-tower of Saint-François-d'Assise in the background make for a lovely picture. Built in 1902, the alley commemorates the Boer War, when France sided, naturally, against the British.

Turn right into rue Compans, left into rue d'Hautpoul and left again into rue de Crimée, which will take you to the entrance to **les Buttes-Chaumont** at Métro Botzaris. Old-time France is ever present on the tree-planted stretch along rue Botzaris, where its representatives gather daily for a game of *boules*.

Les Buttes-Chaumont are unquestionably among the most beautiful gardens in Paris and also among the least polluted. However, a pleasing landscape it was not in 1864, when Napoleon III commissioned his inevitable Alphand to use his creative imagination and turn a dusty wasteland in the newly annexed territory of eastern Paris into a garden worthy of his capital, '*Les Tuileries du Peuple*'. Unlike his wife, the Emperor was sincerely affected by the plight of the underprivileged, but he also hoped to avert social unrest by providing them with a decent environment. It took Alphand seven years to convert the lunar landscape into gardens of dramatic beauty, fit for the most extravagantly Romantic poet; quite a feat, for the site consisted of disused gypsum quarries, cleaned out after a century of intensive activity. The quarries were known as *les carrières d'Amérique* or *du Mississippi*, because their plaster was exported to North America. It took more than 1,000 workmen, 100 horses, 400 small trucks, two steam engines and much dynamite to prepare the ground, after which more than 200,000 cubic metres of earth had to be brought to the site. 5,000 metres of footpaths were then laid out, followed by an artificial lake, fed by the waters of the Bassin de la Villette. Then came a brick bridge, then a suspension bridge, both linking the mainland with a dramatic cliff rising from the water. A grotto and a roaring waterfall followed and, to crown it all, an overpowering folly topping the cliff – a charmingly blatant copy of the Temple of the Sibylle in Tivoli.

Alphand capitalised on the rugged, uneven surface of the gardens and alternated mineral and vegetal matter to achieve his goal, which he defined as follows: 'The stroller can see the landscape change as he goes along. Except for some prominent and open sites, he should be unaware of the city.' What Alphand could not foresee,

Les Buttes-Chaumont

however, were the jarring low-rent high-rises that now mar the otherwise idyllic landscape. Nor did he foresee that his suspension bridge would become a focus for the desperate, the 'suicide's Mecca', according to the poet Louis Aragon, who wrote the following lines: '*Et je reviens vers cette arche jetée vers une île où jadis on cherchait la mort avec ferveur.*' ('And I come back towards this arch thrown out towards an island where death was once fervently sought.') Nowadays the bridge is protected by parapets, which are easily surmountable, but no one comes to jump here any more.

Leave the gardens on their northern side, at **PLACE ARMAND CARREL**. Here stands the festive, confident **Mairie** of Flemish inspiration, built by the Third Republic as a promise of future bounty, a promise which is definitely being fulfilled at present in the vicinity of les Buttes Chaumont. This you will notice as you walk west along the park on rue Manin, along Avenue Mathurin Moreau to your right and into **RUE GEORGES-LARDENNOIS** on your left, home of two public figures of contemporary France – Jean-Paul Goude, the conceptual inspiration of the 1989 Bicentennial splash-happening on the Champs-Elysées, and Patrick Dupont, the director of the Paris Opera Ballet Company. (The street can also be reached up a steep flight of steps between nos 17 and 19 rue Manin, along the park). Jean-Paul Goude's multimillion-franc palatial home is in an elevated position with a spectacular view overlooking Montmartre. How remote it all is from the sinister Place du Combat that lay until 1850 between the present Avenue Mathurin Moreau, rue des Meaux and rue des Chaufouniers, a stone's throw away. It was set up in the late 18th century as an arena for staging animal fights. A vociferous mob, baying for blood, would urge on the most ferocious animals as they tore one another apart: dogs against wolves, dogs against bears, dogs against dogs, most often dogs against bulls. Betting was part of the fun, and even some snobs from western Paris occasionally came here in search of a low-life thrill.

Not much further away, on the corner of the present **AVENUE SECRETAN** and **RUE DE MEAUX** (which can be reached through the pleasant, leafy Avenue Simone Bolivar to your right), on the site of the present **market of La Villette,** was the city's dump until 1850, la Grande Voierie, a cesspool reeking with the stench of the fecal matter of Paris which was turned here into manure called *poudrette.* Furthermore, all the ageing or sickly horses of the capital (up to 15,000 a year!) were brought here to be put down. The poor beasts' hair, bowels and hide were used by tanners, saddlers, violin-string and -bow makers. The rest was left for the neighbourhood's hordes of rats, which meticulously took care of the pickings, leaving the ghastly abandoned carcasses to decay in this abominable seat of disease and infection.

From 1761 this had also been the site of the second gallows of Montfaucon, which replaced the notorious gallows in the 10th arrondissement – four sinister stone pillars surrounded by a moat, where the bodies of those denied Christian burial were also laid by night. With the advent of the guillotine the gallows fell into disuse and was eventually torn down in 1823. Some of the stones were used to build the dump and others for the construction of the parapet of the Canal Saint-Martin.

By 1868, the neighbouring 'arena' on Place du Combat and la Grande Voirie had been gone for nearly 20 years and an iron structure was put up here to shelter a new market, similar to the other market 'pavilions' scattered in Paris by Napoleon III. This one was built by Baltard's collaborator, Jolly, and was saved from demolition in the 1950s by the determination of the neighbours. At present, however, the market seems threatened by its own lethargy, although the passer-by can still enjoy its local colour and surroundings on the leafy Avenue Secrétan, itself a marketplace of sorts, lined with bountiful food stalls and teeming with shoppers. To mingle with these is to share the ultimate experience of being a Parisian.

LA VILLETTE

Our last walk will take us to the newly developed area of La Villette and its gigantic 'urban' park, which, as part of the renovation plan intended to boost the prestige of eastern Paris, has made a considerable public impact, both nationally and internationally. Highly publicised, La Cité des Sciences et de l'Industrie has received on peak days 15,000 and was for a while the second most visited monument of Paris, after the Centre Pompidou. If you can make it on a Sunday morning, you will be part of a crowd of ordinary, genuine French people on a family outing; you may wish to combine your visit with a detour to the Marché de Crimée where buyers and vendors at present are predominantly North and Black Africans.

Make your way to **Métro Porte de Panthin**, where the main entrance to the **Parc de la Villette** is located, just on the site where it stood in the days of the livestock market. Ahead is Girard's fountain, originally commissioned by Napoleon for Place du Château-d'Eau (now République). This was the first of a series of fountains he destined for his capital, meant to outshine those of Rome. It was fed by the water of the new Canal Saint-Martin and looked quite

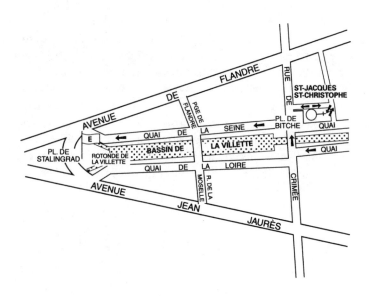

impressive in the intimate Place du Chateau-d'eau of Napoleon's days, but no longer so when Haussmann enlarged it to its present dimensions. Consequently it was replaced by a more spectacular fountain and became available to decorate the entrance to the new livestock market, in good timing for its opening (see also chapters on the 10th and 12th arrondissements).

Across the street, Dagorno, Le Boeuf Couronné and Le Cochon d'Or are still holding their own, huddling against one another – a reassuring presence in a neighbourhood of incessant transformations. Their fare has adjusted to changing times and has been provided with a new environment accordingly, but some of their old dishes can still be enjoyed in specially preserved (and more expensive) areas of the restaurants where time seems to have come to a stop.

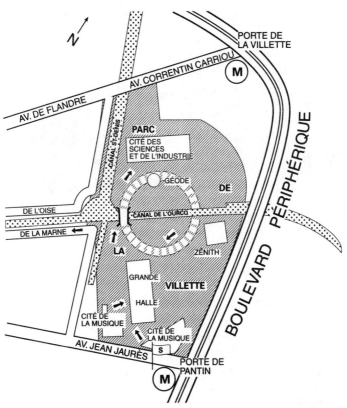

As you enter the park, notice on either side the two buildings of **la Cité de la Musique,** the Music and Dance Conservatory on your left, the first to move here in 1990, the concert halls and a vast café of shiny contemporary design on your right. The music museum, the last of its components, was inaugurated in January 1997.

Although the Cité de la Musique did not benefit from the grandiloquent publicity bestowed on Mitterrand's other *grands projets*, and although it was relegated to the unsavoury north-eastern edge of the city, a remote *terra incognita* ignored by Tout-Paris, and although it turned out to be a laborious venture, both financially and technically (but then, so were the other projects), this has been one of the most successful contemporary constructions in the capital and has brought to the attention of the public an unquestionable young French talent – Christian de Portzamparc – who is

La Grande Halle de La Villette

fast gaining international recognition. Noted for other music and dance schools he has designed, Portzamparc has come to be qualified as a 'musical' architect who refers to architecture in such terms as duration and rhythm. Hence the wave-like shape of the long roof of the Conservatory, evocative of sound waves.

The first valid appraisal of the Cité de la Musique has to come from its occupants and it seems that both students and staff are delighted with their new home. Enjoying the luxury of space, light and modern technology, as against the cramped, outdated premises on rue de Madrid in the congested area of Gare Saint-Lazare, the residents seem more than ready to overlook the drawback of its geographical remoteness. Besides, many of them reside in the comfortable hall of residence located on the site.

Just behind the Cité de la Musique is **La Grande Halle**, a beautiful iron structure bequeathed by Napoléon III, then the livestock auction hall of La Villette. Today it hosts theatre performances, exhibitions, concerts and other cultural events.

As you make your way to the Canal de l'Ourcq, you will see on your right, on the eastern edge of the park, the metal structure of the **Zénith**, the 'shrine' of pop music, highly recommended to the young at heart.

A footbridge will lead you to the new science museum, **La Cité des Sciences et de l'Industrie**, a glass-and-steel building, standing on the site of the old slaughterhouse. **La Géode**, the 'Perfect Sphere' of stainless steel stands next to it, inside which you can embark on a three-dimensional sensory journey. The submarine *l'Argonaute*, anchored close by, will give you the feeling of being leagues under the sea. Once the pride of the navy in Toulouse, rather than let it die when it went out of service, it left Toulouse in spring 1986 and after a six-month voyage by way of Gibraltar, up the Atlantic to Le Havre and down the Seine, it arrived the following October at the Cité des Sciences et de l'Industrie, its new home, where an official inauguration ceremony honoured it on 8 February 1991. The science museum, to our mind, embodies the prevailing confusion between culture and gadgetry. The proliferation of the latter is such that one wonders what the visitor can retain from a brief visit, for example to the exhibit called Explora, which skims over the entire story of mankind, both on earth and in space. Another section, the Inventarium, has the merit of offering children tactile pleasures and a profusion of buttons to press. Children also enjoy the Cité des Enfants, basically a sophisticated playground where fun is meant to be educational. As in the theme gardens outside, everything here seems to have been thought out, leaving little room for spontaneous play. Perhaps this is the deep meaning behind the new concept of '*Parc Urbain*' as the Parc de la Villette has been dubbed. . .

Having scoured the Museum, you may now wish to explore the grounds, which are divided into thematic sections. However, you will not find here any of the intimacy of les Buttes-Chaumont – the future as seen at La Villette seems bleak and uninviting and you may feel no urge to rush into it.

You may decide to end your visit with a walk along the **Canal de l'Ourcq** and the **Bassin de la Villette**. Their junction with the **Canal Saint-Denis** affords a charmingly outdated picture of the latter, on your left.

Continue on the eastern bank of the Canal de l'Ourcq, along QUAI DE LA MARNE until you reach the drawbridge of Crimée. In 1885, when the bridge was built, Paris marvelled at this ingenuous hydraulic system which required a mere 4-kg weight to set the bridge in motion. Today one marvels at the antiquated aspect of this last remaining drawbridge in Paris and at the very fact that it has survived amidst high-rise towers.

If you like market scenes and have come here on a Thursday or a Sunday morning, cross the bridge for a visit of the bustling **Marché de Crimée**. As you cross the bridge, there stands on quai de la Loire, on your left, the last surviving warehouse of a vanished past. An identical building faced it until recently on quai de la Seine, the home of hopeful young artists until a fateful day in 1986, when a mysterious fire all but consumed it. The blackened skeleton remained standing for several years, thanks to the combined energy of locals and artists, who hoped the building would be restored and its artistic vocation maintained. Eventually, however, it was torn down, going the way of so many others.

Ahead is **PLACE DE LA BITCHE** and the **church of Saint-Jacques-Saint-Christophe**, which was built in the early 1840s by Lequeux, also the architect of the suburban church of Batignolles. The market is held on **PLACE DE JOINVILLE**, behind the church, and with its predominantly North African and Black vendors and buyers reflects on the ethnic evolution of the area.

Retrace your steps and continue walking on **QUAI DE LA SEINE**, along the **Bassin de la Villette**. In pre-industrial days jousts were staged here in summer and Russian-style sleighs used to glide on its ice in winter. Of late the Bassin de la Villette has been restored again to recreational activities, such as motorsailing and pyrotechnic laser displays, as befitting modern times.

Continue to the footbridge. From here you can see Nicolas Ledoux's **Rotonde de la Villette**, one of the four surviving monuments he built between 1784 and 1787 to embellish the toll gates of Paris. Seen from here, you will be able to appreciate his talent, particularly at sunrise or sunset, when the rotunda glints in the sunlight and its beautiful sandstone turns pink. At night, when floodlit against the dark, infinite sky and shimmering in the water, it is simply bewitching.

Continue to Place de Stalingrad at the end of the Bassin de la Villette. It commemorates the Russians' decisive victory over Nazi Germany, an appropriate name in what used to be a stronghold of Communism until recently. Rue de Flandre and Avenue Jean Jaurès both fork out from here, once the highways that led respectively to Flanders and Germany. Behind the Rotunda is the elevated Métro line, which runs along the site of the old toll walls. Its vibrations actually damaged the Rotunda and necessitated its restoration before it could be turned into the archaeological department and Museum of Paris. It now houses the city's underground finds and also organises temporary exhibitions.

At no. 11 quai de la Loire, on the opposite bank of the Bassin de la Villette, you can embark on a cruise on the Canal Saint-Martin; in spring and summer you may leave Paris altogether on a day's outing on the Marne. There will be nothing to do aboard except unwind and drift away and enjoy a French meal by the water. In 1837, when boats were first put into service from the Bassin de la Villette to the medieval city of Meaux, they were drawn by horses and could hold 100 passengers. The fare was 1.25 return or 1 franc each way. The company's leaflet provided the following information: 'The speed will be four leagues per hour and the passengers will be placed facing each other with a table in between for their papers and magazines.' Then, with the touch of the poet, it concluded, 'The boat would soar with the velocity of a bird!'

THE 20TH ARRONDISSEMENT

Rues des Haies, des Fougères, des Mûriers, des Amendiers (respectively the streets of hedgerows, fern, mulberry and almond trees), Villa des Bruyères (heather) and Porte des Lilas (lilac) – incongruous celebrations of nature in the sordid heart of plebeian Paris of the Industrial Age. To innocent ears the name Belleville may simply suggest a place of beauty, but to respectable Parisians it sent a shudder down the spine: 'the lowest depths of wretchedness and of hate where ceaselessly seethe the ferments of envy, laziness and anger.' Honest housewives of eastern Paris, determined doggedly to safeguard their respectability, protested vehemently that they were not from Belleville but from Ménilmontant, which was just a little further south but less squalid in reputation. For Belleville was a troublesome neighbourhood which disturbed the peace of mind of the affluent and the secure: 'We hope that tonight Belleville will be willing to let France sleep,' wrote the *Moniteur Universel* following the defeat of the *Commune*. Fortunately, Belleville was tucked away at the easternmost end of the city, clinging to a steep hill 128.5 metres high, a world apart to the relief of bourgeois Paris.

And yet, in pre-industrial days this was a land of bliss, invigorated by fresh air, bathed in sunlight and watered by more rivulets and springs than the world-renowned hill of Montmartre. Early on, these waters were discovered by the congregation of Saint-Martin-des-Champs (see chapter on the 3rd arr.) and were harnessed by means of an aqueduct, an example followed later by the community of Saint-Lazare and later still by the Hôpital Saint-Louis (both in the 10th arr.). In those days Belleville was a land of neat strips of vineyards clinging to its sunny slopes, of fruit orchards and wild flowers, of squat farmhouses and adjoining little gardens known as *courtilles*. A windmill here and there completed the charming picture, which extended all the way south to the village of Charonne. In *Rêverie d'un promeneur solitaire* Rousseau, lover of nature *par excellence*, describes with a journalist's eye a ramble he took on the afternoon of 24 October 1776 along the paths that ran through the vineyards and meadows that separated the villages of Charonne and Ménilmontant. Even in the 19th century, despite the proximity of the city, a lyrical poet spoke of the area's 'green dress and crown of lilacs'.

Nor were these blessed parts spurned by France's topmost families, not even by royalty. Henri IV honoured the housewarming of his friend Martin de Bragelogne with his presence and Richelieu came to visit his friend Barentin in Charonne on several occasions, notably on 12 July 1636, when the *Gazette de France* reported: 'The Cardinal Duc is at Charonne, in the house of Sieur Barentin, where the freshness of the air, the beauty of the air and the good spirits of the host, well please his Eminence.' The Château de Charonne was indeed an admirable place, with rolling grounds beautified by fountains, pools and cascading water courses fed by natural spring water through a sophisticated piping system.

When Mazarin accompanied the 14-year-old Louis XIV here in 1652, he had other considerations in mind than pastoral recreation. Below, to the west, at Faubourg Saint-Antoine, a battle was raging between the rebellious princes led by Condé and the loyalists headed by Turenne, an episode known in history as *La Fronde*. From this vantage-point, Mazarin believed the young King would receive an edifying lesson in government and learn to draw imperative conclusions for the future.

There was also the Château de Bagnolet. At the time of Louis XIV the lady of the manor was his aunt, the Duchesse d'Orléans, wife of Gaston, Louis XIII's brother. In the early 18th century the estate went to the Regent's wife, the legitimised daughter of Louis XIV and of the Montespan. She was so fond of the estate that she was willing to pay three times their value for the adjoining grounds, thus becoming the owner of a huge domain, which she soon set about remodelling. In order to bypass the cumbersome high street of Bagnolet, full of bustling taverns and crammed with wine-laden carts, she opened a beautiful, broad avenue shaded on either side by two rows of trees, and named it l'Allée de Madame (now rue des Orteaux). But although the Duchess avoided the common herd, she could not altogether escape their indiscreet attentions, and soon her headdress was doing the rounds of the village and became the latest fad among its maidens. In 1763 Philippe d'Orléans bought the adjoining property from his neighbour Pinseau, who himself had only recently purchased it from Jean-Baptiste de Sade, father of the more notorious Marquis.

Properties were acquired and dismantled lightheartedly in care-free 18th-century society and a few years later the same Philippe d'Orléans had his estate chopped up and sold off. One of the beneficiaries of the operation was the Baron de Batz-Laumagne, the faithful royalist who, on 21 January 1793, waited for the royal tumbril on the corner of rue de Cléry and the Grands Boulevards (see chapter on the 2nd arr.) in a vain but heroic attempt to abduct the King and save him from the guillotine. It was in this house that the plot was prepared. Some time later the relentless Baron tried to release Marie-Antoinette from the Conciergerie, but this attempt failed too. All that is left of this past beauty is the 18th-century pavilion, le Pavillon de l'Ermitage, now part of a hospice of the Assistance Publique.

Another mansion stood in magnificent grounds further north, the Château de Saint-Fargeau on the heights of Ménilmontant, now in the north of the arrondissement. This was the home of the renowned Le Peletier family and was named after their estate in the Yonne. At the time of the Revolution, its owner, Michel Le Peletier, discarded the privileged life he was born into and became a keen supporter of the Revolutionary cause. Elected to the Convention, he voted for the death of Louis XVI, for which he paid with his own life only eight days after the execution of the King: in the evening of 29 January 1793 he was assassinated in the basement of a café in the Galerie Valois in the Palais-Royal. The motherland mourned him, honoured him with a grand national funeral in the Panthéon and even adopted his daughter, but the magnificent estate of Ménil-montant, together with its French gardens and ornamental pools, was parcelled up and sold, while the *château* – like so many others, alas – was razed to the ground. All that is left are a few venerable trees that cast their shade on the shrunken plot of land that became in 1808 the little cemetery of Belleville.

Throughout the 18th century the area was sought after by Parisians from all walks of life. While the bourgeois built themselves country retreats, the workmen from the Temple quarter and the craftsmen from Saint-Antoine would have to content themselves with a day's outing to one of the area's open-air taverns where, seated at a rough table under leafy bowers, they would quench their thirst with a glass of *guinguet*, a sour wine which had the advantage of being cheap. Eventually the taverns came to be known as *guinguettes*, the most famous of which was Ramponeau in Belleville, or more precisely at La Courtille – the neighbourhood around the toll barrier on the eastern fringe of Paris. As early as the 16th century the meaning of *courtille*, originally a walled-in property, had extended to be synonymous with *guinguette*, and because so many such establishments flourished around the barrier, where they were exempted from tax, it eventually lent its name to the neighbourhood. Thus, in the first half of the 17th century a contemporary claimed that 'to see Paris without seeing La Courtille was like seeing Rome without the Pope.'

Ramponeau, the 'Prince' of the Courtille, founded his establishment in 1750. In no time it gained such fame that the 18th-century chronicler Louis-Sébastien Mercier claimed that it was 'more famous than Voltaire'. Bourgeois, tarts, soldiers and pimps, everyone went to Ramponeau for a bit of fun, or '*ramponner*' as the expression went. During the Restoration Papa Dénoyez's establishment became the new mecca of pleasure, a gigantic place that could seat 2,000. 'One can dance there, dine, make love, swing, spin out love's sweet dreams and sup most pleasantly,' according to an 1828 guidebook.

At dawn on Ash Wednesday, a haggard, drunkard mob of Mardi Gras revellers would arrive at Dénoyez in their dishevelled fancy-dress costumes of Pierrot or Harlequin, having spent a boisterous night at the Opéra, the Variétés or the Ambigu on the Grands Boulevards. Here they would warm up with a bowl of piping hot soup before engaging in the traditional frenzied run, a human avalanche that burst through the toll barrier and swept down Boulevard du Temple to Place du Château-d'Eau (now République). Some were on foot, others clung on to vehicles – thousands of carriages, coaches and carts of different shapes and sizes, all joined in the frenzied *descente de la Courtille*. All of them were wild, vociferous and obscene, hurling eggs and bagfuls of flour at one another.

On Ash Wednesday 1832, at the break of day, a fabulous glittering silver barouche, drawn by six horses, emerged out of a whirlpool of swirling crowds and pulled up in front of Dénoyez.

An immensely tall, red-headed stranger alighted, sporting a black frock coat, sky-blue trousers and a top hat tilted over one ear. With him was a bunch of gay dogs, hangers-on who took advantage of his providential eccentricities. Indeed, Milord d'Arsouille, real name Charles de la Battut, the illegitimate son of a French émigrée and of a wealthy English chemist who bought him the title of Count, had gained notoriety in all the pleasure quarters as an incorrigible, extravagant dandy. Upon arrival at Dénoyez, he showered champagne on all and sundry, along with food, glasses and dishes, even chairs. Having exhausted his normal ammunition, he sent gold coins pouring down through the first-floor window, anticipating the outcome with glee, as he had first taken care to 'fry' the coins in a pan. The frantic mob accordingly burnt their fingers as they pounced on the gold, and in their anger promptly responded by sacking the place. This clearly did not put much of a dent in the finances of Papa Dénoyez – upon his death in 1837 it was discovered that he had left a hoard of one and a half million gold francs! Not so Milord d'Arsouille, the life of the party since 1832, who was soon ruined, unsurprisingly, which marked the end of the *descente* in 1838.

The fun would soon stop altogether, and the unspoilt era in the history of Belleville was about to close. The rural suburbs of Paris would soon be jostled into the Industrial Age, their countryside wrecked and their age-old social stability destroyed. If Charonne to the south was spared for a while and remained a wine-growing village for another generation, Belleville, lying north, was doomed: destitution crept insidiously up its slopes, cleared them of their vineyards and gardens and turned the hill into a nauseating mire, its rivulets into a smelly gutter bordered by hovels, a nest of social unrest. Political militantism followed suit and while the National Guard of Belleville had supported the ultra-conservative Charles X in 1830 against the forces of the Revolution, by 1848 Belleville had shifted its loyalties and sided with the Revolution.

The final blow was dealt in 1860 when the villages of Charonne, a section of Bagnolet, Ménilmontant and Belleville were annexed to Paris as a new arrondissement. The Mayor of Charonne had sensed the disastrous outcome of the annexation in 1859, when the decision had been made, and addressing his local councillors claimed that 'for the suburbs the era of primitive happiness was over . . . their balance will soon be upset.' Indifferent to history and to human ties, the administrative machine sliced implacably into rue de Belleville, the village high street, splitting the village and dividing its 70,000 inhabitants, relegating the north with its church to the 19th arrondissement, the south with the Mairie to the 20th. And as the cost of living rose, due to the new taxes imposed on them as residents of Paris, ever-growing waves of hungry outsiders crammed into Belleville, trying to make a living in its workshops (mostly mechanics, but also leather and later clothing).

Unlike La Villette further north, which was taken over by full-scale factories, resulting in the enslavement of the workforce, most of the Bellevillois worked in family-size workshops, admittedly on dilapidated premises and under makeshift roofs, but with an independent boss at the head of the tiny nucleus and at least the hypothetical prospect that the apprentice might become the boss himself. Thus was forged the free-spirited Bellevillois character, which embodied self-dignity, proletarian pride and solidarity. No wonder the First International opened up three sections in Belleville in the 1860s and the Communist party found a fertile field for new recruits here. In short, just as the Faubourg Saint-Antoine had provided the fuel of the French Revolution, Belleville provided that of the insurrections of the second half of the 19th century, for the simple reason that, with the swelling of its population, Paris was pushing its rejects further east.

On 28 January 1871, Thiers's freshly elected government, which was sitting in Versailles, capitulated to Prussia. Promptly 80% of the companies of the 20th arrondissement joined the ranks of the *Fédérés* and sewed the emblematic red band to their trousers, thus marking their allegiance to the *Commune*. They had become hardened to street riots (after all the Prussian war had been provoked by Napoléon III as an outlet for the all too recurrent riots), but now they were part of a universal cause and stirred by a lofty ideal: 'The world has its eyes riveted on us,' uttered a passionate, lyrical orator. 'From the heights of Belleville the lights of democracy and socialism shine down into the depths of Paris.' This was not the Belleville of terror as perceived by western Paris, but noble Belleville, the beacon of the city. One wallowed in sentimental brotherhood, especially with Montmartre, the other pole of the *Commune*

(see chapter on the 18th arrondissement). The *Times* correspond-
ent was amused by the demonstrations of effusion of the National
Guard, 'in which the French liked to indulge when they were not
shooting at one another.'

These did not last long: like all civil wars, the *Commune* turned
into unspeakable butchery. More than 100,000 men encircled
Belleville for the final assault of 22 May. More than 100 shells fell on
Belleville per minute while its inhabitants cowered in the cellars.
Whipped up to a fury, the Bellevillois clung on to their hill, pursu-
ing a losing battle against all odds. As an ultimate gesture of
desperation they climbed down the hill, stormed the prison of La
Roquette on the edge of the 11th arrondissement and took hostage
52 of its inmates – among them 11 Jesuit priests – irrespective of age,
health or political hue, if any. Trudging uphill two by two, the
victims were led to 85 rue Haxo, a former cabaret turned headquarters of the Ménilmontant-Belleville section, for their mock
trial and consequent execution, attended by a delirious mob who
turned the verdict into a lynching.

The reprisal of the *Versaillais* was terrible. Withdrawing from
central Paris to the cemetery of Père-Lachaise, the *Fédérés* stood
their ground heroically, taking shelter in some of the vaults, but
were dislodged tomb by tomb till finally they had their backs
against the eastern wall of the cemetery. The carnage wreaked in
rue Haxo was now matched by the vengeance of the *Versaillais*,
except that they disposed of greater means – 147 men, women and
children were lined up and shot in front of the cemetery wall. They
were given no sepulchre; instead they were thrown into a common
pit, together with 871 fellow *Communards* who had been shot in the
vicinity. The cherry trees of the Père-Lachaise were yielding their
fruit and the fighters' sweethearts picked some for their lovers to
wear behind their ears, bright red like the *Commune*. It was in their
honour that *Le Temps des Cerises*, the beautiful song written three
years earlier by Jean-Baptiste Clément on the hill of Montmartre,
became the hymn of the *Commune*. The last barricade fell on 12
June on the corner of rues Ramponneau and Tourtille. Only one
National Guard had been left to defend it.

The 20th arrondissement was not to take part in the recovery of
France and her march towards prosperity. Into this seedy neigh-

bourhood streamed the persecuted and destitute of faraway lands – Jews from Eastern Europe, Armenians, Greeks and Turks who made a meagre livelihood in the clothing workshops, and also leather, especially shoes. Bellevile became the centre of the shoe industry and the main supplier of the elegant ladies of the *beaux quartiers*. It was in Belleville that the celebrated platform shoe, the rage during World War II, was invented.

Somewhere in this cesspit, on 19 December 1915, Edith Gassion – better known as Piaf (French slang for sparrow) – was born. Whether she was actually born on the threshold of 72 rue de Belleville, which makes a romantic life story, or more prosaically in the arrondissement hospital, l'Hôpital Ténon, does not alter the fact that she grew up on the streets of Belleville and that she embodied the very essence of plebeian Paris, with its caustic wit, razor-sharp repartee, cocky humour (*gouaille*) and that special *accent de Belleville*, often identified as truly Parisian, somewhat like the Cockney of London. But, whereas the Cockney's rebellion against his plight took the form of humour, often self-targeted, the Bellevillois proclaimed his freedom and independence from the rooftops. Edith learned her trade on the kerbs of Belleville: 'My music school is the streets.'

Edith's father had been a street performer too, a true Bellevillois who claimed to have refused to barter his freedom for a comfortable position with Barnum: 'A man from Paris can't be bought . . . you keep your money and I'll keep my freedom.' Edith followed his typically Bellevillois example: 'No one pushes me around, I'm free, I work when I want to.' The fact that Edith was named after the English nurse Edith Cavell, who had been shot by the Germans two months earlier, also points to the patriotic spirit of Belleville, even though so much foreign blood had been injected into Belleville through constant waves of immigration. The 'truly Parisian' Piaf was in fact half Italian on her mother's side (hence her middle name Giovanna) and her maternal grandmother may have been a Kabyle, which could account for the flamenco-like quality in of Piaf's voice. Her fellow entertainer Maurice Chevalier, a native of neighbouring Ménilmontant, had, like herself, a foreign mother: she was Flemish and came to Paris in the wake of the Prussian war. Yet, Chevalier, like Piaf, was perceived the world over as quintessentially Parisian. During a tour in London towards the end of his life, a critic described him 'as undestructible as the Eiffel Tower', and later the *Times* obituary observed: 'He, too, represented the warmth and the gaiety of shabby back streets and the heart and soul of the great city.'

Ménilmontant, however, was not quite Belleville, albeit only a couple of steps away, but this made all the difference. Maurice was born there on 12 September 1888, at 31 rue du Retrait. His father was a drunkard, who eventually walked out on the family, but his mother, an honest lacemaker, made ends meet as best she could, intent on safeguarding the family's respectability, while his elder brother Paul became his substitute father. Whereas little Edith was left to her own devices, which meant she could wander off as far as the raciest parts of Pigalle, Maurice went to school and was expected to learn a trade like his elder brothers.

Being a Bellevillois also meant living intensely and passionately right from one's guts, as Piaf's love life exemplified, in particular her love and loss of the boxer Marcel Cerdan. The latter died in 1953 in an air crash, along with the famous violinist Ginette Neveu. It was for him that Piaf sang her world-renowned *Hymne à l'amour*, not from her throat or even her heart, but from the deepest well of her being.

The bands of roughnecks of Belleville were also a passionate lot, not like the cynical pimps of Montmartre and La Chapelle. Here a man took out a knife for a girl he really cared for. In 1902 the story of *Casque d'Or* made the headlines throughout Paris, both east and west. Two enemy bands of *Apaches* – a name coined by a journalist inspired by Dumas's *Mohicans de Paris* – sporting their customary insignia of caps, bell-bottom trousers and polka-dotted scarves, had taken to the streets that lay between Belleville and Charonne: les Popincourt headed by the Corsican Leca, les Orteaux by Manda, *'l'Homme!'* The object of their dispute was not territory but a girl called Amélie Hélie, nicknamed *Casque d'Or*, with a stunning, golden-reddish mane. The confrontation turned into a full-scale pitched battle on rue des Haies, in which neither knife blades nor guns were spared. To the inquisitive public prosecutor Manda retorted during his trial: 'We fought each other, the Corsican and myself, because we love the same girl. We are crazy about her. Don't you know what it is to love a girl?' Manda was unquestionably a soulmate of Piaf. . . Condemned to deportation and hard labour – Manda for life, Leca for eight years – the two men met on the island of Saint-Martin-de-Ré. When finally they spoke to each other, it was about *Casque d'Or*. She meanwhile wasted no time bewailing her unfortunate suitors, but turned for solace to the world of entertainment and the company of wealthier men. However, one of Leca's faithful followers had been contemplating revenge and stabbed her one night in the establishment where she sang. Although she survived, she could no longer perform as a singer and it is only thanks to her portrayal by the legendary Simone Signoret in Jacques Becker's movie that she has not fallen into oblivion. The real Amélie Hélie ended by marrying an ordinary workman and died forgotten on 16 April 1933. She was buried in the cemetery of Bagnolet.

In 1966, three years after Edith Piaf's death, Maurice Chevalier came back to the 20th arrondissement to unveil a plaque over the doorway of 72 rue de Belleville which reads: 'On the steps of this house was born 19 December 1915 in the greatest destitution Edith Piaf whose voice would later take the world by storm.' But already the world Piaf and Chevalier grew into was receding into the past.

With economic prosperity boosting her self-confidence, France was determined to catch up on lost time and replace rickety shacks with soaring high-rises. Nobody thought the planning through however, so the relentless bulldozers ploughed through Belleville and metamorphosed it into a vertical jungle of concrete, obstructing the horizon, obliterating the picturesque slopes and the quaint steep flights of steps at the bends of cobbled alleys. Those early high-rises of the Cité des Fougères, built back in the late 1950s, are already threatening to collapse. . .

Gone was also the spirit of Belleville. New waves of immigrants now crammed into the new anarchical high-rise towers, coming predominantly from the south – Black Africans, as well as North Africans (both Arabs and Jews). The *Titi parisien* ('Parisian urchin') was gradually pushed out, together with the old bistrots and workshops, and couscous became the daily fare around Boulevard de Belleville.

However, tucked away behind leafy, pocket-size courtyards or gardens, some vestiges of the past remain, so far overlooked by developers, and sometimes still occupied by the last survivors of pre-war Belleville. Of late they have attracted the eye of a new generation of ecologically-minded Parisians on the look-out for a morsel of greenery. Among them are many artists – 400 in all – grouped in an association which opens its doors to the public on specific days and tries to salvage what is still left of old Belleville. Some of these hidden havens conceal enough charm to persuade even the occasional celebrity to move to the 20th arrondissement. Most Parisians, however, still perceive it as remote and unappetising.

Not so the dead. From the start, those very proper Parisians, who when still alive had taken up residence on the opposite side of the city and would have never set foot in these accursed parts, were ready to pay astronomical prices for a share in the most prestigious cemetery in Paris, le Père-Lachaise, a spectacular necropolis, basically constituting the only museum the 20th arrondissement has to show for itself. Here the last two centuries of the history of France and Paris are on display and the ghosts of Tout-Paris enjoy the setting of the largest garden in the capital – 44 hectares – rising above the world of the living to the west, on a lofty hill and that much closer to heaven. . .

In order to make a commercial success of the venture, the 19th-century bourgeoisie had to be persuaded to allow their remains to be transferred to the eastern edge of Paris – not yet a place of evil reputation but certainly remote. The Prefect of the Seine Frochot resorted to an astute promotional campaign which, by playing on vanity, naturally worked: by putting up for sale in perpetuity land grant property, he was sure to arouse interest among self-engrossed Parisians, and by setting prices so high that only the upper crust could afford them, he made the new cemetery both desirable and fashionable (one of the rare fashions that have not worn out in nearly 200 years!). And when Frochot further transferred to this site the remains of glorious past celebrities – notably those of the medieval lovers Abélard and Héloïse and those mistaken for La Fontaine and Molière's – Everyone was taken in by it, including Frochot himself, who rests in division no. 19, Brogniart, the architect of the new cemetery and of the Paris stock exchange, and Godde who built the cemetery gate. Jacques Baron, the previous owner of the 17-hectare grounds of the cemetery also lies here, and at a very high price: the poor man, who had been squeezed out of his grounds by the hard-bitten Frochot for a pittance, had to pay 300 times the amount for his own little plot of 5 square yards!

Balzac, who had buried here his characters, was brought here in his turn, despite his biting account of the place and of its clients:

> This is a disgusting comedy! this is once again Tout-Paris with its streets, its signs, its industries, its *hôtels*; but seen through the wrong end of the spyglass, a microscopic Paris, reduced to the small dimensions of shadows, of larva, of the dead, a human race that has nothing great left but its vanity.
>
> *Ferragus*

Or as Georges Brassens put it summarily in one of his songs:

> *Les gens avaient à coeur*
> *De mourir plus haut que leur cul.*
>
> People had set their hearts
> On dying higher than their arse.

both had in mind the extravagant monuments erected for the dead in a delirium of self-aggrandisement. The best artists of the day, the very same who were commissioned to embellish Paris – Percier, Fontaine, Viollet-le-Duc, Garnier, Visconti, Davioud – were now recruited to inflate the egos of the deceased and build for them bombastic mausoleums.

The Jews were also allotted a sector in the new cemetery, since they had been emancipated during the Revolution, but the Muslims were only granted a section in 1856 by Napoléon III who was seeking a *rapprochement* with Turkey. The defeated *Commune* was also granted a share at Père-Lachaise, though more reluctantly. In 1883 the Third Republic, by then secure in its victory, could afford the magnanimous gesture of offering the working classes this tragic wall as a shrine to mourn their frustrated ideals. They called it Le Mur des Fédérés.

The cemetery of Père-Lachaise has been extended several times since it was first acquired by Frochot on behalf of the city of Paris in 1804. Part of the site was in the 15th century the splendid property of a wealthy spice merchant, Régnault de Wandonne, who himself had bought the grounds from the Bishop of Paris, the owner of large stretches of land on the periphery of the city, notably the entire area of today's 8th arrondissement. In 1430 Régnault de

Le Père-Lachaise

Wandonne built himself a *folie* (from *feuillu* meaning leafy, not the 18th-century meaning of a frivolous monument).

The estate was still known as La Folie-Régnault two centuries later, when the Jesuits bought it as a country retreat from their city dwelling on the busy rue Saint-Antoine. They renamed it Mont-Louis, in homage to the Sun King who had given the Jesuits his full support and had chosen his own confessor from among their ranks, the Reverend Father François d'Aix de la Chaize – hence the name Père-Lachaise given to the estate later. The Jesuits did not sustain their influence over the licentious Louis XV and were expelled from France altogether in 1763, following which the Mont-Louis was bought up by private people and fell eventually into the hands of the Baron family.

It would be impossible to list the celebrities who rest here – Chopin, Piaf and now Yves Montand are certainly among the favourites, as well as Jim Morrison, whose fans – the sort that make respectable middle-class people shudder – used to gather around his grave for psychedelic and other uplifting ceremonies, until a closer watch was recently put on the site. The Anglo-Saxon community pays its respects to Oscar Wilde, just as frowned on in his day. Some visit Isadora Duncan's grave, fewer Sir Richard Wallace's. Distinguished representatives of the fine arts and science, music and dance, literature, architecture, the stage and the screen, the armed forces and politicians are gathered here under the shade of 12,000 venerable trees, alongside more ordinary Parisians. As befitting the orderly French, they have chosen to complete their earthly journey in the 20th arrondissement, at the end of the snail-shell-like layout of Paris. The streams of daily visitors (this is the sixth most visited site in the capital) enjoy recognising the original bearers of so many street names down below by stopping at their graves, thus perpetuating their memory and piecing together fragments of the history of Paris.

WHERE TO WALK

FROM BAGNOLET THROUGH CHARONNE TO PERE-LACHAISE

Early spring (late April into May) would be an ideal time to explore these parts, when the lilac blossoms in the rare surviving leafy enclaves recall a long-gone pastoral life.

Unlike Belleville and Ménilmontant, which had already fallen victim to the proliferating industries north-east of Paris in the first half of the 19th century, the old villages of Charonne and Bagnolet in the southern part of the arrondissement benefited from a reprieve and maintained their rural nature until their annexation to Paris in 1860. This will be the territory of our first walk.

Start from **PLACE DE LA PORTE DE BAGNOLET** on the eastern edge of the circular Boulevards Extérieurs, also known as the Boulevards des Maréchaux after the twenty military heroes they commemorate. This is a busy junction dense with traffic, but it is also a pleasant spot of greenery, especially if you look north and

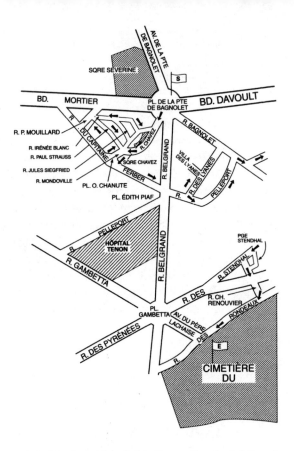

ignore the unsightly blocks of flats behind you. On the left-hand side, a charming row of terrace houses, standing on a ridge, their pocket-size gardens lush with bushy vegetation, belies the stereotyped image of all you have been told about the infamous arrondissement. A substantial flight of steps leads you to a compound of 89 houses called **La Campagne à Paris**, one of the rare examples of successful council housing in Paris, where aesthetics and the environment were given careful thought.

Although Napoléon III was the first to grasp the importance of environment as a weapon to defuse social discontent, and contributed greatly to the embellishment of Paris by way of gardens and tree-lined avenues, he failed to solve the proletarian housing problem and swept it under the carpet, pushing the poor further and further away from the centre of the city, and out of his sight. But some 50 years later, Paul Strauss took the bull by the horns and set out to prove that the labourer of eastern Paris was not an unbridled

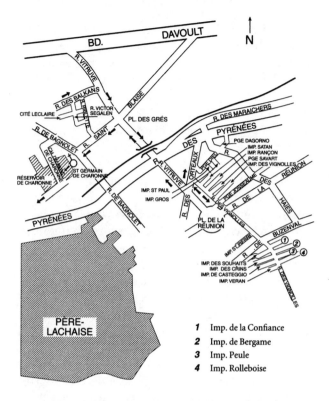

1	Imp. de la Confiance
2	Imp. de Bergame
3	Imp. Peule
4	Imp. Rolleboise

murderous brute bent on terrorising his social betters, but an honest citizen – provided he was allotted decent housing.

The hill on which the houses were built is actually artificial, for until 1875 this had been the gaping hole of a gypsum quarry, possibly the last one in Paris. Its owner, unable to find a buyer, filled it up with rubble from the newly opened eastern section of the Avenue de la République, Avenue Gambetta, rue Belgrand and rue des Pyrénées. He planted acacia and plane trees to retain the soil of the new hillock and gave it the pretty name of l'Ermitage Gambetta. In 1907 the newly formed philanthropic society La Campagne à Paris, a subsidiary of a charity founded to combat tuberculosis, took over the tree-shaded hill and built on it houses. However, work came to a halt with the outbreak of World War I, which delayed the completion of the project until 1926.

The official inauguration ceremony on 20 June was honoured with the presence of the Mayor as well as Paul Strauss, Irénée Blanc and Jules Siegfried, the three promoters of this happy initiative who are commemorated in the three street names of this housing estate. Monsieur Sully Lombard, chairman of the society, gave an address in which he said the site was 'worthy of being sung of by a Virgil or a Ronsard. It is enough for us,' he went on, 'to look at these 89 houses, to contemplate this little village, in the heart of Paris, this village where we feel good, despite some of the inconveniences of the countryside, despite the early morning crowing of the cock, the inordinate barking of the dogs, the nasal sound of phonographs which can be heard from the very first summer evenings. It is enough for us to see this string of houses with their gardens and flowers, to note the considerable progress achieved in France in the field of hygiene and social welfare.' Looking towards the future he continued: 'May the whole of France be covered with low-cost houses and we shall have no cause to envy those ancient times when, it is said, simplicity of manner reigned, when neither the unwhole-some thirst for pleasure nor greed had yet consumed the hearts of men. Isn't the family 'cottage' a guarantee of health, temperance and morality just as the hovel is a cause of disease, wretchedness and all the shame that comes from lack of willpower?'

Their example was not followed and France was not covered with little cottages surrounded by pretty gardens. Instead, from the 1950s on, a new generation of town planners set out to wreck Paris, and indeed France at large, by creating dehumanised urban and suburban ghettos, edgy and ready to explode. But here, as you stroll through these quiet streets, you will be enchanted by the unaffected good taste of the houses, where Art Nouveau and Art Deco have left their subtle mark.

After meandering through rues Irénée Blanc, Jules Siegfried and Paul Strauss walk down the steps towards the Place Chanute and left into rue du Capitaine Ferber to **PLACE EDITH PIAF**, one of those shaded refreshing spots, somewhat provincial yet so Parisian, graced with one of Sir Richard Wallace's fountains, one of Paris's trademarks. There is also a sculpture of Edith Piaf here, but it is stuck to a drab slab of concrete and does justice neither to the square, nor to Piaf, despite its attempt to convey the extraordinary expressiveness of her tiny face and hands. Only the faded flower laid by an anonymous admirer in the singer's vibrating hands redeems the sight. Place Edith Piaf is situated next to the Hôpital Tenon, where Edith was probably born (although some claim she was born on the threshold of 72 rue de Belleville, as reported above).

Walk down rue Pelleport, past rue des Lyanes. Ahead, at 148 RUE DE BAGNOLET, lies the lovely garden of the Hospice Debrousse, a home for the elderly and the blind opened in 1892, a shrunken remnant of the Orléans's Château de Bagnolet, which, in 1719, became the property of Marie-Bourbon, Duchesse d'Orléans, wife of the Régent and the legitimised daughter of Louis XIV and of Madame de Montespan.

Having extended the estate, in 1734 she proceeded to build the gemlike **Pavillon de l'Ermitage** in front of you, which had access through a regal gate. The gate had two oval medallions which bore the coats of arms of the Orléans family. The Duchess entered her estate, however, through another gate, which was located beyond the present Boulevard Davout and was reached by way of the tree-lined Allée de Madame (now rue des Orteaux), as mentioned earlier. Her grandson Louis-Philippe d'Orléans inherited the property in 1763. Louis-Philippe was a devout man, deridingly nicknamed *le Pieux*. Offended by the delicate murals that decorated the oval vestibule of the pavilion, representing the Temptations of Saint Antoine, he had them all washed out, leaving only the hermit intact!

The Baron de Batz became the landlord of the *château* in 1787 and it was here that his aborted plot to abduct the royal couple was hatched. Having got wind of the scheme, the police came to search the place on 30 September 1793 and arrested those present at the Ermitage, all of whom ended up on the guillotine, including the Baron's mistress Marie Badin de Grandmaison, a former actress at the Comédie Italienne. The Baron, on the other hand, by a double stroke of luck, came out of the Terror unscathed, having managed to slip away when the rescue attempt failed on the Grands Boulevards, and happening to be away during the search at the Ermitage.

The Ermitage Pavilion is the only vestige of that past beauty, a meagre reminder of the extensive estate. Unfortunately, as often in Paris, it is locked bolted, depriving outsiders from seeing a lovely example of an 18-century interior.

Village Saint-Blaise

Turn left into **RUE DES BALKANS**. Behind the arcades at no. 19 looms the old church tower of Charonne. At no. 13 the old branches of wistaria, burdened with purple blossoms in early spring, have become one with the iron railing of the fence and add pleasantly to the weight of time.

Rue Victor Segalen has to date preserved its old shacks – a humble spot yet not devoid of charm with its bits of ceramic decoration on the corner house of rue Riblette. **RUE VITRUVE**, at the end of rue des Balkans to your right, borders a unique enclave, the **Village Saint-Blaise**, shining white with the gentrified farmhouses of the former village of Charonne (the surrounding high-rises must, of course, be ignored). A charming garden lies at the back of the houses, boasting bright rosebushes, a soothing fountain and one ancient tree.

Rue Vitruve leads to **PLACE DES GRES**, once the old village square. As such this was where justice was dispensed by the lords of Charonne (except for hangings and beheadings, which took place on rue de la Justice further north, just south of the reservoir of Ménilmontant). A post was set up here to which the condemned would be tied with an iron collar, his offence billed on his chest and back as a deterrent for all to see. Thus the square was previously known as Place du Carcan ('iron collar') and Place du Poteau ('post'). The lords of Charonne were hardly tender-hearted: in

1770, for having stolen some seeds one night, Louis-Claude Milcent, a poor vine grower from the hamlet of Petite Charonne (near the present Place de la Nation), was brought here after mass and tied to the post until 2 in the afternoon. He was then birched and branded on his right shoulder with the letters GAL, which stood for *galère* ('galley'). The poor wretch was condemned to the King's galleys for three entire years, while his wife was made to watch her husband being chastised and to pay a fine of three pounds, following which she was banished from her village for the three years he was away. Two decades later, the relentless overlords of France's downtrodden peasantry would pay heavily for their historical shortsightedness. Today a modern sculpture of a couple stands on the old square, now renamed Place des Grés. Could the artist have had in mind poor Milcent, the vine grower, and his wife from the village of La Petite Charonne?

If you wish to be among the last to see the seamier side of old Paris before it is relegated to the historical archives, and your feet are up to it, continue along **RUE VITRUVE** as far as **RUE DES ORTEAUX**, then turn left. To your right, on either side of **RUE DES VIGNOLES** – whose name alone evokes the vinegrowing past – lie several narrow streets, lined with crumbling houses and hovels, which have retained the exact layout of the vineyards they have, regrettably, replaced. Here too, concrete is fast devouring the little crumbling houses, whose ill-fated tenants were poets and wits. The first alley to your right on rue des Orteaux, beyond rue de Vignoles, has been dubbed **Impasse Dieu**, not to mark some spiritual yearning but just to honour the memory of one of the inhabitants of Charonne, a certain Monsieur Dieu.

A bunch of rascals was quick to give tit for tat with **Impasse Satan!** – first to your left along rue des Vignoles. And if the parallel **Impasse Rançon** ('ransom'), reflects the presumably shady goings-on in these parts, **Impasse des Souhaits** ('wishes') and **Impasse de la Confiance** ('confidence', 'trust' or 'faith'), on either side of rue des Vignoles a little further down, add a touch of optimism to an otherwise desperate world. So does the happy, sunbathed roof terrace at no. 86 rue des Vignoles, bursting with flowers among its crumbling neighbours.

Retrace your steps and turn left (right if you have left out the above detour) into the pedestrian RUE SAINT-BLAISE – a picturesque sight with its cobbled paving, belly-potted houses and the rustic church of Charonne beckoning you from the top of the street. As you make your way up towards it, notice the house at no. 25, once the premises of a tavern where guests could turn up with their victuals and do their own cooking. With so much charm, the street could not have escaped the attentions of trendy Parisians, who opened various shops and eating places here during the optimistic 1980s, but one café-tabac has survived the clean-up on rue de Bagnolet to your left. Its dark, warm walls are covered with posters that look old even when they are not, and among them are two paintings of the obviously fondly regarded church of Charonne, across the street. The bakery shop next door, which has preserved its genuine 1900 decoration, also deserves a glance.

The church of Saint-Germain-de-Charonne is not as old as it looks and has been largely altered over the centuries, but it has a lovely antique feel and a harmonious structure, even though only the lower part of its tower is medieval, dating back to the latter part of the 13th century. The rest of the church was built in the second quarter of the 15th century, which is pretty old for Paris, but was altered several times in the 18th and 19th centuries. It was probably because of a fire in the first half of the 18th century that the entrance, hitherto located on the western side as customary, was moved to its present location on the southern side, facing you charmingly from the top of the hill, as you approach it.

The origin of the church is so remote as to be shrouded in mystery. Legend has it that the famous Saint Germain, the Bishop of Auxerre, to whom were also dedicated the churches of Saint-Germain-l'Auxerrois, opposite the Louvre in the 1st arrondissement, and Saint-Germain-des-Prés on the Left Bank in the 6th, came to these parts in the year 429, during his saintly journey that took him as far as England, spreading the Gospel wherever he went. It is here that his first encounter with the six-year-old Geneviève is said to have taken place, an event that was to determine the calling of the future patron of Paris. Historically, however, it seems doubtful that the Bishop should have chosen such a detour to go into the capital, especially since this spot was

Rue Saint-Blaise

particularly steep. And what cause was there for a little girl from Nanterre, north of Paris, to be visiting these out-of-the-way parts?

Be that as it may, it is probably thanks to its remote position that the church escaped the fury of the Revolution and that it has preserved its parish churchyard – the only such case in Paris apart from the churchyard of Saint-Pierre-de-Montmartre – attributable to the fact that until 1860 both churches lay outside the city boundaries. They were therefore unrestricted by the law of 1804 that required the closure of all parish cemeteries in Paris. On the very far left of the churchyard is the sober grave of André Malraux's two sons, tragically killed in an accident. Also buried here is the infamous Robert Brasillac, sentenced to death on 19 January 1945 for his pro-German writings, 'who had loved Germany . . . and wished for the victory of some of her principles'. Despite protests on the part of writers François Mauriac, Paul Claudel and Paul Valéry, Brasillac was executed on 6 February 1945.

Before leaving, walk to the top left of the graveyard for a final glorious glimpse of the church, hopefully followed by a snapshot – nobody will believe it was taken in Paris!

Leave the graveyard on its northern side, at the top of the central alley and turn left into LE CHEMIN DU PARC DE CHARONNE, a discreet reminder of the fabulous grounds and the Château de Charonne, now totally wiped off the face of the earth. It is quite extraordinary that after a series of amputations and mutilations no eye witness left a record of the final demolition of the building, although it occurred only in the 19th century. Paradoxically, we do have records of it from the 17th century as reported earlier (see p. 263). The water reservoir of Charonne is now situated on its site, invisible behind a solid wall overhung by green boughs.

Turn right into rue Stendhal, along the western side of the reservoir, left into rue Charles-Renouvier, right into rue des Rondeaux to its junction with the AVENUE DU PERE-LACHAISE. This is the main entrance to the Cemetery of Père Lachaise, the largest cemetery of Paris and also its largest stretch of greenery. It lies partly on the site of the Folie-Régnault, one of the three magnificent domains of the area. But would it have survived had it not been converted into a cemetery?

With the help of a leaflet at the entrance, you will find the location of the tombs you are interested in. Many Parisians like to come to le Père-Lachaise for a stroll, and tourists like to include it on their cultural visits to the French capital. Some visitors may feel uncomfortable among the thick forest of forlorn family vaults, bought in perpetuity, yet now abandoned for lack of caring descendants. It is a gloomy setting at the close of a late November day, an implacable reminder in a territory largely taken over by cats of the uselessness of man's vanity. With the ever-increasing number of unclaimed vaults, it has been decided to put them back on the market, to prevent their dangerous collapse. The remains of their occupants are piled up in boxes in a secret catacomb under the War Memor-

Saint-Germaine-de-Charonne

ial. Its existence, however, is unknown to most visitors, and its entrance is barred even to the cemetery's guards.

The pompousness of the 19th century has given way in modern times to a more sober style, even when commemorating the most tragic events of our century. Hence, the various memorials to the deportees and Resistance members of World War II, which express the horror and anguish poignantly but with no florid pathos. A beautiful piece of mosaic in the memorial to Communist members of the Resistance brings a patch of colour to the place.

Naturally Le Père-Lachaise is a propitious site for those attempting to communicate with the beyond, whether by psychedelic means around the tomb of Jim Morrison, or through a trance by the tomb of Allan Kardec. Kardec, real name Denizard-Hippolyte Rivail, was a pedagogue and science teacher who lived in the 19th century. He was too rational a fellow to be taken in by such nonsense as turning tables and mediums, ideas freshly imported from the United States. Scoffing at his more gullible contemporaries, he said, 'I'll believe it when I see it' – which was precisely what happened when he eventually agreed to attend a session. He went on to publish the *Book of Spirits* using the pen name Allan Kardec. This was supposedly the name he had borne in the ancient times of the Druids, when he and the spirit Zéphyr had roamed the forests of Gaul and picked the holy mistletoe with a golden sickle. Having exhausted his savings to publish the book, which he claimed was dictated by the spirits of Socrates, John the Evangelist, Fénelon, Benjamin Franklin, Hahnemann (the inventor of homeopathy), Swedenborg and Napoleon, he soon recovered all his expenses, made a nice profit, and was even showered with glory, his book having become one of the bestsellers of the time. Today, the bookshop at 10 Avenue du Père-Lachaise still carries his works.

Other visitors more concerned with the life of now and its continuation focused their attention on the tomb of Victor Noir, the journalist who on 10 January 1870 was shot dead by Napoléon III's cousin Pierre Bonaparte in the latter's home in Auteuil, in the heat of a political dispute over the capitulation to Prussia. The murder was followed by a gigantic funeral, attended by 100,000, and led to a riot on the Champs-Elysées. A strikingly realistic sculpture of the man at the moment of his assassination surmounts his tomb: dressed in his morning coat, he lies on his back, his top hat next to him, where it has dropped off. For some unfathomable reason this bronze effigy became the object of a fetishistic cult induced by the belief that caressing it would cure women of sterility. The shiny patch you may notice around the protruding phallic region of the bronze sculpture is the result of years of tactile devotion. There was a long-stemmed red rose in the palm of his hand on our last visit and a white chrysanthemum in the top buttonhole of his trousers fly.

You may think Le Père Lachaise is not the place to crack a joke, but the humorist Pierre Desproges would surely disagree. Knowing himself to be terminally ill when only in his forties, he braved death as best he could with this piece of advice to the living: 'Commit suicide while you are still young – you will have more time to enjoy death.' One assumes Desproges is enjoying his, for he lies close to several great musicians – Chopin, Cherubini, Bellini, Ginette Neveu – who are surely enlivening his stay here and uplifting his soul.

BELLEVILLE AND MENILMONTANT

This walk to the northern part of the 20th arrondissement will take you to the quintessentially Parisian villages of Belleville and Ménilmontant, the respective birthplaces of Edith Piaf and Maurice Chevalier. With so many high-rises around, the two singers would find it hard to recognise the streets of their childhood and we in the late 20th century have to rely on our memories of old French films to recreate that fast disappearing world.

If you want to combine this walk with a plunge into present-day ethnic Paris at the end, you should start out early on a Tuesday or a Friday morning so as to wind up later at the open-air market on Boulevard de Belleville.

We start at **Métro Télégraphe** at the top of the hill and walk along **RUE DU TELEGRAPHE** named after the telegraph installed by Claude Chappe in September 1792 just south of the site of the main gate of the **Cemetery of Belleville**, a spot he had chosen for his first experiment because of its notable altitude (128.5m). France was engaged in a patriotic republican war against the monarchies of Europe and a successful conclusion of Chappe's experiment would allow the capital to communicate with the provinces. But the *sans-culottes*, suspecting Claude Chappe of communicating with the royal family incarcerated at the Temple, proceeded to wreck his brilliant invention and Chappe had to run for his life. He waited for the people's fury to abate before trying out his invention again on the 25th of the following July, when he sent a telegraph to Ecouen, covering the distance of 35.5 km. Communication with Lille was successfully established soon after, which enabled Paris to be informed instantly of the capitulation of the Austrian garrison. The connection with Lille was transferred to the northernmost hill of Montmartre, while Strasbourg, lying to the east, was connected with Belleville.

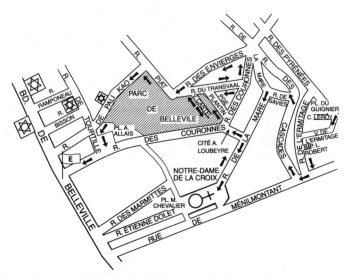

The cemetery of Belleville did not exist at the time and rue du Télégraphe ran along the beautiful estate of Ménilmontant, Le Saint-Fargeau, whose landlord, Louis-Michel Le Peletier, was assassinated at the Palais-Royal for having voted for the death of the King, as mentioned above. When the estate was parcelled up, the municipality of Belleville bought a share of the land and opened a cemetery in 1804, after the closure of all the cemeteries of Paris. This is a small, intimate place which boasts few celebrities, except however for Léon Gaumont, the early promoter of motion pictures who, at the dawn of the 20th century, offered the poor inhabitants of Belleville an escape by means of his '*usine à rêves*' ('factory of dreams').

Continue past the **reservoir of Belleville**, which stands on the site of the actual mansion of Saint-Fargeau, le Grand Château. Turn left into rue du Borrégo and right into **Passage Gambetta**. Gambetta is honoured amply in these parts because he was the deputy of

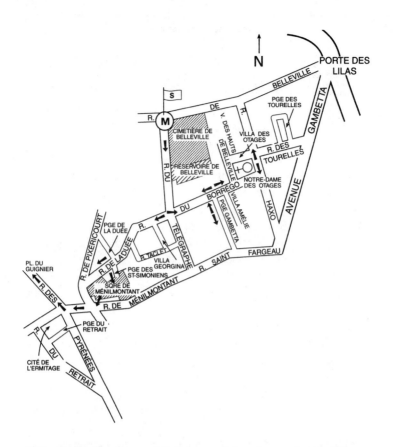

Belleville during the troubled times of 1870, hence also the Place Gambetta in front of the Mairie, the hub of the arrondissement. The Bellevillois had gone all out to have him elected in 1869, and he in his turn stood up at the National Assembly the following year and announced eloquently: 'We declare that Louis-Napoléon Bonaparte and his dynasty have ceased forever to reign over France!' As the war degenerated, however, Gambetta was reproached for his lukewarm attitude and lost the initial enthusiastic support of Belleville.

Passage Gambetta provides a rare example of modern urban renovation in good taste, blending discreetly into a leafy, traffic-free environment. The old lampposts have been preserved, adding a charming touch to the serene alley.

Continue along rue du Borrégo and turn left into **RUE HAXO**. On your left is the **church of Notre-Dame-des-Otages**, behind

289

which, at no. 85, once stood a *café-concert*. In May 1871 it was converted into the headquarters of the Belleville section of the *Commune*, where 52 hostages were massacred by the *Communards* on 26 May, as reported on p. 268 – not that the hostages were necessarily enemies of the *Commune*, but their assailants were too excited to bother to find out. As it happened, 11 were Jesuit priests and 36 were Gardes Républicains. After an exhausting uphill march in quick time from the prison of La Roquette, from where they had been snatched, the churchmen hindered further by their skirts, the hostages arrived on rue Haxo where an enraged crowd, most of them women, were waiting, baying for blood. Insulted, jostled, beaten by the mob, they entered the courtyard dishevelled and haggard and before the order of execution could be read from the balcony, a crazed 18-year-old woman pulled the trigger of her gun and shot down the Abbé Planchat, the founder of the youth club of Charonne. This was the signal for the carnage to begin. An onlooker who protested against the savagery was pushed among the ranks of the victims before he had time to retract; so by mistake was one *Communard*. Following the bloody week of May 1871 Dumas fils wrote: 'the women who followed the red flag were hags with the appetites of tigresses and vampires.' Even the *Commune* leader Jules Vallès, condemned the massacre of rue Haxo and the shrew who had instigated it. Yet he had genuinely sided with Belleville, proclaiming: 'I had resolved to live among these people and to choose this dark corner as my motherland.'

The Jesuits bought the site the following year and built on it an oratory in memory of the victims, which they replaced first by a chapel and in 1936 by the present church (open on weekday afternoons only). They also founded a charity, *l'Oeuvre des Otages*, to bring the Gospel to this accursed neighbourhood through social and educational work with children.

In the second half of the 19th century, a prestigious establishment was situated east of rue Haxo. It was named Le Saint-Fargeau, after the former estate of the Le Peletier. It had an artificial lake, an island and a *guinguette* and was a favourite place for functions and an attraction for pleasure-seekers. It was also a gigantic establishment – with grounds extending roughly from Passage des Tourelles to the Avenue Gambetta and as far as rue de Belleville – enabling Belleville to uphold its tradition of fun on a large scale (and also to provide space for political meetings held by the likes of Gambetta and Jules Ferry). People came here in such great numbers that the Paris transport network, in those days the Omnibus Company, decided to extend the line that connected the Louvre and the church of Belleville as far as Saint-Fargeau. The Company even agreed to adopt the name of this popular landmark for its new terminus – Lac Saint-Fargeau – and to display this name on its vehicles, providing for the celebrated establishment further publicity; in exchange for which the Saint-Fargeau lent the company some office space free of charge. Thus the horse-drawn omnibus that plodded up the hill, then trotted downhill jauntily, was the ancestor of the Métro Levallois-Porte des Lilas, now line no 3. Today the lake has disappeared both in fact and in name, and also from Parisian memory. Who now remembers that up until World War I, people came here for the boating and fishing, or that Stendhal, George Sand, Alfred de Musset and Alexandre Dumas would cross the entire city to enjoy a bucolic meal on the enchanting shore of the lake of Saint-Fargeau?

Retrace your steps on rue du Borrégo and turn left into rue de la Duée, named after one of Belleville's water courses. To the right, the Passage de la Duée is the narrowest alley in Paris – an 0.80-m crevasse – and is not devoid of shabby charm. Rue des Rigoles ('rivulets'), just beyond it to the left, is another reminder of the waters of Belleville.

Retrace your steps and turn right into the **Villa Georgina**, filled with flowers and birdsong and with the inebriating smell of honeysuckle. Retrace your steps and turn left into Passage des Saint-Simoniens which leads to the pleasant **Square de Ménilmontant**, once the property of the Saint-Simoniens. The drab block of flats overlooking the garden was erected here in the 1960s in place of the lovely house of the Saints-Simoniens, surrounded at the time by a neat vegetable garden, a magnificent fruit orchard and lilac trees.

In 1832 the 36-year-old Prosper Enfantin, the son of a wealthy banker and an alumnus of the prestigious Ecole Polytechnique which still trains France's topmost mathematicians and engineers, renounced the privileges of both birth and personal merit and retired with forty disciples to this water-blessed spot. He had inherited the house from his father who, like other bourgeois of the time, had built himself a country retreat in hilly Belleville. Inspired by the doctrine of the philosopher the Comte de Saint-Simon, this bunch of enlightened idealists wished to promote the notion of justice and brotherhood through a life of simplicity, close to the soil. So as to ensure brotherly cooperation and mutual aid among the members of the group, they wore red waistcoats that buttoned at the back, along with white trousers and purple tunics. They also grew venerable beards and accompanied their garden labours with chants about equality and the rebirth of a new man, which they sang to the music of their friend, the well-known composer, Félicien David. Overflowing with the milk of human kindness, they threw open their property to the public on Sundays, many of whom came to scoff at those rich Daddy's boys with their ridiculous attire and dainty white hands playing at ploughmen.

The police, on the other hand, did not find them at all amusing but a cause for great concern. Alarmed by their eccentricities, by the subversive ideas they peddled and, above all, by the fact that they allowed women in as fully-fledged members of the human race, they accused the brotherhood of causing an outrage to public decency. The following December each member of the sect was sentenced to one year's imprisonment and a fine of 100 francs. Their pleasant house was put on sale and a beautiful experience was nipped in the bud. The doctrine lived on, however, thanks to the intellectual level of its disciples, and had a great following throughout the 19th century. Their adherents included such sympathisers as Pereire, Victor Hugo and even Napoléon III (!) who, unlike his wife, had a penchant for the socialist ideal. In view of the other Utopian communities that developed into more threatening political forces, perhaps the police forces of Louis-Philippe had a point after all.

Once released, Prosper Enfantin travelled to Egypt where he stayed for four years. Here the brilliant engineer came into his own, befriending Mehmed Ali, viceroy of Egypt, and conceiving the idea of the Suez Canal, a project which he did not live long enough to carry out, but which would be taken over by his disciple, de Lesseps.

Exit the gardens into **RUE DE MENILMONTANT** and turn right. Continue to the corner of rue des Pyrénées. Two blocks down rue de Ménilmontant, on your left, a provincial red-tiled roof of a one-storeyed house contrasts with the anarchical concrete towers of the arrondissement. It is the gatepost to a quiet side street, appropriately named rue du Retrait where, at nos. 29/31, Maurice Chevalier was born on 12 September 1888. At present this is a vast empty building-site, where another concrete tower will soon protrude into the sky. No sign is left of the world of honest workmen among whom Maurice grew up.

Turn right into **RUE DES PYRENEES**, the main thoroughfare of the 20th arrondissement. The street was opened by Haussmann to offer its more privileged residents a leafy and airy environment, but, like elsewhere, it was also built to give the police forces quick access into a troublesome area. Walk up to **PLACE GUIGNIER**, whose pink and white houses, shady trees and subdued light grace it with provincial charm, especially on market days (Thursdays and Sundays).

Retrace your steps and turn right into **Cité Leroy**, a characteristic, humble dead-end alley. Walk to the next alley, **Villa de l'Ermitage**, a lovely nook where wild flowers mingle with vines. Turn left into rue de l'Ermitage which will take you back to rue de Ménilmontant.

From the corner of rues de l'Ermitage and Ménilmontant you will enjoy a sweeping view of Paris with the Tour Saint-Jacques rising ahead against the sky and, to its left, the bright blue piping of the Centre Pompidou. This will give you a measure of the distance the inhabitants of Belleville had to cover before 1635 in order to attend mass at the church of Saint-Merri (next to the Centre Pompidou) and, especially, of the climb back home up the steep hill, shivering on a cold winter Sunday or slipping on the ice. Not until 1635, at long last, were they allowed to build themselves a parish church (on the northern side of rue de Belleville, in today's 19th arrondissement).

Continue downhill along rue de Ménilmontant. On your right is the **Cité de l'Ermitage**, a surviving pocket of old Belleville which has preserved its cobblestones, bungalows, flower blossoms and a touch of the old atmosphere.

Turn right into **RUE DES CASCADES**, whose name brings to mind once more the abundance of water that once blessed Belleville. As you walk down the steps and ramp at no. 13, exquisitely

293

fragrant with lavender, you will reach a well restored inspection-hole shelter – **le Regard des Messiers** – a vestige of the days when the aqueduct of Belleville supplied water to the city. Another such construction – **le Regard de la Roquette** – is situated at no. 41. In the 17th century endless law cases were brought against the religious community of La Roquette for its excessive use of the hill's water. A final shelter (*regard*) is located on the corner of rue de Savies, **le Regard Saint-Martin**. It was used by the congregation of Saint-Martin-des-Champs which harnessed the water of a local spring, known as la Fontaine de Savies. The legend of the holy man sharing his coat with a pauper is carved on the wall above the door but is barely recognisable. The monks also built a small aqueduct which they connected to the main aqueduct of Belleville. It was in fact the congregation of Saint-Martin that set out to harness the water of Belleville back in the 13th century and supply the Marais area, including the royal residence of Saint-Pol, a century later. Today, after a wet spell, you may still hear the happy trickle of water.

Continue into **RUE DE SAVIES** – so called after the early name of the village of Belleville. Plunging downhill, its bumpy paving may not make for an easy walk but it is certainly picturesque. Note the two old houses at nos. 42 and 44, which seem about to collapse. In 1951 Jacques Becker chose this street as the location for some of the scenes of *Casque d'Or*, featuring the legendary Simone Signoret (see above).

Ahead is rue de la Mare ('pond'), which led downhill to a pond. Today it leads to the church of Notre-Dame-de-la-Croix, which boasts a splendid Cavaille-Coll organ and superb acoustics, and which overlooks the charming Place Maurice Chevalier to the west. If you have explored the street all the way down, retrace your steps and turn left into Cité A. Loubeyre, across rue des Couronnes, then up the steps to **Passage de Plantin**, a pocket-size alley, bordered by cosy, little houses, all huddled up together and drowning in wonderfully untidy vegetation. On rue du Transvaal turn left and immediately left again into **Villa Castel** – if unlocked – the backdrop for some scenes of another French classic, François Truffaut's *Jules et Jim*. Nothing much seems to have altered since the 1950s and somebody has even hung up a string of colourful electric bulbs among the trees, as if to echo a 14th-of-July celebration by René Clair or Jacques Tati.

Back on rue du Transvaal turn right and left onto **RUE DES COURONNES** where, roughly on today's no. 45, was a well-known cabaret, le Pistolet. On the night of 20 October 1721, the 28-year-old Louis Dominique Bourgogne, better known as the notorious bandit Cartouche, was surprised here while sound asleep by the police who had found his remote hiding place thanks to the denunciation extorted from his accomplice Duchâtelet. To secure the capture of this most dangerous enemy of society, at once elusive and ubiquitous, who had been giving the authorities the slip for several years, 30 soldiers were sent to Belleville. Duchâtelet showed them the way and disclosed the passwords. The unsuspecting tavern owner showed them into Cartouche's room, where he was pounced upon, tied up and whisked off. A brief trial ensued, after which Cartouche was brought to Place de Grève (now Hôtel-de-Ville) on 28 November and put to death by quartering.

Continue to the junction of rues des Envierges, de la mare, des Cascades and Levert, a countrified spot with one-storeyed houses, a garden wall overflowing with Virginia creeper and an old-time *tabac*. Turn left into **RUE DES ENVIERGES** and walk into the gap between no. 25 and 27. You will penetrate a patch of genuine woodland, from which wafts the exquisite fragrance of untamed nature.

Rue des Envierges will lead you to the top of the **Parc de Belleville** that rolls down the hillside. Thanks to the steepness of the slope and the instability of the soil, the neighbourhood was spared the eyesore of yet another cluster of high-rises, and instead was granted a recreation area, including a tiny vineyard to commemorate the pastoral past of Belleville. Nothing, however, has survived of the Impasse Piat, a narrow, steep, cobbled alley that ran down this slope prior to the opening of the gardens, nor of the rickety bistro, Le Repos de la Montagne, used at times as a film set for low-life thrillers featuring such actors as Jean Gabin and Alain Delon. A commanding view of the skyline of Paris unfolds instead, its monuments old and new radiating in the sunshine.

Follow the slope downhill towards **BOULEVARD DE BELLE-VILLE**, where a human tide will engulf you and the accents of North Africa, which have of late replaced the native accent of Belleville, will urge you on to the market stalls. As you are swept along, willy nilly, you will be astonished by the irresistibly low prices of the goods on display and also by the fact that the native French have become a rare species in these parts. Across the Boulevard and spilling into the side streets, it is the Jewish community of North Africa that has taken over. Their predecessors from Russia, Poland and Lithuania have by now either left the area or blended into the native population. Their North African successors – obviously in their element in this Mediterranean atmosphere – have lined the Boulevard with couscous restaurants, while their grocery shops climb up the hill, notably along rue Ramponeau. Less conspicuously, artists too have been living and working here for the past twenty-odd years, but they operate quietly in the background and have to be sought out, except on special annual occasions when their galleries are open to the public. However, the true atmosphere of today's Belleville is right in front of you, exposed in broad day light. Why not finish your walk with a couscous at La Lumière de Belleville, also known as Chez Charlot, served with the sunny smile of its Tunisian hosts?

EPILOGUE

Passent les jours, passent les années
Sous le Pont Mirabeau coule la Seine

Pass the days, pass the years
Under Mirabeau bridge flows the Seine

Guillaume Apollinaire

Paris emerged from the Seine at its intersection with the south-north road. It could have chosen the busy road, through which travelled copper, pewter, iron, amber and furs as far as the Pyrenees or the Rhine. It chose the river instead. Today, long after it has been dethroned by the railway, then the automobile, the boat the early merchants used to ply its waters still represents the city's emblem. Unlike the peaceful present, marred only by zooming car traffic on either shore, quick blood ran through this artery in earlier times, reflecting on the nature of the turbulent city, throbbing with a life of intense activity, of territorial and economic struggles, of fun and crime, ravaged periodically by the floods of the swelling river.

In 1760, a time of intense commercial activity, the banks of the Seine were crowded with as many as 20 ports: wine at La Râpée, fruit and vegetables at the Arsenal, coal at the Ile Saint Louis, fodder and fishponds at Pont Marie, corn at the Grève (Hotel-de-Ville); a long succession of tiles, bricks, wood, coal, apples and chestnuts faced them across the river, while oils, wines, flour, oysters, codfish and herring overflowed at the foot of the Louvre – a bustling, crammed territory where traders, especially the timber dealers, fiercely elbowed one another out of the way for extra space. There was similar wrangling over the water itself. At that time, when bridges were few and threatened by floods, the ferrymen enjoyed a monopoly and a right to levy a toll, a privilege granted by Louis XIV, which the city authorities tried to grab for themselves. Even leisure boats such as those which took passengers on a 6-hour journey to Sèvres were not allowed to cross the river from bank to bank. (The 8-hour ride back would necessarily follow the shore, the boat then being horse-drawn upstream). But the real threat to the ferrymen came from the passing of time: Paris was growing and the construction of new bridges could not be postponed for long.

It was only in the 12th century that the first stone bridge was built, le Petit Pont between Notre Dame and the Left Bank, surmounted by houses, which, it was hoped, would give it more weight to resist the floods – to no avail: the Petit Pont was swept away in 1280, 1296 and 1325. The Pont Notre-Dame, between the island and the Right Bank, was also built of stone but it collapsed in 1499, together with its 65 houses. A new bridge replaced it in 1512, complete with 68 houses of equal height and harmonious proportions, considered at the time the most beautiful bridge in Europe. The Grand Pont connected the island with the Châtelet prison, just a little further west; it became the Pont au Change when Louis VII started to levy rents there. It went up in flames in 1620 and was replaced by another bridge soon after. But it was on the brand new Pont Neuf, now the oldest bridge of Paris (1578–1604), that the city's lifeblood pulsated: 'Le Pont Neuf is to the city what the heart is to the human body,' wrote the 18th-century chronicler Louis-Sebastien Mercier. This was the stamping-ground of beggars and tramps, rogues and charlatans, such as the notorious would-be 'dentist' Grand Thomas, who, again in the words of Mercier,

> . . . with his panache
> Is the best of charlatans
> A toothache he relieves
> By pulling out all one's teeth.

Street performers also congregated here, such as Tabarin, who in the 17th century delighted his audience with crude jokes from the top of his trestles. The boat jousts at the foot of the bridge, opposite the Louvre, were of better taste. The Pont Neuf was also the hunting ground of the police, teeming with spies in search of those on the run, and with the military hired to abduct recruits for their ranks. This was no place for ladies of society, which is why the Pont Royal was built in 1652 opposite the Tuileries, an indispensable link with the budding Faubourg Saint Germain across the river. The Pont Marie and the Pont de la Tournelle became a necessity, too, when the elegant Ile Saint Louis was being constructed about the same time.

The construction of bridges accelerated in the 19th century. Like many inhabitants of mainland Paris at this time of economic revolution, the ferryman lost his trade. Steamboats took over from 1830 on, and were boosted by the 1867 Universal Exposition, when they became an ideal mode of transportation to the Champ-de-Mars, where the fair was held. Following a contest, the boat selected for the fair was the '*mouche*', so called because of its propeller. Others claim it owes its name to the 'flea' (*puce*)-boats on the Thames, which some French engineer mistook for 'fly' (*mouche*). Be that as it may, it remains the most famous of Paris's pleasure boats to this day. With 3.5 million passengers plying the water aboard the *bateaux-mouches* in 1867, the Seine resembled an aquatic motorway. In 1874 their number was 9 million but by then one had to fend off fierce competition from the '*hirondelles*' which had stepped in in 1874. Worse was to come in 1883, when the *bateaux-express* offered a non-stop crossing of the city, sweeping off 850,000 passengers within 100 days! From now on it was free competition for all and in 1889 33 million passengers took a ride on the Seine.

The boats, of various shapes and sizes, have never lost their appeal, carrying back and forth their loads of visitors. The loud commentaries they spit out in several languages do not exactly enhance the experience, but the beauty of the banks of the Seine as one glides along is irreplaceable, and magical when floodlit by night. So much so that on 10 September 1992 the section between the Pont de Sully and the Pont d'Iéna was listed by UNESCO as international heritage 'of exceptional universal value'.

The Pont Mirabeau, albeit the work of Résal, the architect of the lavish Pont Alexandre III, was excluded from this honour – sculpted mermaids and all; so was the third island of Paris which lies between it and the Eiffel Tower, a narrow leafy, uninhabited strip, barely 11 metres wide, blessed with the name of l'Ile aux Cygnes – the Island of Swans. Of course, it does not have the glamour of l'Ile de la Cité, nor the sparkle of l'Ile Saint-Louis. Besides, it has no swans and never had any (these belonged to another island at the time of Louis XIV, further east, and which no longer exists). Rather, it is an artificial construction, built for functional reasons as part of the Port de Grenelle, stretching opposite the unappetising concrete compound of Le Front de Seine (Beau Grenelle), a

painful example of what should have been avoided in urban planning.

Yet this third island of Paris has the special charm of all secret places, disclosing its poetry only to the few that seek them out. You can make your way to the island by way of a flight of steps down the bridge of Bir Hakeim. The right bank of the river has been turned into a fast motorway which you will do best to ignore, but on the left bank is a sprawl of installations belonging to the port of Paris, the

fifth largest in France: clusters of barges with their laundry flutter-
ing on the line, cranes, containers, warehouses. . . As you make
your way west among rows of serene poplars, limes and chestnut
trees, you can see the tower-dented skyline of modern Paris. Facing
it on the tip of the island is a small-scale version of the Statue of
Liberty, an unexpected sight, indeed – rising above the water as a
reminder to all passing boats that the torch of liberty first shone
forth from here; this is why the people of America offered this
replica to Paris as a gift (see also chapter on the 17th arr.). The odd
stroller, a couple of joggers, a loner soaking in the sun or engrossed
in a book on a bench under a shady tree, the lapping water, the
occasional cries of circling seagulls – l'Ile aux Cygnes is a world set
apart, yet surrounded by characteristic, disparate reflections of
present-day Paris, at the foot of the ubiquitous Eiffel Tower.

INDEX

AROUND AND ABOUT PARIS
VOLUMES 1, 2 & 3

Volume 1 takes you from the 1st to the 7th arrondissement, the territory of Paris before the French Revolution.

Volume 2 covers the 8th to the 12th arrondissements which were annexed to Paris in 1795.

Thirza Vallois brings Paris to life in a way that enthralls her readers and provides them with a detailed knowledge of the city which exceeds that of most Parisians, while her fast moving style disguises a depth of historical fact that is normally only found in academic tomes.

ORDER FORM

To order your copy, either check or insert the number of copies you want in the appropriate box and return this order form (or a photocopy of it) along with your cheque to the address below. Alternatively you can phone your order through on (+44/0) 973 325 468 and pay by credit card.

Volume 1: From the Dawn of Time to the Eiffel Tower
Arrondisements 1 to 7 £14.95 ☐

Volume 2: From the Guillotine to the Bastille Opera
Arrondisements 8 to 12 £14.95 ☐

Volume 3: New Horizons: Haussmann's Annexation
Arrondisements 13 to 20 £15.95 ☐

Add £2.90 per copy for post and packing

Send your order to:
Iliad Books, 5 Nevern Road, London SW5 9PG

Name: _____

Address: _____

_____

_____

Enclosed is my cheque payable to Iliad Books, amount: _____

Please bill my credit card. Specify type of card _____

Card No _____ Expiry date _____

Signature _____